Charles Darwin and
The Origin of Species

Charles Darwin and *The Origin of Species*

KEITH A. FRANCIS

Greenwood Guides to Historic Events, 1500–1900
Linda S. Frey and Marsha L. Frey, Series Editors

GREENWOOD PRESS
Westport, Connecticut • London

Library of Congress Cataloging-in-Publication Data

Francis, Keith A.
    Charles Darwin and The origin of species / Keith A. Francis.
        p. cm. — (Greenwood guides to historic events, 1500–1900, ISSN
1538-442X)
    Includes bibliographical references.
    ISBN 0-313-31748-8 (alk. paper)
    1. Darwin, Charles, 1809–1882. On the origin of species. 2. Darwin,
Charles, 1809–1882. 3. Evolution (Biology). I. Title.
QH365.O8F73 2007
576.8′2092—dc22   2006029478

British Library Cataloguing in Publication Data is available.

Library of Congress Catalog Card Number: 2006029478
ISBN-10: 0-313-31748-8
ISBN-13: 978-0-313-31748-4
ISSN: 1538-442X

First published in 2007

Greenwood Press, 88 Post Road West, Westport, CT 06881
An imprint of Greenwood Publishing Group, Inc.
www.greenwood.com

Printed in the United States of America

The paper used in this book complies with the
Permanent Paper Standard issued by the National
Information Standards Organization (Z39.48–1984).

10   9   8   7   6   5   4   3   2   1

CONTENTS

Photographs follow chapter 6.

SERIES FOREWORD

American statesman Adlai Stevenson stated, "We can chart our future clearly and wisely only when we know the path which has led to the present." This series, Greenwood Guides to Historic Events, 1500–1900, is designed to illuminate that path by focusing on events from 1500 to 1900 that have shaped the world. The years 1500 to 1900 include what historians call the early modern period (1500 to 1789, the onset of the French Revolution) and part of the modern period (1789 to 1900).

In 1500, an acceleration of key trends marked the beginnings of an interdependent world and the posing of seminal questions that changed the nature and terms of intellectual debate. The series closes with 1900, the inauguration of the twentieth century. This period witnessed profound economic, social, political, cultural, religious, and military changes. An industrial and technological revolution transformed the modes of production, marked the transition from a rural to an urban economy, and ultimately raised the standard of living. Social classes and distinctions shifted. The emergence of the territorial and later the national state altered man's relations with and view of political authority. The shattering of the religious unity of the Roman Catholic world in Europe marked the rise of a new pluralism. Military revolutions changed the nature of warfare. The books in this series emphasize the complexity and diversity of the human tapestry and include political, economic, social, intellectual, military, and cultural topics. Some of the authors focus on events in U.S. history such as the Salem witchcraft trials, the American Revolution, the abolitionist movement, and the Civil War. Others analyze European topics, such as the Reformation and Counter-Reformation and the French Revolution. Still others bridge cultures and continents by examining the voyages of discovery, the

Atlantic slave trade, and the Age of Imperialism. Some focus on intellectual questions that have shaped the modern world, such as Charles Darwin's *Origin of Species*, or on turning points such as the Age of Romanticism. Others examine defining economic, religious, or legal events or issues such as the building of the railroads, the Second Great Awakening, and abolitionism. Heroes (e.g., Meriwether Lewis and William Clark), scientists (e.g., Darwin), military leaders (e.g., Napoleon Bonaparte), poets (e.g., Lord Byron) stride across the pages. Many of these events were seminal in that they marked profound changes or turning points. The Scientific Revolution, for example, changed the way individuals viewed themselves and their world.

The authors, acknowledged experts in their fields, synthesize key events, set developments within the larger historical context, and, most important, present well-balanced, well-written accounts that integrate the most recent scholarship in the field.

The topics were chosen by an advisory board composed of historians, high school history teachers, and school librarians to support the curriculum and meet student research needs. The volumes are designed to serve as resources for student research and to provide clearly written interpretations of topics central to the secondary school and lower-level undergraduate history curriculum. Each author outlines a basic chronology to guide the reader through often-confusing events and presents a historical overview to set those events within a narrative framework. Three to five topical chapters underscore critical aspects of the event. In the final chapter the author examines the impact and consequences of the event. Biographical sketches furnish background on the lives and contributions of the players who strut across the stage. Ten to fifteen primary documents, ranging from letters to diary entries, song lyrics, proclamations, and posters, cast light on the event, provide material for student essays, and stimulate critical engagement with the sources. Introductions identify the authors of the documents and the main issues. In some cases a glossary of selected terms is provided as a guide to the reader. Each work contains an annotated bibliography of recommended books, articles, CD-ROMs, Internet sites, videos, and films that set the materials within the historical debate.

Reading these works can lead to a more sophisticated understanding of the events and debates that have shaped the modern world and can stimulate a more active engagement with the issues that still affect us. It has been a particularly enriching experience to work closely with such dedicated professionals. We have come to know and value even more highly the authors in this series and our editors at Greenwood, particularly Kevin Ohe and Michael Hermann. In many cases they have become more than colleagues; they have become friends. To them and to future historians we dedicate this series.

Linda S. Frey
University of Montana

Marsha L. Frey
Kansas State University

PREFACE

In 1985, the Italian scientist Antonella La Vergata remarked that the "Darwin's-place-in-history approach" dominated writing about Darwin and the development of the theory of evolution before 1960. Darwin was the colossus who stood above every other scientist in the nineteenth century when it came to developing a theory about the origin of life. La Vergata's argument was that historians and scientists who used this approach ignored the important contributions made by Darwin's contemporaries as well as other scientists who preceded and followed him. Even worse, this approach ignored the large number of people to whom Darwin wrote letters either to discuss the research he was doing or to obtain the answers to questions he had. Darwin should be viewed as part of a community even if he was the central figure in this community.[1] While acknowledging La Vergata's criticism, this book is a Darwin's-place-in-history book.

Darwin's community of correspondents—which included scientists, cattle breeders, explorers, and government officials—was important but, first and foremost, the story of *The Origin of Species* is the story of Charles Darwin's research and writing. Darwin could not have written *The Origin of Species* without the help of many people—his friends Charles Lyell and Thomas Hooker, for example—but, ultimately, Darwin was the sole author. An introduction to *The Origin of Species* cannot ignore this fact. It is foolish to pay insufficient attention to the community who helped Darwin and it is equally foolish to gloss over the singular genius of Darwin.

Darwin covered a large number of subjects in *The Origin of Species*. He did not propose every aspect of the theory of evolution, but Darwin was able to develop his theory because he was proficient in several scientific disciplines. Without boasting, Darwin could claim to be an expert in zoology, botany, geology, and embryology. He read widely and wrote prolifically. His scientific interests ranged from animal psychology to plant tropism.

Despite the genius of the man and book, it is possible to read *The Origin of Species* without having any prior knowledge of zoology or paleontology or the history of the biological sciences. Darwin's argument in the book is clear and easy enough to follow. Darwin called it "a long argument" in the final chapter, but it is also a straightforward one.[2] Furthermore, Darwin's intended audience for *The Origin of Species* was the general public. He wanted not only specialists to read the book, but also ordinary people.

Because there were six editions of *The Origin of Species* published during Darwin's life, the question of which is the best edition to read is an important one. In this book, most of the references will be to the first edition of 1859. As the British historian John W. Burrow and the American evolutionary biologist Ernst Mayr suggest, the first edition of *The Origin of Species* was the cleanest, freshest, and most revolutionary.[3] (And this edition is readily available in the Penguin Classics book series.)

The edition of 1859 was the result of twenty-plus years of thinking by Darwin. When Darwin forced himself, under pressure from his friends and the work of Alfred Russel Wallace, to finish *The Origin of Species* he said what he wanted to say. In the next five editions, Darwin was addressing criticisms of the first edition. By the time he finished the revised and definitive sixth edition, published in 1876, Darwin was reacting rather than stating: in a sense, he said what others provoked him to say. Equally important, some of the concessions Darwin made were unnecessary. For example, scientists who did research on chromosomes and genes in the late-nineteenth and early twentieth centuries demonstrated that Darwin was closer to explaining how and why natural selection worked in the first edition of *The Origin of Species* than in subsequent editions. Furthermore, in Darwin's other major works, his position on evolution by natural selection seems closer to the one he took in the first edition. In the first edition of *The Origin of Species*, Darwin was as right as he could be without knowing about genetics.

Charles Darwin is one of the great minds of the last five hundred years because his work transformed the way humans think about themselves. His work is important because the discussion about this transformation and its effects continues today. Given this debate, it is accurate to call *The Origin of Species* a seminal work of world literature. It is equal in importance to the writings of Confucius or the sayings of the Buddha: it is a must-read book whether or not the reader agrees with Darwin. Like any genius, Darwin was not always right. As one of Darwin's biographers put it, we should "express our admiration and pick our quarrels, discovering his greatness at one time, his limitations at another."[4] I hope that readers of this book will enjoy reading about Darwin and *The Origin of Species* as much as I did.

Notes

1. Antonella La Vergata, "Images of Darwin: A Historiographic Overview," in *The Darwinian Heritage*, ed. David Kohn (Princeton, NJ: Princeton University Press, 1985), 904.

2. *On the Origin of Species by Means of Natural Selection, or the Preservation of Favoured Races in the Struggle for Life* (London: John Murray, 1859), 459.

3. John Barrow, "Note on This Edition," *The Origin of Species* (London: Penguin Classics, 1985), 49; Ernst Mayr, "Introduction," *On the Origin of Species by Charles Darwin: A Facsimile of the First Edition* (Cambridge, MA: Harvard University Press, 1975), xxiv.

4. Peter Brent, *Charles Darwin* (London: Heinemann, 1981), 522.

CHRONOLOGY OF THE LIFE OF CHARLES DARWIN AND IMPORTANT EVENTS IN THE DEVELOPMENT OF IDEAS ABOUT EVOLUTION

Before 1882, Darwin's age at the time of a particular event is included in brackets. After 1882, the number of years since Darwin's death that the event occurred is included in parentheses.

1809	12 February: Born in Shrewsbury, England.	
1817	Spring: Begins attending the Reverend G. Case's day school in Shrewsbury.	[8]
1818	Summer: Begins attending Shrewsbury School.	[9]
1825	22 October: Begins studying at the University of Edinburgh.	[16]
1827	15 October: Admitted to Christ's College, Cambridge.	[18]
1830	July: First volume of Charles Lyell's *Principles of Geology* published.	[21]
1831	26 April: Graduates from Cambridge with a B.A.	[22]
	30 August: Receives an invitation to sail on the *Beagle*.	

	27 December: HMS *Beagle* sails from Plymouth.	
1833	April: Third and final volume of Charles Lyell's *Principles of Geology* is published.	[24]
1835	26 March: Darwin is bitten by Benchuca insects in Argentina.	[26]
	September/October: Visits the Galapagos Islands.	
1836	2 October: *Beagle* lands at Falmouth.	[27]
	November: Elected Fellow of the Geological Society.	
1837	July: Begins his first notebook on the transmutation of species.	[28]
1838	28 September: Starts to read Thomas Malthus's *Essay on the Principle of Population.*	[29]
1839	24 January: Elected Fellow of the Royal Society (F.R.S.)	
	29 January: Marries Emma Wedgwood at Maer, Staffordshire.	
	March: Elected Fellow of the Zoological Society.	[30]
	August: *A Journal of Researches into the Geology and Natural History of the Various Countries Visited by H.M.S.* Beagle *under the Command of Captain FitzRoy, R.N. from 1832 to 1836* is published.	
	27 December: His first child William Erasmus Darwin is born.	
1841	2 March: Anne Elizabeth Darwin is born.	[32]
1842	May: *Structure and Distribution of Coral Reefs* is published.	[33]
	June: Writes "a very brief abstract" of his species theory (35 pages).	
	17 September: Moves to Down House, Downe, Kent.	
	23 September: Mary Eleanor Darwin is born.	
	16 October: Mary Eleanor Darwin dies (at three weeks old).	
1843	25 September: Henrietta Emma Darwin is born.	[34]

1844	July: Darwin writes an longer version of his species theory (230 pages).	[35]
	October: Robert Chambers's book *Vestiges of the Natural History of Creation* is published anonymously.	
	November: *Geological Observations on the Volcanic Islands, Visited During the Voyage of H.M.S. Beagle, together with Some Brief Notices on the Geology of Australia and the Cape of Good Hope* is published.	
1845	9 July: George Howard Darwin is born.	[36]
	August: Second edition of *A Naturalist's Voyage Round the World* is published.	
1846	October: *Geological Observations on South America* is published.	[37]
1847	8 July: Elizabeth Darwin is born.	[38]
1848	16 August: Francis Darwin, Darwin's first biographer, is born.	[39]
1850	15 January: Leonard Darwin is born.	[40]
1851	23 April: Anne Elizabeth Darwin dies (at ten years old).	[42]
	13 May: Horace Darwin is born.	
	June: *A Monograph on the Fossil Lepadidae, or, Pedunculated Cirripedes of Great Britain* is published.	
	December: *A Monograph on the Sub-Class Cirripedia, with Figures of All the Species: The Lepadidae; or Pedunculated Cirripedes* is published.	
1853	30 November: Awarded the Royal Medal of the Royal Society.	[44]
	Tenth edition of *Vestiges of the Natural History of Creation* is published.	
1854	August: *A Monograph on the Sub-Class Cirripedia, with Figures of All the Species: the Balanidae, (or Sessile Cirripedes); The Verrucidae, etc., etc., etc.* is published.	[45]

September: *A Monograph on the Fossil Balanidae and Verrucidae of Great Britain* is published.

1855   September: Alfred Russel Wallace's article "On the   [46]
        Law which has regulated the Introduction of New
        Species" is published in the *Annals and Magazine of
        Natural History*.

1856   14 May: Darwin begins to write a complete version   [47]
        of his theory on species.

        6 December: Charles Waring Darwin is born.

1858   18 June: Receives from Alfred Russel Wallace "On   [49]
        the Tendency of Varieties to Depart Indefinitely
        From the Original Type," an essay that postulated a
        theory of evolution by natural selection similar to
        Darwin's.

        28 June: Charles Waring Darwin dies (at 18 months
        old).

        1 July: The Secretary of the Linnean Society, John J.
        Bennett, reads the joint paper of Darwin and
        Wallace entitled "On the Tendency of Species to
        form Varieties; and on the Perpetuation of Varieties
        and Species by Natural Means of Selection" at the
        Society's meeting. The paper is actually a short
        essay on the origin of species and natural selection
        by Darwin, Darwin's letter to Asa Gray of
        September 5, 1857, and Wallace's paper "On the
        Tendency of Varieties to Depart Indefinitely from
        the Original Type."

        20 July: Darwin begins to write *The Origin of Species*.

1859   19 March: Finishes writing and begins to prepare   [50]
        The Origin of Species for publication.

        1 October: Finishes correcting proofs of *The Origin
        of Species*.

        24 November: *On the Origin of Species by Means of
        Natural Selection or the Preservation of Favoured
        Races in the Struggle for Life* is published (1,250
        copies printed).

26 December: Review of *The Origin of Species* published in *The Times*; from the beginning of the article up to the section "What is a Species?" is written by a journalist from *The Times*, Lucas, but the majority is written by Thomas Huxley.

1860   7 January: Second edition of *The Origin of Species* is published (3,000 copies printed).

30 June: Meeting of the British Association for the [51] Advancement of Science at Oxford: *The Origin of Species* is defended aggressively by Huxley against the attack of Bishop Samuel Wilberforce.

July: Bishop Wilberforce's review of *The Origin of Species* is published in *Quarterly Review*.

1861   April: Third edition of *The Origin of Species* is [52] published (2,000 copies printed).

1862   15 May: *On the Various Contrivances by which* [53] *British and Foreign Orchids are Fertilised by Insects, and on the Good Effects of Intercrossing* is published.

September: William Henry Flower demonstrates that apes have a characteristic of brain physiognomy originally thought unique to man at a meeting of the British Association for Advancement of Science held at Cambridge.

1863   February: Charles Lyell's *Antiquity of Man* and [54] Thomas Huxley's *Evidence as to Man's Place in Nature* are published.

1864   30 November: Awarded the Copley Medal by the [55] Royal Society.

Herbert Spencer's *Principles of Biology* is published. Spencer uses the term "survival of the fittest" in the book.

1865   8 February: Gregor Mendel presents the first part of his paper on heredity to the Brünn Society for the Study of Natural Science.

8 March: Gregor Mendel presents the second part [56] of his paper on heredity to the Brünn Society for the Study of Natural Science.

1866   15 December: Fourth edition of *The Origin of* [57] *Species* is published (1,500 copies printed).

Mendel's article "Experiments with Plant Hybrids" ("*Versuche über Pflanzenhybriden*") is published in the journal of the Brünn Society for the Study of Natural Science.

1868   30 January: *The Variation of Animals and Plants* [58] *under Domestication* is published (1,500 copies printed).

1869   7 August: Fifth edition of *The Origin of Species* is [60] published (2,000 copies printed).

1871   24 February: *The Descent of Man, and Selection in* [62] *Relation to Sex* is published (2,500 copies printed).

August: Sir William Thomson gives the presidential address at the British Association meeting in Edinburgh. Based on the cooling of the Earth's crust, he argues that the Earth's age is one hundred million years or less.

1872   19 February: Sixth edition of *The Origin of Species* [63] is published (3,000 copies printed).

26 November: *The Expression of the Emotions in Man and Animals* is published (7,000 copies printed; 5,267 sold).

1874   Second edition of *The Descent of Man* is published. [65]

1875   22 February: Sir Charles Lyell dies. [66]

2 July: *Insectivorous Plants* is published.

September: *The Movements and Habits of Climbing Plants* is published.

1876   5 December: *Effects of Cross and Self Fertilization in* [67] *the Vegetable Kingdom* is published.

The revised and definitive sixth edition of *The Origin of Species* is published.

1877	9 July: *Different Forms of Flowers on Plants of the Same Species* is published.	[68]
	17 November: Receives an honorary doctoral degree from Cambridge University.	
1878	5 August: Elected a Corresponding Member of the Académie des sciences.	[69]
1879	19 November: *Life of Erasmus Darwin* is published.	[70]
1880	22 November: *The Power of Movement in Plants* is published.	[71]
1881	10 October: *The Formation of Vegetable Mould, Through the Action of Worms, with Observations on their Habits* is published.	[72]
1882	19 April: Darwin dies at Down House.	[74]
	26 April: Darwin buried in Westminster Abbey.	
1884	6 January: Gregor Mendel dies.	(+2)
1885	9 June: Thomas Huxley presents a statue of Darwin to the Natural History Museum, London.	(+3)
1890	1 December: Newly created Darwin Medal of the Royal Society is presented to Alfred Russel Wallace.	(+8)
1895	29 June: Thomas Huxley dies.	(+13)
1896	1 October: Emma Darwin dies.	(+14)
1900	German botanist Carl Erich Correns, Dutch botanist Hugo de Vries, and Austrian botanist Erich Tschermak von Seysenegg, working independently, obtain results similar to Mendel's and confirm his thesis about heredity.	(+18)
1905	23 September: Albert Einstein, in his article "On the Electrodynamics of Moving Bodies" in the German physics magazine *Annalen der Physik*, postulates the special theory of relativity and, by using quantum physics, raises the possibility of a long age for the universe.	(+23)
1906	January: Henri Poincaré's essay on the dynamics of the electron is published: written independently of Einstein, it confirms the special theory of relativity.	(+24)

1909	William Bateson coins the term genetics.	(+27)
1913	7 November: Alfred Russel Wallace dies.	(+31)
1925	February: Raymond Dart names a fossil he obtained *Australopithecus africanus*: he claims it is an intermediary between humans and apes.	(+43)
	10 July: Scopes Trial opens.	
	14 July: Scopes Trial ends.	
1929	17 January: Edwin Hubble demonstrates that the universe is expanding, the founding idea for the "Big Bang" theory, and confirms the idea that the universe is billions of years old.	(+47)
1942	March: Julian Huxley's book *Evolution: The Modern Synthesis* is published; it becomes one of the standard works on Neo-Darwinism.	(+60)
1952	15 March: Robert W. Briggs and Thomas J. King, working at the Institute for Cancer Research in Philadelphia, announce they have developed a technique for transplanting the nucleus from the cell of one frog to the cell of another frog. The technique becomes the basis for the process used to clone animals in the 1990s.	(+70)
1953	25 April: James Watson and Francis Crick announce their findings about the structure of DNA in the journal *Nature*; the article is entitled "A Structure for Deoxyribose Nucleic Acid."	(+71)
	30 May: Watson and Crick's article "Genetical Implications of the Structure of Deoxyribonucleic Acid" is published in *Nature*.	
	June: Edward O. Wilson's article "The Origin and Evolution of Polymorphism in Ants" is published in the *Quarterly Review of Biology*.	
1972	Stephen Jay Gould and Nils Eldredge propose the theory of punctuated equilibrium to explain evolution.	(+90)

1974	24 November: A team led by Donald Johanson finds the oldest hominid skeleton in the Afar region of Northern Ethiopia. The fossil, classified *Australopithecus afarensis* and nicknamed "Lucy," is 3.2 million years old.	(+92)
1976	Richard Dawkins publishes *The Selfish Gene*; the book popularizes the work of evolutionary biologists.	(+94)
1978	July–August: A team led by Mary Leakey discovers a series of *Australopithecus* footprints near Laetoli in Tanzania: this discovery provides evidence that Australopithecines walked upright. The footprints are over 3.6 million years old and are made by hominids similar to "Lucy."	(+96)
1997	23 February: Announcement of the successful cloning of "Dolly," a sheep, by a team of scientists at the Roslin Institute near Edinburgh, Scotland, led by Ian Wilmut.	(+114)
2000	26 June: Joint announcement at the White House by the Human Genome Project and Celera Genomics that the human genome has been mapped.	(+118)
2001	15–16 February: Results published by the Human Genome Project in the journal *Nature* and Celera Genomics in the journal *Science* show that the human genome contains approximately 30,000 genes, much fewer than the 100,000 estimated by most scientists.	(+119)
2003	June: A team that includes the U.C. Berkeley anthropologist Timothy White announces that it has discovered the skeletal head of the oldest *homo sapiens* in Ethiopia in a dig in 2002.	(+121)

CHAPTER 1

Overview: The Impact of Charles Darwin

Why Charles Darwin Is Important

Charles Darwin is one of the most important men of science of the last five hundred years. In his book, *On the Origin of Species by Means of Natural Selection, or the Preservation of Favoured Races in the Struggle for Life*, published in 1859,[1] Darwin proposed what is now called the theory of evolution. This book, along with its best-known companion *The Descent of Man, and Selection in Relation to Sex*, published in 1871, precipitated a major change in scientific thinking about the origin of life, particularly in the field of biology. (Both books are known popularly by their shortened titles *The Origin of Species* and *The Descent of Man*, respectively.) Darwin was not the first scientist to propose a theory of evolution nor was he the foremost thinker on the subject in 1859. More important, his theory had some significant flaws: it did not convince everyone of its validity, not even every scientist. Darwin tried to answer his critics by revising *The Origin of Species*, but he was not completely successful. Darwin is an important man of science not because his theory was foolproof, but because he solved a problem that had baffled scientists and philosophers for centuries.

What was this problem? Put simply, it was the difficulty of finding enough convincing evidence to prove that one species could change into a completely different one. Scientists and philosophers called the significant changes that a plant or animal experienced mutations (whether permanent or not); if an animal, for example, became a completely new animal, scientists and philosophers called this transmutation. The question troubling some was whether transmutation ever occurred. Most people who thought about the question before the widespread dissemination of *The Origin of Species* believed transmutation could not and never had occurred. The species were fixed: the same number and type existed at the present time as had existed one or two thousand years earlier. Each species had appeared or been created at a fixed point in time. Most likely, so the thinking went, all species had been created at the same time. Special creation and the fixity of the species, as these ideas were called, were the standard explanations in the Western world for the origin and existence of life on Earth until the late-nineteenth century.

It may have been the traditional view of the origin of life, but the plausibility of the fixity of the species had also been challenged. Was it really possible for thousands of years to have passed and organic life to remain exactly the same? Had nothing changed? To answer these two questions "yes" seemed to defy logic. Thinkers as far back as the Ancient Greeks discussed the merits of the theory. As Darwin noted in his Historical Sketch at the beginning of *The Origin of Species*, Aristotle (B.C.E. 384–322) wrote in one of his best-known books that, "In cases where a coincidence created a combination which seems as though it might have been arranged on purpose, the creatures, it is urged, having been suitably formed by the operation of chance, survived; otherwise they perished, and still perish. . . ."[2] Darwin, who was told about the statement by the British philologist Claire Grece (1831–1905), latched on to the fact that Aristotle recognized that some change occurred in nature.[3] In fact, Darwin had misunderstood Aristotle: Aristotle was quoting a philosopher with whom he disagreed. Aristotle was no proponent of evolution. He was better known for his theory of "The Great Chain of Being," the idea that living organisms could be organized from the simplest to most complex and that no organism could change its place in this ladder of progression.

By the beginning of the nineteenth century, the fixity of the species was a major problem in science. Geologists and paleontologists had discovered fossils of animals and plants but could not find contemporary living examples of these organisms. Scientists such as Georges Cuvier (1769–1832), who worked on classifying the species, grouping similar and related species into families and subfamilies, calculated that some species were extinct. Perhaps it was stretching credulity to argue that all life on Earth remained as it had been six thousand years before.[4]

In the 1830s, the authors of the Bridgewater Treatises tried to counter challenges to the fixity of species idea by arguing that God allowed a "useful and purposeful decline" in nature. The publication costs of these books were paid for by the Reverend Francis Henry

Egerton, the Earl of Bridgewater (1756–1829), and the authors were chosen by Davies Gilbert (1767–1839), the president of the Royal Society (which was the most important scientific society in Britain). The treatises were supposed to use the latest scientific knowledge to demonstrate "the power, wisdom, and goodness of God as manifested in the creation."[5] Recognizing the debate among scientists at the time, each of the eight authors addressed the question of decline or decay in his treatise. Talking about superfluity in the physiology of animals, Thomas Chalmers (1780–1847), professor of divinity at the University of Edinburgh, asked the question: "Now what inference shall we draw from this remarkable law in nature, that there is nothing waste and nothing meaningless in the feelings and faculties wherewith living creatures are endowed?"[6] Commenting on geological decay, William Kirby (1759–1850), a clergyman in the county of Suffolk, asserted

> It is not moreover at all improbable that while its population
> was concentrated, many regions when uninhabited, God so will-
> ing, by diluvial, volcanic, or other action of the elements, might
> be materially altered, new mountain ridges might be elevated,
> mighty disruptions take place and other changes to which there
> could be no witnesses, but which can only be conjectured by
> the features such countries now exhibit.[7]

William Buckland (1784–1856), professor of geology at Oxford University, stated that extinct species provide a "chain of connected evidence, amounting to demonstration, of the continuous Being, and of many of the highest Attributes of the One Living and True God."[8] The comments were cautious and conservative. These authors did not defend the fixity of the species, nor did they abandon the idea that God controls nature.[9]

Darwin was different. He questioned the conclusions of the prominent scientists of his era. More significant, he did not accept the orthodox explanation for the decay and extinction of species: a flood, as described in the Bible, or a similar kind of catastrophe. In *The Origin of Species*, Darwin argued that transmutation had occurred. Over a long period of time, and particularly in reaction to changes in their living conditions, different species had experienced small but significant mutations. The accumulation of these small mutations eventually led to transmutation. And why did the small mutations remain permanent? Darwin argued that the mutations had helped the plant or animal to adapt to its environment better than its competitors for resources such as food. Natural selection, as Darwin called it, was the process by which those plants or animals that adapted better to their environment survived and those that did not adapt became extinct. Natural selection was not obviously visible because it took place over long periods of time, far longer than the life of a human. On the other hand, Darwin drew attention to the ability of pigeon-fanciers to produce different varieties of pigeon or breeders to produce different types of dogs as practical examples of selection at work. In contrast to natural selection, these were cases of artificial selection. In nature, the selection occurred on a grander scale.

Charles Darwin and Evolution

Bentley Glass, one of the editors of the book *Forerunners of Darwin*, calls Darwin's solution "a magnificent synthesis of evidence." Glass argues that Darwin's forerunners had worked out every aspect of the broad details of a theory of evolution but Darwin's solution was, and this is the important point, "a synthesis so compelling in honesty and comprehensiveness that it forced men such as Thomas Huxley to say: How stupid not to have realized that before!"[10] Darwin's solution was so simple that, in the words of the evolutionary biologist Richard Dawkins, "the human brain finds it hard to believe."[11]

Natural selection and evolution are not the same. Natural selection is the mechanism that enables evolution to occur. Because Darwin was more interested in dealing with the question of mutability and whether mutation could occur, he did not concentrate on evolution in *The Origin of Species*. But it was not too difficult to draw out the implication of Darwin's arguments about natural selection. The controversy that erupted after the publication of the book occurred, in part, because a theory of evolution was too easy to deduce from what Darwin wrote. In *The Descent of Man*, Darwin stated the obvious: all animal life has a common ancestor. Animals, for example, were attracted to members of their own species who exhibited characteristics (that is, mutations) that enabled them to survive better: Darwin called this process sexual selection. Life on Earth started with the simplest organisms whose mutations resulted in them becoming more complex organisms. Therefore, humans were not created at a specific time but descended from an aquatic wormlike organism (and ultimately from a single-celled organism, although Darwin did not say this). Natural selection made this descent or evolution possible and that is why *The Origin of Species* is, as the historian Michael Ruse says, "the key work in the whole organic origins controversy."[12]

Charles Darwin was not the only scientist writing about the origin of life in the first half of the nineteenth century. This is important to remember. Darwin was a product of his time. In the year of his birth, 1809, Britain was still fighting France for hegemony in Europe and George III was the king of Britain. Even though there were several prominent French scientists formulating theories of evolution, two factors worked against them: the dominance of opponents such as Georges Cuvier in the French scientific community and the upheavals in France during the French Revolution and the Napoleonic Wars. Georges-Louis Buffon (1707–1778), Jean-Baptiste Lamarck (1744–1829), and Étienne Geoffroy Saint-Hilaire (1772–1844) did not develop their ideas into a full-blown theory of evolution as a result. In the newly independent United States, scientists were more interested in studying indigenous flora and fauna than the larger question of their origins. Their work was, nonetheless, significant. The research of the botanist Asa Gray (1810–1898) was critical in helping Darwin to develop his ideas about the relationships between species spread far apart geographically: Darwin's conclusions became an important component of his theory of evolution.

When Darwin died in 1882, Victoria had been queen of Britain for forty-five years. Darwin died a Victorian. During his lifetime, the British had abolished the slave trade, enacted major reforms of the voting system in 1832 and 1867, and enlarged the empire. It is not surprising then that Darwin quarreled with Captain FitzRoy about slavery while voyaging on the *Beagle* or that Darwin was involved in a government-sponsored expedition to map the coast of South America, or that friends of Darwin such as Thomas Huxley (1825–1895) were able to make a professional career in science in a Britain where democracy and meritocracy enabled the middle class to play a more active role in society.

The professionalization of knowledge, particularly in the natural sciences, was an important development that made it possible for a Charles Darwin to produce a theory of evolution. The coining of the term "scientist" in Britain in the 1830s to describe a person interested in investigating the material world was an example of the new emphasis placed on the study of nature for its own sake. The formation of organizations such as the Geological Society of London (1807) and the Entomological Society of London (1833) was an example of the building of scientific communities to bring together research on specific areas of science.[13] (The Royal Society, founded in 1660, was still the preeminent scientific society in Britain, but its existence did not prevent the growth of more specialized societies.) The increase in the number of professorships at universities in subjects such as geology and the creation of research jobs such as "curator of the botanical gardens" were signs that scientific study was no longer the purview of dedicated aristocratic or clerical amateurs. Darwin was doing his research and writing at the time of these changes. Despite the competition with other scientists who were trying to earn a reputation, Darwin became one of the preeminent scientists of his era.

Darwin, who had an unassuming personality, acknowledged the importance of the research of fellow scientists, professional and amateur. Darwin never boasted about the uniqueness of his ideas. *The Origin of Species* may be one of the most innovative works of science, particularly in the way the argument is put together, but Darwin was careful to give credit to all the breeders, scientists, and philosophers upon whose ideas he built his theory. In fact, *The Origin of Species* is a veritable who's who of scientists in the eighteenth and nineteenth centuries. Some of these men—Darwin does not mention any women—although famous at the time are forgotten except in books dealing with the history of science. The work of men such as John Ray (1627–1702), Antoine Laurent Jussieu (1748–1836), and George Bentham (1800–1884) was critical in the development of a system for classifying plants, but that fact is probably only appreciated among a small group of scientists today.[14] Darwin, on the other hand, recognized and applauded their work. Darwin knew that he was a member of a community of scientists; he knew that this social network made it possible for him to work out his theories.

Darwin's use of the research of fellow scientists is one of the most fascinating features of *The Origin of Species*. Darwin quoted from their work even if they did not support a theory of evolution. Louis Agassiz (1807–1873) and Richard Owen (1804–1892), both outspoken opponents of applying evolutionary theories to organic life, were mentioned a combined twenty-eight times in *The Origin of Species*. What these men had to say about comparative anatomy was important, and Darwin did not ignore it or brush it aside. Knowing something of the ideas and research of Darwin's contemporaries makes it easier to understand *The Origin of Species*. The genius of Darwin was that he took a wide and seemingly unrelated group of ideas and molded them into an overarching thesis: the theory of evolution.

The Impact of Charles Darwin's Theory

But Charles Darwin was not simply a clever scientist: he is a symbol. Darwin's name is associated closely with the theory of evolution just as Christopher Columbus is associated with the discovery of America. Columbus was not the first European to set foot on the continent and there were thriving civilizations in the Americas before he arrived, but these facts have not undermined the significance of the man Columbus. Alfred Russel Wallace (1823–1913), who might have published a theory of evolution first had circumstances been different, is not the symbolic figure associated with the new thinking about biology in the nineteenth century: Darwin is. Darwinism is the term used interchangeably with the theory of evolution; it is inaccurate to think of the two as the same, but everyone is familiar with the term Darwinism. No one ever talks about "Wallaceism."

Charles Darwin may also be the best-known scientist of the last five hundred years. In an informal survey taken among college freshmen in a world history course, Darwin was the only scientist whom everyone recognized, and 96 percent of the group could identify correctly the reason why Darwin is famous. Even more telling, 73 percent could identify correctly the century in which Darwin lived: the next highest figure was 35 percent for Nicolas Copernicus.[15] While the controversies surrounding other important scientists have come and gone—few are willing to argue about the ideas of Galileo or Isaac Newton as people did in the seventeenth and eighteenth centuries—Darwin's name and Darwin's ideas can still provoke heated debate.

Twentieth-century scientists modified Darwin's ideas and theories, but Darwin is still the scientist most associated with the theory of evolution. The present theory of evolution is a combination of Darwin's ideas and those of a nineteenth-century Austrian monk, Gregor Mendel (1822–1884). It is more accurate to call the contemporary understanding of evolution "Neo-Darwinian" rather than "Darwinian" and yet people taking issue with the theory of evolution are likely to think of Darwin as their opponent. Darwin may not have been completely right, but he is still the most important scientist associated with the theory of evolution. A search in the catalog of the British Library reveals that Darwin's writings have been translated into dozens of languages, including Hebrew and Serbo-Croatian. No other scientist, including experts in evolutionary science as well as all other scientific disciplines, has had his or her ideas disseminated so widely.

Why were Darwin's ideas so controversial if so many people read and agreed with them? Put in nineteenth-century language, Darwin demonstrated that the natural world of organisms on Earth was subject to laws in the same way as the inorganic world or the world of planets and stars. The study of biology was just as scientific as the study of chemistry or physics. This conclusion is not particularly shocking today—and this fact suggests that Darwin's ideas are common knowledge, which are accepted by most—but in the nineteenth century, these ideas revolutionized scientific thought and the field of biology. Before Darwin, most people in the West believed that all forms of plant and animal life were created by a single creator who had a specific purpose in mind. There was nothing accidental about this creation: random mutations or variations could not explain the appearance of species. If those same people were asked to explain what they meant by a "purposeful creator," they would have replied that the God of the Bible had created the world as a home for humans or something similar. Darwin presented evidence that contradicted the thesis about the activity of a creator; he argued that life on Earth was the result of the same kinds of laws that cause the attraction of one object in the universe to another. There was no person "running the show." There were simply laws of nature at work.

Darwin's explanation for the origins of life is a naturalistic one (hence, the philosophy associated with it is called naturalism). Instead of relying on forces outside of or beyond human knowledge, Darwin proposed that scientists investigate processes and laws that humans could identify. In *The Origin of Species*, natural selection is the process that enables various forms of life to change from a particular form to a different one. (Darwin called these changes "descent by modification" rather than evolution.) In *The Descent of Man*, sexual selection is the means by which various species preserve characteristics that will enable them and their descendants to survive. In 1905, Hugo de Vries (1848–1935), one of the botanists who discovered the forgotten work of Gregor Mendel on heredity, summarized the importance of Darwin this way:

> Newton convinced his contemporaries that natural laws rule the whole universe. Lyell showed, by his principle of slow and gradual evolution, that natural laws have reigned since the beginning of time. To Darwin we owe the almost universal acceptance of the theory of descent. This doctrine is one of the most noted landmarks in the advance of science. It teaches the validity of natural laws of life in its broadest sense, and crowns the philosophy, founded by Newton and Lyell.[16]

Through his theories, Darwin completely rearranged humanity's place in the universe. While Darwin made no claims to be a philosopher, his theory about the origin of species had major implications for the way in which people in the nineteenth century viewed themselves and the world around them. (One way to think about this change is to imagine Darwin saying, "Let's just imagine life beginning

in a way that humans can explain, let's ignore the supernatural. . . .")
Darwin did not just revolutionize science or the field of biology;
accepting his theory forced most people to make a fundamental shift
in the way they approached religion and philosophy.

Because everyone has wondered where they came from at one
time or another, Darwin's assertion that the origin of species had
nothing to do with a creator god was stunning. Darwin was British
and, in the nineteenth century, the British thought of their country
as Christian. The "creator god" was the God of the Bible: to argue
anything else seemed fanciful at best and heretical at worst. There already was an answer to the origin of species. Accepting Darwin's
theory required a radical rethinking of every Christian idea. (What
should a person make of the text in the book of Genesis where it
says that humans are created in the image of God, for example?[17]
When exactly did that "creating" occur? Or, more problematic, if the
first humans came from a common ancestor, when exactly did they
commit the bad act, the "sin," that resulted in the Christian doctrine
of the fall of humans and the need for someone to rescue them from
the consequences of their bad acts?) Because the whole Western
world thought of itself as Christian in the nineteenth century, from
Australia to the United States to Germany, church leaders and theologians had to confront Darwin's ideas if for no other reason than to
reject them.

Alternatively, not even every scientist who read *The Origin of
Species* accepted Darwin's ideas at once; in fact, some scientists were
quite skeptical and some reviews of the book were very critical.
Charles Lyell (1797–1875), Darwin's friend and mentor, was not
completely convinced about Darwin's theory until a year after *The
Origin of Species* appeared in print. Richard Owen, one of the best-
known scientists in Britain, wrote a harsh review in *The Edinburgh
Review*.[18] Nevertheless, the way Darwin put his argument together,
using a large number of examples from the natural world, opened
new avenues of research for most scientific fields, particularly in
biology. For example, if Darwin's transmutation theory was correct,
then there should be evidence of these changes: one obvious place to
look was the fossils in the Earth. If there were fossils that looked
like, in a phrase Darwin used frequently, the "transitional forms"
between one species and another, this would be proof of the validity
of Darwin's theory. The attempt to prove or disprove Darwin's theory
spurred research in the relationship between fossils; completing the
fossil record, the name scientists give to the list of all fossils and
their various relationships, is a major component of the sciences of
paleontology and paleobiology. "Darwin established so broad a basis

for scientific research," wrote Hugo de Vries in 1904, "that after half a century many problems of major interest remain to be taken up."[19] The research stimulated by Darwin's work is still being done today.

That Darwin's idea about natural selection affected the study of such sciences as zoology, botany, paleontology, and geology is unsurprising. Darwin's theory relied on the passage of long periods of time. Mutations in different species occur slowly, and it might take thousands of years for a particular species to develop into a completely different one. In the same way, it would take thousands of years for the sea to wear away a cliff face and create a new geological phenomenon. But Darwin's work did not just affect research in the natural sciences and the physical sciences. *The Origin of Species* had a profound effect on the social sciences, as subjects such as history and sociology were being called in the late nineteenth century. As a mundane example, before the nineteenth century, historians did not talk about "pre-history"; if all life was created in a short space of time or the Earth was a few thousand years old, such a term would make no sense. After the acceptance of Darwin's theory, this term became part of everyday vocabulary.

What Darwin said about the development of larger numbers of a particular species was critical for stimulating study in anthropology and sociology, both of which began to become distinct disciplines in the nineteenth century. For example, if sexual selection was a critical factor in the survival of a species, social scientists who studied the ways in which members of a group interacted would be able to better understand the process of sexual selection. Researching the rules and laws that were the bases of group interaction became the new discipline of anthropology. Finding out which groups survived the best and what they did to ensure their survival—how they organized themselves—became one of the bases of the new discipline of sociology.

Darwin's ideas affected more than scientific thinking and research. Questions about the origin of life are as much religious and philosophical as they are biological. Because Darwin's ideas are so ingrained in contemporary thought, it is easy to forget the many other areas in which Darwin's theories have had an impact. For example, the idea of evolution is littered throughout contemporary language. If someone talks about an institution "evolving" or an idea as "evolutionary," the other people participating in the conversation will know that the speaker is talking about something that is progressing or moving forward. Darwin was not the first to use such language—he hardly ever used the term "evolution" in his books— but it is largely because of him that the idea of human society or human institutions progressing or evolving into something better has become a central idea in Western thought.

Given the centrality of the idea of evolution in Western (and world) thought, it is surprising to note that Darwin's reputation has suffered since his death. Darwin has been both overrated and underappreciated. On the one hand, there is the tendency to associate all ideas about evolution with Darwin. That is incorrect. For example, Darwin did not discover the significance of genes. The credit for this discovery belongs to men such as Mendel, de Vries, and William Bateson (1861–1926). Darwin's ignorance about chromosomes and genes meant that he was never able to explain logically and convincingly why natural selection worked. The changes in the successive editions of *The Origin of Species* were partly an attempt by Darwin to "fix" this problem. In the end, Darwin seemed to be following the theory of the French naturalist Jean-Baptiste Lamarck who suggested that characteristics of organisms were transferred whole from the parent to the progeny. (For example, the characteristic of "long-neckness" would be transferred from one generation to the next with the latter becoming a giraffe.) Knowledge about chromosomes and genes demonstrated that Lamarck and the later Darwin were wrong. Darwin did not develop the whole theory of evolution.

Conversely, it is equally inaccurate to think of Darwin as one of many scientists who developed the theory of evolution. As Darwin complained in his autobiography, some people thought, and some still do, that Darwin was simply a synthesizer of other scientists' research.[20] But Darwin received one of the highest recognitions for research in geology, the Wollaston Medal of the Geological Society of London, in 1859, seven years before Charles Lyell, one of the greatest geologists of the nineteenth century. The fact that he received the highest recognition from the Royal Society, the Copley Medal, in 1864 for "researches in geology, zoology, and botanical physiology" proves that Darwin was considered an important scientist in his own right.[21] When contemporary opponents of evolution, such as creationists and supporters of Intelligent Design, complain about the impact of Darwin, they are targeting the right person. Darwin's theory is the preeminent idea in the theory of evolution.

In contrast to the treatment of scientists such as Galileo, many of Darwin's contemporaries appreciated the importance and impact of his ideas. When Darwin died in 1882, he was immediately recognized as one of the great minds of his and any other generation. Darwin was buried in Westminster Abbey, one of the two most important churches in Britain, next to the memorial to Sir Isaac Newton. In Italy, students at the University of Naples held a meeting in Darwin's honor in May, the month after he died. In Germany, a wax figure of Darwin was placed in the Berlin Panopticon, the famous German waxworks. Darwin was a national and international figure.

To study the life of Darwin then is to study one of the great figures of science and of the Modern Age. "Charles Darwin is one of the greatest among the creators of modern science," according to Theodosius Dobzhansky (1900–1975), the American geneticist and evolutionary biologist.[22] In its historical context, *The Origin of Species* is not only the explanation of a scientific theory, it is one of the bases of modern science. Darwin's ideas represent a key component of scientific thought specifically, and Western thought in general. It is no wonder that the historian John Barrow called *The Origin of Species* "a pioneering work."[23]

Notes

1. The publisher John Murray suggested changing the title of the sixth English edition, which was published in 1872, to *The Origin of Species by Means of Natural Selection, or the Preservation of Favoured Races in the Struggle for Life*. The binding of the fifth English edition already had the shortened title.

2. See Philip H. Wicksteed and Francis M. Cornford, trans., *The Physics* (Cambridge, MA: Harvard University Press, 1957), I: 171. Aristotle wrote *The Physics* in B.C.E. 350.

3. Charles Darwin, *On the Origin of Species by Means of Natural Selection, or the Preservation of Favoured Races in the Struggle for Life*, 4th edition (London: John Murray, 1866), xiii [Penguin Classics, 53–54].

4. In Europe and North America, most people believed that the Earth and life on it was approximately six thousand years old. The first four thousand years before the Christian or Common Era were calculated by adding the genealogy lists found in the Bible. See Genesis 11:10–26, 1 Chronicles 1:1–8:39, and Matthew 1:1–17.

5. This phrase was used in the title or the preface of each book.

6. Thomas Chalmers, *On the Power, Wisdom and Goodness of God as Manifested in the Adaptation of External Nature to the Moral and Intellectual Constitution of Man* (London: William Pickering, 1833), II: 128.

7. William Kirby, *On the Power, Wisdom and Goodness of God as Manifested in the Creation of Animals and in their History, Habits and Instincts* (London: William Pickering, 1835), I: 388–389.

8. William Buckland, *Geology and Mineralogy Considered with Reference to Natural Theology* (London: William Pickering, 1837), I: viii.

9. The elimination of a discussion of natural theology or God-inspired design from most contemporary scientific books is one example of the impact *The Origin of Species* had on science.

10. Bentley Glass, Owsei Temkin, William L. Straus, Jr., eds., *Forerunners of Darwin, 1745–1859* (Baltimore: Johns Hopkins University Press, 1959), vi.

11. Richard Dawkins, *The Blind Watchmaker* (New York: W. W. Norton, 1996), xv. Dawkins is the Charles Simonyi Professor of the Public Understanding of Science at Oxford University.

12. Michael Ruse, *The Darwinian Revolution* (Chicago: University of Chicago Press, 1979), xii.

13. These societies are now known as the Geological Society and the Royal Entomological Society.

14. The Ray Society was founded in 1844 in honor of John Ray: it publishes research in the natural sciences (see www.jri.org.uk/ray/ray_society.htm). Jussieu has a metro station in Paris named after him: it is near the French museum of natural history, which Jussieu helped to found.

15. Survey taken by author. In the last fifty years, regular debate and controversy about human origins—particularly in the United States—has kept Darwin's name in the public consciousness.

16. Hugo de Vries, *Species and Varieties: Their Origin by Mutation*, ed. Daniel Trembly MacDougal (London: Kegan Paul, Trench, Trübner and Co., Ltd., 1905), 1.

17. Genesis 1:26–27.

18. *Edinburgh Review* 111 (April 1860): 487–532. As with all reviews in the journal at that time, the author's name was not given. After the review appeared, it became common knowledge that Owen was the author.

19. De Vries, *Species and Varieties*, 1.

20. See Francis Darwin, ed., *The Life and Letters of Charles Darwin, Including an Autobiographical Chapter* (London: John Murray, 1887), I: 87–88, 103–104.

21. See "Copley Archive Winners 1899–1800," Royal Society, www.royalsoc.ac.uk/page.asp?id=1743 (accessed 3 November 2005).

22. In Paul H. Barrett, ed., Foreword to *The Collected Papers of Charles Darwin* (Chicago: University of Chicago Press, 1977), I: xi.

23. "Editor's Introduction," *The Origin of Species* [Penguin Classics], 14.

CHAPTER 2

THE LIFE OF CHARLES DARWIN

The Ordinary and Extraordinary Life of Charles Darwin

Charles Robert Darwin was born on 12 February 1809 in Shrewsbury, an ancient market town near the Welsh border in the county of Shropshire, the most westerly county in the West Midlands. Before Darwin, the town's most famous resident was Robert Clive, the man who led the British conquest of India in the eighteenth century. In the first twenty years of the nineteenth century, the town had a population of approximately 16,000. Shrewsbury, although it had a comparatively small population, was the county town of Shropshire, the most rural of the English counties. The rural character of the county and Shrewsbury's importance were two of the reasons why Darwin's parents chose to live there. By the time Darwin was born, Darwin's father had a flourishing medical practice that covered the town and the surrounding area. Darwin's interest in and love of nature can be traced to the surroundings of his early childhood.

These simple facts about Darwin's life are well known. In fact, so much is known about Darwin's life that it is easy for anyone reading his life story for the first time to be overwhelmed and underwhelmed. Darwin was an extraordinary man and a great scientist. He was the author of the best-known theory in biology and he did all of this without completing a university degree or any extended formal training in science. And yet there is much about Darwin that was very ordinary; in fact, some aspects of Darwin's life are so ordinary as to be banal. He lived for many years in a small village outside London; compared with the hustle and bustle of the city, he lived in the middle of nowhere. He worried about the health of his children and grandchildren. He enjoyed listening to his wife read novels aloud. He acquired a penchant for playing billiards. Darwin was very much a common man.

Any biographer of Darwin faces the difficulty of capturing the greatness and the ordinariness of his life. His biographers know, for example, what Darwin was reading on certain days of his life because he kept a log. They know how Darwin felt about his family, his friends, his work, and the criticisms of his theories because he wrote hundreds of letters. They know what Darwin was writing and when because he kept a log of that, too. They know when Darwin was or felt too ill to work because he also kept track of his health, sometimes in minute detail, in his diary. They even know how much Darwin loved his favorite dogs, Bob and Polly, because he wrote about it in two of his books, *The Descent of Man* and *The Expression of the Emotions in Man and Animals.*[1] Biographers of Darwin have a great deal of material at their disposal.

One reason why his biographers know so much about Darwin is due to Darwin himself. Darwin wrote a short autobiography for his wife and children in 1876, which he added to in 1881. Then there are his more than twenty major books. Add to these more than a hundred articles and the numerous letters he wrote and received. This is an impressive corpus from which biographers can find plenty of details about Darwin's personal life and his scientific thought.

While he was alive, feature articles written about his life and work appeared in popular journals and magazines, such as *Contemporary Review, Edinburgh Review, Punch*, and *Vanity Fair*; soon after his death, Darwin's relations starting writing about him as well. Francis Darwin, who had worked with his father on his research into the movement of plants in the 1870s, became the first major editor of Darwin's works. The first published copy of Darwin's autobiography appeared in the three-volume *The Life and Letters of Charles Darwin, Including an Autobiographical Chapter* (1887).

Nora Barlow (1885–1989), Darwin's granddaughter, continued the family tradition. Most notably, she put back the material taken out by her uncle in the first autobiography; the "new" book was published in 1958 with the title *The Autobiography of Charles Darwin, 1809–1882*. Other books such as *Charles Darwin and the Voyage of the Beagle* (1945) and *Darwin and Henslow: The Growth of an Idea. Letters, 1831–1860* (1958) expanded the knowledge of the wider scientific community in which Darwin operated.

And then there are the biographies of Darwin, short and long, written by a wide range of people from journalists to historians of science. Whether it is Sir Gavin de Beer's analysis of Darwin's life as a man of science or Adrian Desmond and James Moore's detailed picture of Darwin as a man of the nineteenth century or Janet Browne's evocation of sailing as a metaphor for his life, there is no shortage of biographies of Darwin.[2] Add to these biographies the numerous books written for the anniversaries of Darwin's birth and death, and the anniversary of the publication of *The Origin of Species*, and the material becomes mountainous, literally.

Because Darwin is a symbol, almost shorthand, for the theory of evolution, there is almost no end to the number of books written about his ideas, the reasons why he wrote them, and why his theories are good or bad (both in a scientific and moral sense). This kind of writing started while Darwin was alive and has proliferated since his death. The books dealing with "Darwin" and "evolution" run into the thousands—and that is just in the English language.[3]

Perhaps it is possible to limit a description of Darwin's life to his scientific work, a person new to his story might say. This is impossible. Ignoring the fact that Darwin's theory of descent by modification, the origin of species, is such a big idea that Darwin himself worked on it for most of his life, the man and the scientist cannot be separated. Darwin was an amateur scientist in the sense that he did not teach at a university or work for a scientific institution: his house and garden were his laboratory. His home life was his scientific life and vice versa. Furthermore, Darwin's writing was definitely a reflection of the character of the man. His tentativeness and unwillingness to be combative, the large amount of evidence he used to support his ideas, the numerous authorities he quoted, and the wide-ranging nature of his syntheses are as much descriptions of Darwin's personality as his work as a scientist. It is a difficult task to encapsulate such a life and such a body of work.

The Family Background of Charles Darwin

What should a first-time reader know about Darwin? Apart from the obvious details such as when and where he was born, the first significant detail someone new to his story should know is that the Darwin family and the Darwin name were famous before Charles Darwin was born. Robert Waring Darwin (1766–1848), Darwin's father, had married Susannah (1765–1817), the daughter of Josiah Wedgwood, the famous pottery magnate, in 1796. Darwin had four sisters and one brother: Marianne (1798–1858), Caroline (1800–1888), Susan (1803–1866), Erasmus (1804–1881), and Catherine (1810–1866). Darwin was the fifth child of the six. Because the family was wealthy, the Darwins belonged to the Shropshire gentry. Darwin grew up in a family whose wealth enabled him to become a gentleman, a man of means who did not need a career to support himself or his future family.

Apart from his wealth, Darwin was fortunate in another way: he had distinguished recent ancestors on both sides of his family. As well as a famous grandfather on his mother's side, Josiah Wedgwood (1730–1795), Darwin's paternal grandfather was Erasmus Darwin (1731–1802), the renowned doctor, scientist, poet, and entrepreneur. Erasmus Darwin and Josiah Wedgwood also distinguished themselves as leading figures in the British Industrial Revolution of the eighteenth century. Together with men such as James Watt (1736–1819); Matthew Boulton (1728–1809), the manufacturer who build Watt's steam engine; John Whitehurst (1713–1788), the pioneering geologist; and Joseph Priestley (1733–1804), the famous chemist, they formed a club called the Lunar Society of Birmingham. The club was partly social and partly business. The members, who were all close friends, held their meetings in the 1770s near the date of the full moon so that, as the story goes, they could stagger home drunk without hurting themselves. The Lunaticks, the nickname they gave themselves, discussed new inventions, particularly technological ones such as Josiah Wedgwood's pyrometer (which measured high temperatures), and considered ways to promote these technological innovations so that they could become viable business ventures. Even before he became famous as the author of *The Origin of Species*, Darwin had a high standard to emulate.

When Darwin was sixteen, he seemed to have little direction and drive in his life. His father made the following caustic comment about him: "You care for nothing but shooting, dogs, and rat-catching and you will be a disgrace to yourself and all your family."[4] The comment is easier to understand if Darwin's family background is taken into account. Robert Darwin had continued the family tradition of brilliance: he became a fellow of Royal Society at the age of twenty-two and, like his father, had a well-respected medical practice. The son of Robert Darwin was privileged in ways that meant much was expected of him.

From Early Childhood to Cambridge University

Being privileged provides no insurance against disappointment or tragedy. This was true of Darwin's childhood (as well as his adult life). His mother died when Darwin was eight years old: it is the first specific event that Darwin recorded in his autobiography. Darwin claimed to have little recollection of her—not a surprise given how young he was—but the event probably marked a coming of age for Darwin. As his father was kept busy by his practice, his older sisters became surrogate parents. Darwin learnt self-sufficiency at an early age. He also become fond of activities that did not require the company of others: long, solitary walks; fishing; and collecting eggs, shells, and minerals. To say Darwin was destined to be a naturalist is putting too much emphasis on his childhood habits, but his interest in natural history began at an early age.

At the age of nine, Darwin became a student at Shrewsbury School. Although the school was less than two miles from The Mount, his home, Darwin was a boarding student. He could run home from school, and frequently did, but, as was his father and mother's original plan, he was forced to live at the school. This was unfortunate for Darwin because the main subjects taught at the school were the classics, Latin and Greek language and culture. These subjects supposedly turned boys into gentlemen, but Darwin was uninterested in the classics. "Nothing could have been worse for the development of my mind," was Darwin's assessment of his school days.[5] The experiments he and his brother did in their small chemistry laboratory at the back of their house were far more interesting. When Darwin left Shrewsbury School in 1825, the most that could be said of his abilities was "ordinary."[6]

His father recognized that Darwin needed more purpose in his life and took him out of school two years early. Darwin's elder brother Erasmus was going to Edinburgh University to complete his studies in medicine: Robert Darwin decided that Charles ought to accompany his brother. Their father's plan was for Charles to attend the medical lectures with his brother and when Charles was old enough he too could take the appropriate examinations for his degree.

The plan seemed sensible enough. In the summer before he went to Edinburgh, Darwin had taken care of about twelve of his father's patients. He enjoyed the work and his father thought Darwin would make a successful physician. Counterbalancing this was the fact that Robert Darwin was doing exactly the same as his father Erasmus Darwin. The grandfather forced the father to become a doctor and the father intended to do the same for the son. Robert Darwin submitted, grudgingly, to his father's authority: Charles Darwin, who soon realized that his father would provide financial support sufficient to last his whole life, was less subservient. Darwin found the lectures at Edinburgh "intolerably dull" and the sight of human blood made him physically sick.[7] He fled from one particularly stomach-churning operation on a child—the regular use of anesthetics did not occur until the 1850s—and his efforts at studying were dilatory at best. Darwin felt no call or inclination to become a doctor when he actually had to study medicine.

His time at Edinburgh University was not a complete waste. In his first year, he went regularly on long Sunday walks with his brother Erasmus. Darwin acquired the habit of picking up and collecting marine life such as sea slugs. John Edmonstone, a freed black slave living in Edinburgh, taught him how to stuff and mount birds. He joined the Plinian Society, a group of students who met regularly to discuss papers on natural history. He took a course in geology and zoology from Robert Jameson (1774–1854), professor of natural history at the university, in which he learned the basics of annotating rock strata and had free access to the fourth largest natural history museum in Europe. He also befriended Robert Grant (1793–1874), a physician who had abandoned medicine so that he could study marine life and who later became professor of zoology at London University. Darwin accompanied Grant on field trips to the Firth of Forth, and Grant encouraged Darwin to study marine invertebrates.

Darwin was studying natural history. Although he went on the *Beagle* voyage around the world at the seemingly tender age of twenty-three, by his twentieth birthday, Darwin was learning both the skills of a naturalist and some of the controversial ideas debated by scientists of the time.

These developments did not please Robert Darwin. The news of Darwin's lack of interest in medicine, obtained through Darwin's confessions in letters to his sisters, was bad enough, but Darwin's trips around the countryside to see various friends during the summer of 1827 and his obsession with shooting suggested to Robert Darwin that his son would become a dilettante—a wealthy son squandering his father's money on trivial pursuits. Robert Darwin intervened in his son's life again: Charles Darwin would go to Cambridge University and study to become a clergyman.

The Cambridge Years, 1827–1831

If Robert Darwin believed that his son would settle into a less dissolute life at Cambridge, he was mistaken. Looking back on his years at the university, Darwin claimed that "my time was wasted, as far as the academical studies were concerned, as completely as at Edinburgh and at school." Darwin may have been too hard on himself—he was in his early twenties and he was not the first nor the last person to find extracurricular activities more interesting than studying for his degree—but he thought that his time at Cambridge was "worse than wasted."[8] There is no doubt that his father was exasperated by the fact that Darwin continued his shooting, hunting, and riding in the countryside while at Cambridge. Even worse, Darwin also added drinking, "jolly singing," and playing cards to his leisure activities.[9]

Although Darwin was not an outstanding student at Cambridge, he was beginning to apply himself to studying more seriously than before. He worked with a private tutor in Shrewsbury between October and December 1827 to bring his Greek up to the standard necessary for Cambridge. Although he found the lectures boring and generally only attended the compulsory ones, he learned the classics and mathematics well enough to pass the necessary examinations comfortably. And he read thoroughly *A View of the Evidences of Christianity* and *The Principles of Moral and Political Philosophy* by the British theologian William Paley (1743–1805). A knowledge of both books was required to pass the degree examination: Darwin knew the arguments in *Evidences of Christianity* so well that he could write and explain every one in the book. Darwin placed tenth out of 178 students who did not take an honors degree, the more difficult course of study: not impressive but creditable nonetheless.

The irony of Darwin's stay at Cambridge was his career goal. He was studying to become a clergyman. Darwin was not pious. His mother and sisters were, but Darwin was more like his father and grandfather in religious temperament: there were too many problems with religion in general and Christianity in particular to take either too seriously. Darwin persuaded himself that he should accept the doctrines of the Church of England fully and did not think too deeply about the literal truth of the Bible or the foundational premises of Paley's arguments.

In the end, neither Darwin's partying, nor his supposed lack of application to his studies, nor the strength of his religious convictions mattered. At Cambridge, Darwin took the first steps toward becoming a naturalist; in today's language, a practicing scientist. He began collecting beetles. In fact, he became so obsessed with this that, as Darwin recounted,

> one day, on tearing off some old bark, I saw two rare beetles and seized one in each hand; then I saw a third and new kind, which I could not bear to lose, so that I popped the one which I held in my right hand into my mouth. Alas it ejected some

intensely acrid fluid, which burnt my tongue so that I was forced to spit the beetle out, which was lost, as well as the third one.[10]

Knowing his obsession well, one of his friends at Cambridge, Albert Way (1805–1874), drew a cartoon of Darwin riding a large beetle and swinging a net like a deranged cowboy.[11] But there was a method to Darwin's madness. He became skilled enough at recognizing new species of beetle that some of his finds were recognized in *Illustrations of British Entomology*, a well-known guidebook at that time.[12]

Darwin, through introductions made by his cousin William Darwin Fox (1805–1880), made acquaintances with several of the science professors at Cambridge. Two men in particular had a profound effect on the direction of Darwin's life: John Stevens Henslow (1796–1861), a botanist and geologist, and Adam Sedgwick (1785–1873), a geologist. Darwin and Henslow became friends even though Darwin was a student. Darwin was a frequent dinner guest at Henslow's home and regularly accompanied Henslow on walks in the countryside, so much so that professors called him "the man who walks with Henslow."[13] It was Henslow who encouraged Darwin to turn his interest in science into serious study. He suggested that Darwin start studying geology. Darwin followed Henslow's advice and, as part of his education, went with Sedgwick in August 1831 on a tour of North Wales to examine the rocks of the area. Under Sedgwick's guidance, Darwin learned the basics of the discipline: Darwin became knowledgeable enough to be the ship's geologist during the voyage of the *Beagle*.

It was at Cambridge that Darwin realized what he wanted to do with his life. In his last year at the university, he read *Personal Narrative of Travels to the Equinoctial Regions of the New Continent, During the Years 1799–1804* by the German naturalist and explorer Alexander von Humboldt (1769–1859) and *A Preliminary Discourse on the Study of Natural Philosophy* by the English astronomer Sir John Herschel (1792–1871). This "stirred up in me a burning zeal to add even the most humble contribution to the noble structure of Natural Science," wrote Darwin.[14] Darwin wanted to become a scientist. All he had to do was break the news to his father.

The Voyage of HMS *Beagle*

Waiting for Darwin when he returned home from Wales was the letter that changed his life. Henslow had written,

I have been asked by Peacock [a professor of astronomy at Cam-
bridge] ... to recommend him a naturalist as companion to Capt
Fitzroy, employed by Government to survey the S. extremity of
America. I have stated that I consider you to be the best qualified person I know of who is likely to undertake such a
situation....[15]

Peacock had hoped that Leonard Jenyns (1800–1893), Henslow's
brother-in-law, could go, but Jenyns was unavailable.[16] Henslow
thought Darwin was "amply qualified" because of his passion for collecting and his observational skills, particularly at noticing new phenomena.[17] Darwin, who had been planning a scientific expedition to
the Canary Islands, even learning Spanish (but not telling his father),
was excited by the offer. His father was not impressed.

Robert Darwin initially believed that the proposed voyage on
the *Beagle* was another attempt by his son to avoid adult responsibilities. How could a future clergyman become involved in such a "wild
scheme" and "useless undertaking"?[18] Or, even worse, perhaps the
Admiralty, the arm of the government that ran the Navy, had organized the expedition poorly and intended to send out an unseaworthy
vessel—hence the offer to an unknown naturalist.[19]

Here again Darwin showed the difference between his and his
father's personality. Rather than acquiescing to his father's wishes, as
Robert Darwin had done in becoming a doctor, Charles Darwin
attempted to circumvent his father. Robert Darwin had left a small
opening for his son: he would give his permission if Charles could
find a sensible person who thought the voyage was a good idea.
Charles Darwin sought the help of his favorite uncle, Josiah Wedgwood (1769–1843). Wedgwood wrote to Robert Darwin on 31
August refuting his cousin's objections to the voyage point by point.
Wedgwood also drove to Shrewsbury so that father and uncle could
discuss the voyage. After talking to his cousin, Robert Darwin "con-
sented in the kindest manner," according to Darwin.[20] Darwin con-
soled his father by pointing out that he would have to be extremely
clever to overspend his allowance while on the *Beagle* to which
Robert Darwin replied, "But they tell me you are very clever."[21]

Everything was not settled yet. FitzRoy interviewed Darwin to
see whether he was suitable—whatever Darwin's scientific qualifica-
tions, he and FitzRoy were going to share a cabin for nearly five
years. (Later Darwin found out that FitzRoy had nearly rejected him
because FitzRoy did not like the shape of Darwin's nose.) And Robert Darwin had to pay the passage, the fare: a crew member on a
ship like the *Beagle* had to work (under very harsh conditions) or
pay in order to avoid the work and naval discipline. FitzRoy was not

offering a free ride. Darwin's statement in the introduction to *The Zoology of the Voyage of the H.M.S. Beagle* that "in consequence of Captain FitzRoy having expressed a desire that some scientific person should be on board, and having offered to give up part of his accommodations, I volunteered my services" downplays the machinations that occurred.[22] In fact, there was an element of farce about the events in Darwin's life between August and December 1831. And in the first few days of the voyage, Darwin discovered that the boat's motion made him violently seasick, adding a further element of tragi-comedy.

When the *Beagle* set sail on 27 December, according to one of Darwin's biographers, "a new chapter in the history of science began."[23] This is true. Darwin wrote in his autobiography that "the voyage of the *Beagle* has been by far the most important event in my life, and determined my whole career."[24] On 5 September, when Darwin had his father's permission and was soon to meet FitzRoy, he wrote to Henslow that "*Gloria in excelsis* is the most moderate beginning I can think of."[25] Darwin was excited about his upcoming adventure, and the research he did in the years between 1831 and 1836 established him in his career as a scientist and led to the writing of one of the most important books in the history of science. (All talk about Darwin becoming a clergyman was quietly dropped by 1836.) But the voyage of the *Beagle* must be placed in a larger historical context: it was not simply Darwin's voyage.

The nineteenth century was the high point of the British Empire, but this dominance was built on information and a calculated use of resources. In South America, for example, there were many opportunities for trade as new governments formed that had liberated themselves from Spain and Portugal between 1790 and 1830. But British businessmen needed to know exactly what was in South America before investing money there. The Royal Navy sent ships to survey the area: mapping the shoreline, recording the weather conditions, and looking for good places for ports and refueling stations. This was the *Beagle* crew's task. In addition to rechecking the survey information for Patagonia, modern-day Argentina, and Chile, FitzRoy and his crew would circumnavigate the world, giving them the opportunity for further exploration in places such as Australia.

But an empire is built on more than safe harbors. Knowing what was available for trade was critical to British success in the nineteenth century. And this is why naturalists were necessary additions to the British explorations of the time. Discovering and mapping new natural resources was as important as finding good ports and mapping shorelines. FitzRoy wanted a naturalist to share his quarters to counteract the likelihood of depression on a long voyage—the previous captain of the *Beagle*, Pringle Stokes, shot himself in August 1828 during the ship's previous voyage—and, given his interest in science, FitzRoy thought a naturalist would be stimulating company. In fact, several of FitzRoy's crew were bona fide naturalists. Initially, Darwin was one naturalist among many on the ship. Darwin became the premier naturalist of the *Beagle* because he proved himself the best at doing what Britain needed: collecting and identifying important and new specimens of plant and animal life.[26]

The voyage of the *Beagle* is significant because, during it, Darwin began to think about some of the important and unanswered questions in science. Darwin's voyaging was not unique: this was the era of David Livingstone (1813–1873), the great Scottish explorer and missionary who discovered Victoria Falls and opposed the slave trade in Africa. A naturalist making his name by participating in a voyage to South America or Australasia was also not uncommon. Darwin had been inspired by the adventures of Alexander von Humboldt and Aimé Bonpland (1773–1858), the French botanist, in South America.

Following Henslow's suggestion, Darwin took a copy of the first volume of Charles Lyell's *Principles of Geology*: the early entries in the diary he kept while on the voyage show that Darwin was thinking like a geologist.[27] Darwin did not join the *Beagle* because he intended to solve the problem of the origin of species.

But the miles covered and the places visited by the *Beagle* and her crew provided an excellent opportunity for a naturalist aspiring to fame, as Darwin was. The voyage from England to Cape Verde, off the West African coast, and the east coast of South America occupied most of 1832. Exploring Patagonia, the Falkland Islands, and Tierra del Fuego took all of 1833. In 1834, the crew explored Lower Patagonia, the Straits of Magellan, the Falkland Islands, again, and the west coast of South America. The crew continued on the Pacific Ocean side of South America during 1835 and sailed to the Galapagos Islands in September, where they stayed for just over a month; they traveled to Tahiti by November and the North Island of New Zealand by the end of December. They arrived in Sydney, Australia, in January 1836 and in the next eight months sailed to Hobart, Tasmania (February), King George Sound, South Australia (March), the Keeling Islands in the Indian Ocean (April), the islands of Mauritius and Réunion (April/May), the Cape of Good Hope at the southern tip of Africa (May), the islands of St. Helena and Ascension in the mid-Atlantic (July), the coast of Brazil and Cape Verde (August), the

Azores, the mid-Atlantic off the coast of Portugal (September), and back to Falmouth, England, on 2 October. Most of the voyage was spent in and around South America, forty-two out of fifty-seven months; nonetheless, Darwin saw a significant portion of the world. He returned to England a changed man. "Why, the shape of his head is quite altered," exclaimed his father when he first saw Darwin, adding a phrenological explanation to the maturity he perceived.[28]

The change in Darwin was not difficult to explain. During the voyage, he had become a scientist. Although Darwin did not recognize it at the time, this process began when he started a daily journal. At first he was self-conscious about putting his observations and reflections on paper, but he found that writing in the journal helped him to make sense of each day's events: he started a habit that he would continue for the rest of his life. One day he read parts of the journal to FitzRoy who was impressed by the detail of Darwin's observations. FitzRoy suggested that the journal was worth publishing and the compliment made Darwin even more careful about observing his surroundings and recording what he encountered. The edited version of the journal was published as *Journal of Researches into the Geology and Natural History of the Various Countries Visited by the H.M.S. Beagle* (1839). And Darwin's observations of the geology of the places he visited were published in three books: *The Structure and Distribution of Coral Reefs* (1842), *Geological Observations on the Volcanic Islands, Visited During the Voyage of H.M.S. Beagle, together with some Brief Notices on the Geology of Australia and the Cape of Good Hope* (1844), and *Geological Observations on South America* (1846). The books formed three parts of a series Darwin titled "The Geology of the Voyage of the *Beagle*."

Darwin also wrote a large number of letters. He wrote to his father, sisters, and cousins, the Wedgwoods, who found his adventures fascinating. He wrote to Henslow, who read some of the letters to the Philosophical Society of Cambridge on 16 November 1835 and arranged to have them printed so that other members of the Society could read them. He also wrote to naturalists such as Thomas Campbell Eyton (1809–1880) and Frederick William Hope (1797–1862). By the time Darwin returned home, his adventures were already well known: his family, former professors, and interested naturalists had seen to this.

Most important, Darwin observed, collected, and analyzed. At Punta Alta, in Argentina, Darwin discovered seven sets of fossil bones, including the head and a tooth of two Megatherium, a giant mammal related to present-day armadillos. This discovery and other fossil bones that Darwin sent back to England "excited considerable attention amongst palæontologists," noted Darwin later.[29] In the Galapagos Islands, he found (and collected specimens of) twenty-six different species of land birds: all except one could only be found in the Galapagos. There were also the "curious finches" of the Galapagos. The ornithologist John Gould (1804–1881) later identified thirteen different species and four new subgenera from the specimens.[30] In places like Tahiti, Darwin found "useful wild plants" such as sugar cane, arum, and yam: specimens of these were sent back to England for analysis.[31]

The more he observed and collected, the more Darwin reflected on the significance of his observations and his specimens. Why were some animals and plants found in one location but not in another, even though the distance between the two locations was not large? Why were the same types of animals and plants found in the same latitude but in completely different countries? Why were some varieties of species unique to islands separated by long distances from any continent? Darwin wrote his thoughts on biodiversity and biogeography to friends such as Henslow. His reflections and comments ranged so widely—from the formation of coral reefs to the ways in which seeds could be transported over the Pacific Ocean—that many naturalists were eagerly awaiting the publication of Darwin's findings from the voyage. Voyaging on the *Beagle* turned Darwin's life toward a career in science. Writing the papers, articles, and books based on his research during the five-year voyage made Darwin famous. Charles Darwin was a well-known scientist fifteen years before *The Origin of Species* was published.

From the Voyage of the *Beagle* to *The Origin of Species*

The popular myth is that Darwin had a "eureka moment" about the theory of evolution while observing the unique species on the Galapagos Islands: this was not the case. However, it is true that Darwin's observations in the Galapagos and in the other countries he visited had a profound effect on his thinking. Darwin began to think about the relationships among the facts he was accumulating. Was there a larger thesis that would accommodate all of the disparate pieces of information he had gathered? For example, was there a connection between the formation of mountain ranges and the locations of particular species? In July 1837, less than nine months after landing at Falmouth, Darwin began writing down his thoughts on the relationship and origins of species in a notebook.

Although Darwin is best remembered for *The Origin of Species,* the work on "Species," as Darwin called it in his diary, was not his sole occupation after 1836. To take advantage of his newly won fame, Darwin had to socialize. In March 1837, he rented an apartment on Great Marlborough Street, in the center of London, and "went a little into society."[32] He attended dinner parties and met famous men of the day such as the writer and historian Thomas Carlyle (1795–1881). He even met his idol Alexander von Humboldt while having breakfast with the eminent Scottish geologist Sir Roderick Murchison (1792–1871): because von Humboldt was the best-known scientist-explorer of the day, this meeting was the highlight of this period. He read papers at the meetings of the Geological and Zoological societies. And he met and befriended Charles Lyell, a friendship that would continue until Lyell's death in 1875.

Equally important to Darwin, he married Emma Wedgwood, his cousin. He had always enjoyed the company of the Wedgwoods: Josiah Wedgwood was his favorite uncle; Frances and Emma were his favorite female cousins; and Maer Hall, where the Wedgwoods lived, was a second home to him. Emma and Charles found that they were both interested in being more than just companions and, to the delight of both families, the couple married on 29 January 1839.

The domestication of Darwin was complete. In less than a decade, he had changed from Cambridge reveler to a family man. The Darwins' first child, William, was born in 1839 and they had nine more children. Seven of the ten children survived into adulthood: William (1839–1914), Henrietta (1843–1927), George (1845–1912), Elizabeth (1847–1926), Francis (1848–1925), Leonard (1850–1943), and Horace (1851–1943). George and Francis became distinguished scientists themselves.

A wife (and children) meant responsibilities that Darwin was happy to accept. The Darwins moved to a house on Upper Gower Street, London, and, in September 1842, to a sprawling house in the village of Downe in Kent. Darwin learned to live on a budget and became an expert at it. Darwin also became concerned about the state of his family. He worried as much about his children's health as he did about his scientific work. The death of his daughter Anne, affectionately known as Annie, in 1851, was one of the most traumatic events of his life.

His marriage, the move to the countryside, and the friends he made are all reminders of the ordinariness of Darwin. It was Darwin who wrote, when thinking about his future,

> My God, it is intolerable to think of spending ones whole life,
> like a neuter bee, working, working & nothing after all.—No,

no won't do.– Imagine living all one's day solitarily in smoky dirty London house.—Only picture to yourself a nice soft wife on a sofa with good fire, & books & music perhaps—Compare this vision with the dingy reality of Grt. Marlbro St. Marry–Mary–Marry Q.E.D.[33]

Darwin's ordinariness was also manifested in his suffering from a malady typical of many famous Victorians: unexplained sickness. Like Thomas Carlyle, Herbert Spencer (1820–1903), who coined the term "survival of the fittest," and Florence Nightingale (1820–1910), the prominent reformer of the nursing profession, Darwin was sick a great deal. In his autobiography, phrases like "I lost time because of illness" or "my health was not strong" appear regularly. The phrases even appear at the beginning of some his books, including *The Origin of Species.*[34]

These bouts of sickness were not minor incidents. Violent vomiting attacks lasted for hours. Wrenching stomach aches with fits of flatulence made Darwin too embarrassed to leave his house. Incessant coughing persisted through the night. Intense tiredness left him unable to do anything else but lie down. Fevers could not be quelled. These episodes necessitated drastic action and, following another habit common among famous, sick Victorians, Darwin went to a health spa. These visits were significant. For example, Darwin was resting at a hydropathic institution near Ilkley, Yorkshire, when the first edition of *The Origin of Species* was published. Also of significance, and to Darwin's greater regret, he was unable to attend his father's funeral in November 1848 because he was too unwell. Any excessive "excitement," as Darwin called it, was likely to make him violently ill.

Darwin's contemporaries, his biographers, and numerous commentators have tried to explain why Darwin was ill so often after he returned from the *Beagle* voyage. According to his son Francis, Darwin once attributed his poor health after 1836 to a severe fever he contracted in September 1834 while in Chile.[35] Some commentators have suggested Darwin's illnesses were caused by repressed guilt about the ideas in *The Origin of Species*. His illnesses were partly psychosomatic, as Darwin himself acknowledged, but unlikely to be related solely to his feelings about his radical theory of evolution or the reaction to it: he was in poor health in 1837 before he had begun to formulate a theory to explain his various findings about the diversity of species. Perhaps the bite of the Benchuca beetle (*Triatoma infestans*), "the great black bug of the Pampas," as Darwin referred to it, caused his illnesses.[36] People with Chagas' disease, the result of infection by the protozoan *Trypanosoma cruzi*, which the Benchuca frequently carries, manifest some of the symptoms Darwin had.[37] In 1903, George M. Gould, a doctor, even suggested Darwin's illnesses were caused by eye strain.[38]

Whatever the cause of Darwin's illnesses, the important fact is that they prevented him from working. Darwin's literary output is impressive. It is even more impressive when put in the context of his frequent bouts of sickness.

Darwin continued to work hard despite his poor health. In 1846, after he finished editing the volumes on the geology and zoology of the *Beagle*, Darwin began writing about barnacles (Cirripedia). After eight years of research, Darwin published two large books on living barnacles and two small books on extinct barnacles. By 1855, Darwin was a world authority on barnacles. His research on the Cirripedia also helped him with his musings about another problem in biology: the relationship between species.

The Birth of *The Origin of Species*

"From September 1854 I devoted my whole time to arranging my huge pile of notes, to observing, and to experimenting in relation to the transmutation of species." This is one of the most auspicious statements in Darwin's autobiography. Darwin did not need to write *The Origin of Species* to establish his credentials as a naturalist or to become famous: he had already done both. His travelogue on the voyage of the *Beagle* was a best seller. His volumes on the geology and zoology of the voyage of the *Beagle* were highly praised and valued by scientists around the world. He had done pioneering research on the origins and structure of coral reefs. He was the world expert on barnacles. In 1853, he was awarded the Royal Medal by the Royal Society in recognition of the work he had done: the medal was one of the highest awards a scientist could receive. His father would have been proud. No one could call Darwin a wastrel now.

However, even while he was working hard on his other projects, Darwin was musing over some of the phenomena he had seen, particularly in South America: the fossils he had discovered, the geographical distribution of closely related animals, and the slight differences between species on each island of the Galapagos. What was the significance of these facts? The facts "could only be explained on the supposition that species gradually became modified," thought Darwin. "The subject haunted me," he wrote.[39] His explanation ran counter to established scientific thinking, but Darwin did not drop his idea. He continued to collect information. He did not formulate a theory; he made observations and he took notes.

In October 1838, he read *An Essay on the Principle of Population* by Thomas Malthus (1766–1834) and it gave Darwin an idea. Malthus, an English economist, suggested that competition for limited resources, particularly food, was a major reason for disputes and wars between groups of humans. As Darwin put it, "here then I had at last got a theory by which to work."[40] Applying Malthus's idea to species, Darwin surmised that those animals and plants that were best adapted to their environment would survive the competition for resources, the struggle for existence: those species that adapted poorly would die. In 1842, after more thinking and research, Darwin wrote a thirty-five-page explanation of his theory. In 1844, he wrote out his theory in more detail, penning an essay of two hundred and thirty pages.

In 1844, Darwin also began an important friendship—with Joseph Dalton Hooker (1817–1911). Hooker's father was Sir William Jackson Hooker (1785–1865), the first director of the Royal Botanic Gardens at Kew in London, an important contact for Darwin in his research on plants. (Kew Gardens, like the Jardin des Plantes in Paris, had a large collection of plants from around the world.) Hooker and Darwin shared a common interest in the geographical distribution of plant species and, equally important, both knew the thrill that came from conducting research while on a long sea voyage. On 11 January, Darwin wrote to Hooker, whom he hardly knew at the time, saying, "I am almost convinced (quite contrary to the opinion I started with) that species are not (it is like confessing a murder) immutable." Darwin worried that Hooker might think his "presumption" crazy.[41]

In fact, Darwin had been a little coy. In his book *The Expression of the Emotions in Man and Animals* published in 1872, he wrote, "At the above date [1838] I was already inclined to believe in the principle of evolution, or the derivation of species from other and lower forms."[42] Later, in his autobiography, he wrote that "as soon as I had become, in the year 1837 or 1838, convinced that species were mutable productions, I could not avoid the belief that man must come under the same law."[43] Perhaps the cause of Darwin's reticence was the fact that Hooker was not a confidante. Darwin expressed relief when Hooker wrote back, saying that he would be "delighted" to hear Darwin's theory rather than condemning him.[44]

And then Darwin dropped the matter. Or, more precisely, the urgency to publish his theory dissipated as he concentrated on completing other projects such as his work on barnacles. Ten years passed before Darwin turned his full concentration to his work on species.

Some of Darwin's biographers have drawn attention to Darwin's concern about publishing his theory about the origin of species. These biographers suggest that Darwin realized that his theory was so heretical (in the Christian sense of the word), so opposite to the prevailing view about the origins of life that he deliberately delayed publishing his ideas publicly. This suggestion has some merit. His "confession" to Hooker is proof that Darwin was worried. And it did take more than twenty years before Darwin's first musings about transmutation became the book *The Origin of Species*.

Darwin did worry about the furor that his theory might cause, but it is inaccurate to blame only this concern for the "delay" in publication. Darwin disliked controversy: "I rejoice that I have avoided controversies," he wrote in 1881, "and this I owe to Lyell, who many years ago ... strongly advised me never to get entangled in a controversy, as it rarely did any good and caused a miserable loss of time and temper."[45] Furthermore, a controversy had already erupted in 1844 over the origin of species. The book *Vestiges of the Natural History of Creation* was published that year. The author was unknown: only posthumously was Robert Chambers (1802–1871), a Scottish publisher and amateur geologist, revealed as the author. The book's support for transformism—the idea that the evolution of species was proof that society could progress to become more egalitarian, for example—did cause a furor, particularly as the scientific evidence Chambers gave for evolution was not convincing.[46] Equally important, Darwin was concerned about his wife Emma. He did not want to upset her by publishing a theory that seemed to oppose or undermine the Christian explanation of the origin of species. Emma, like Darwin's sisters, was very religious.

But it is too easy to focus on these concerns because they fit so well into a story of the outbreak of the "war" between science and religion. Without doubt, the delay in the completion of *The Origin of Species* was mainly due to the character of the man. Darwin was a cautious person. He was certainly of a very different temperament from Alfred Wallace who could work out a theory of natural selection during three days of torrid thinking and write down his conclusions in an essay immediately. Darwin's method of work was slow and methodical. He preferred to accumulate facts over a long period of time, think about the ways these facts related to each other, and then fit them together into a large synthesis. This approach was not the kind that would produce an academic paper or a book in a week, a month, or even a year. "I gained much by my delay in publishing from about 1839, when the theory was clearly conceived, to 1859," Darwin wrote in this autobiography, "and I lost nothing for it, for I cared very little whether men attributed most originality to me or Wallace; and his essay no doubt aided in the reception of the theory."[47]

Looking no further than Darwin's other major books provides proof that his modus operandi rather than his religious sensibilities explain the long period of gestation for *The Origin of Species*. Darwin began collecting facts for what would become *The Descent of Man* while working on *The Origin of Species* in the 1850s. *The Descent of Man* was not published until 1871. Other books such as *The Various Contrivances by which British and Foreign Orchids are Fertilised by Insects*, *Insectivorous Plants*, and *The Formation of Vegetable Mould, through the Action of Worms, with Observations on their Habits* were equally long in the making: fifteen, twenty, or more years.

In 1856, at the urging of Charles Lyell, Darwin decided "to write out my views pretty fully."[48] Lyell had good reason to push Darwin. In September 1855, an article written by Alfred Russel Wallace (1823–1913), a Welsh naturalist who was doing research in the Malaysian archipelago at the time, appeared in *Annals and Magazine of Natural History*: its title was "On the Law which has regulated the Introduction of New Species." Lyell was worried that another naturalist might preempt Darwin—and receive the praise and honor for doing groundbreaking research—even though Darwin had been working on his "Species" for more than twenty years.

Some time before 1856 Darwin had a eureka moment. He was certain transmutation occurred, but how? The answer, he realized, was that organic beings became more and more different from each other as they underwent more modification. The species were not so different that it was impossible to see the relationship between wolves and dogs, for example; but their evolutionary paths were different enough that a wolf would not be mistaken for a lion. Darwin was so excited about his insight that he wrote, "I can remember the very spot in the road, whilst in my carriage, when to my joy the solution occurred to me."[49]

On 14 May 1856, Darwin began to write a complete explanation of his theory. He called it his "big book" on species.[50] This writing occupied most of his time until June 1858. He wrote a chapter, sent it to a scientist for comment, usually Hooker or Lyell, and revised it—sometimes at the same time as working on a new one. What survives of this manuscript amounts to about 225,000 words, a book of well over five hundred pages.[51] The full manuscript was never published.

On 18 June 1858, Darwin received an essay from Alfred Wallace: it changed Darwin's life. The essay was entitled "On the Tendency of Varieties to Depart Indefinitely From the Original Type." In it Wallace outlined a theory of transmutation based on the idea that the more varieties of a species became modified the more they differed from their common ancestor and from each other. Wallace sought the opinion of a well-known and well-respected scientist, Darwin; he wanted to know whether his theory was plausible and worth publishing.

Darwin was horrified. "I never saw a more striking coincidence. [I]f Wallace had my M.S. sketch written out in 1842 he could not have made a better short abstract! Even his terms now stand as Heads of my Chapters," he wrote to Lyell.[52] What should he do? He could not suppress Wallace's essay: he could not deny its existence. Even worse, if he published an article or a book on the origin of species it would look as though he had stolen the idea from Wallace. "All my originality, whatever it may amount to, will be smashed," Darwin complained.[53] How could he claim to have thought of the idea first when he had not published anything about his theory? There appeared to be no good options.

To characterize Darwin's comments to Lyell and Hooker as angst-ridden is too kind. Darwin's tone sounded as if his whole life had been turned upside down by Wallace's essay. Why was Darwin so disturbed? The answer reveals something of Darwin's character—it is not possible to be definitive because Darwin was so emotional about the turn of events—and the importance of scientific discovery in the nineteenth century.

Darwin had been thinking about the problem of transmutation seriously since his travels in South America and had been working steadily to prove the validity of his theory. Darwin wanted scientists to be convinced by his arguments and proofs: he did not want any part of his argument to be easily disputable. He did not want his work to be dismissed the way *Vestiges of the Natural History of Creation* was. Despite all of his care, however, he had been preempted. Even worse, Wallace had "discovered" the theory of transmutation without investing years of research and was willing to publish it immediately. Wallace seemed so much bolder and smarter to Darwin: perhaps the younger man should receive the credit for this important discovery. But it was still agonizing to concede that someone else had thought of "his" idea. Darwin was cautious, but he was also ambitious: he wanted his fellow scientists to be impressed by his scholarship.

Furthermore, the rewards for authorship of an important scientific theory or discovery were more than academic in the nineteenth century. There was recognition by important scientific bodies, but that was just the beginning. The author's name would be attached to the theory: thus, "Darwinism" is associated with the theory of evolution. The author would probably receive a knighthood: Charles Lyell became "Sir Charles" and Joseph Hooker became "Sir Joseph." Then there was the name recognition, which meant the likelihood of book sales and invitations to lecture in Britain and other countries. Furthermore, the author could be certain of invitations to sit on important government commissions and to professorial chairs at the most prestigious universities. Fame, money, and prestige awaited the pioneering scientist in the nineteenth century. Should Darwin give up all of these possibilities just because Alfred Wallace had written an essay on the origin of species (compared with Darwin's five hundred pages)?

Darwin decided to let Hooker and Lyell take care of the matter. He had good reason to do so. His family needed his attention. A outbreak of scarlet fever swept through the village of Downe affecting nearly every child. His youngest son, Charles Waring Darwin, who was eighteen months old, died from the disease on 28 June. His daughter Henrietta had diphtheria, another deadly disease for nineteenth-century children.

Hooker and Lyell decided that Darwin should receive the bulk of the credit for the theory about the origin of species. Their reasoning was simple: Darwin had worked out the theory first. Descent by modification through natural selection, the best description of the theory of evolution as Darwin and Wallace conceived it, was Darwin's "baby." Hooker and Lyell took a copy of a letter Darwin had written to Asa Gray on 5 September 1857, in which Darwin outlined his theory—a critical piece of evidence that Darwin had written down his theory before Wallace—and added Wallace's essay plus an essay written by Darwin entitled "On the Variation of Organic Beings in a State of Nature; on the Natural Means of Selection; on the Comparison of Domestic Races and True Species." Hooker and Lyell sent the three papers to the Linnean Society, a prestigious scientific society, to be read at its next meeting. Hooker and Lyell gave the joint paper the title "On the Tendency of Species to form Varieties; and on the Perpetuation of Varieties and Species by Natural Means of Selection." The secretary of the Linnean Society, John Bennett (1801–1876), read the joint paper on 1 July—even though he received it on 30 June, such was the status of Hooker and Lyell as scientists—to approximately thirty "nonplused fellows."[54]

More surprising than the reaction of the Linnean fellows was the attitude of Wallace. He conceded without a fuss that Darwin should publish a major work on evolution by natural selection. Wallace was happy to let Darwin take the credit; in later years, Wallace was one of staunchest defenders of Darwin's theory of evolution. David Knight, a historian of science, suggests that Wallace was so amenable because "he was a modest man, and conscious of his social and scientific position... [who] recognized that Darwin had got there first."[55] Perhaps neither the Linnean fellows nor Wallace recognized at the time the significance of the ideas in the joint paper.[56]

Others did. Lyell and Hooker urged Darwin to write a shorter version of his large manuscript on natural selection. The publisher John Murray offered to publish the forthcoming summary before seeing any of the manuscript. Murray had published Lyell's *Principles of Geology*, a best-selling book explaining the geological theory of uniformitarianism: Lyell's recommendation smoothed the path for Darwin.

On 20 July 1858, Darwin began to write the book that would become *The Origin of Species*. Spurred by the knowledge that he had no choice about whether to publish his theory, Darwin continued writing until he finished the manuscript on 10 May 1859. (Wallace was still in the Malaysian Archipelago, but prudence suggested that Darwin could not expect Wallace to be completely silent about his own research.) Darwin finished editing the proofs of the manuscript on 1 October: thirteen months and ten days of writing. Including his notebooks of the 1830s, his two essays of the 1840s, and his manuscript on natural selection, *The Origin of Species* was Darwin's fourth major attempt at explaining his theory about the transmutation of species. *The Origin of Species* was also the most successful piece of writing Darwin ever did.

The rumor that Darwin was writing a major book about the transmutation of the species spread rapidly through Britain, the rest of Europe, and the United States between July 1858 and November 1859. Scientists and others interested in the idea of evolution eagerly anticipated the book's appearance. All 1,250 copies of *The Origin of Species* had buyers by the first day of publication, 24 November. On the same day, John Murray wrote to Darwin asking him to prepare a second edition of the book. Whatever controversy *The Origin of Species* might precipitate, it was destined to be a best seller.

Life after *The Origin of Species*

Darwin's life did not "end" after the publication of *The Origin of Species*. His name is so inextricably linked with the theory of evolution and the best-known exposition of that theory, *The Origin of Species*, that it is tempting to forget about Darwin after 1859. He did write *The Descent of Man*, but that book seems like a sequel to *The Origin of Species*: a sequel is easily overlooked.

The main reason Darwin's life is ignored after 1859 is that he was not personally involved in the controversy surrounding the ideas in *The Origin of Species*. Because he was the author, Darwin did not write any reviews of the book. He did not write letters to the prominent newspapers and journals to defend the book. He did not attend any of the meetings of scientific societies at which his ideas were discussed. The names associated with the furor after the publication of *The Origin of Species* are men such as Thomas Huxley, nicknamed "Darwin's bulldog" because he defended Darwin's ideas so aggressively; Joseph Hooker; Charles Lyell; Richard Owen (1804–1892); Asa Gray; Louis Agassiz (1807–1883); and Ernst Haeckel (1834–1919). Darwin seemed to disappear.

In fact, it is more accurate to think of Darwin's life, his life in the public eye, as beginning in 1859. He was already a famous scientist but *The Origin of Species* vaulted Darwin to the level of most important naturalists and scientists. Darwin was the man responsible for a "big" theory in natural history. He was a well-known figure worldwide with the extra burden this status entailed. This meant that he was quoted, consulted, argued with, and even demonized: Darwin's life was no longer private. He was a frequent subject for nineteenth-century cartoonists, for example. In 1864, Darwin received the Copley Medal of the Royal Society, the highest award from the most prestigious scientific society. To nineteenth-century society in Europe and the United States, Darwin and his ideas were very much at the forefront. The socialist thinker Karl Marx (1818–1883) considered Darwin one of his heroes, to Darwin's bemusement, and sent him an autographed copy of *Das Kapital* in 1873. Marx was one of many admirers.

Darwin's continuing research kept him in the limelight. Excluding *The Descent of Man*, Darwin wrote eight major scientific books: five on botany; one on zoology; one on domesticated species combining zoology and botany; and one that combined zoology, psychology, sociology, and anthropology. Between the publication of *The Origin of Species* and *The Descent of Man* Darwin had three other books published: *On the Various Contrivances by which British and Foreign Orchids are Fertilised by Insects, and on the Good Effects of Intercrossing* (1862), *On the Movement and Habits of Climbing Plants* (1865), and the two-volume *The Variation of Animals and Plants under Domestication* (1868). These books were so popular that

Darwin had to prepare a second edition of each one. In addition to the books, Darwin also wrote more than ninety articles that were published in scientific journals and natural history magazines.[57] Darwin was a busy researcher and author.

Darwin did retire in one way: he lived in a small, rural village. (Even today the village of Downe is not easy to reach from London.) His country life and country location enabled him to escape or be a little removed from the controversies in London, Cambridge, or Oxford. He could concentrate on his research and writing in the quiet of his home and gardens. Even vacations he found too stressful.

Darwin's public life did not even end after 1871. The publication of the *Descent of Man* was not the climax of Darwin's work and certainly not the end of his research and writing on the theory of natural selection. To use a game-playing analogy, reading through Darwin's books and articles written after 1859 is like watching a game of chess develop. *The Origin of Species* was more like the first piece moved in the game. Continuing with this analogy, *The Descent of Man* was another piece played in the game, not the final move.[58] Books such as *The Expression of the Emotions in Man and Animals* (1872) and *Insectivorous Plants* (1875) were all part of his larger strategy of showing that the modification of species is a slow process based on natural selection, descent or sexual selection, and adaptation to the surroundings. He even managed to use some of the material from his manuscript on natural selection in these later books. *The Origin of Species* may be one of the most important books in the history of science, but if ever a person deserved recognition for his lesser-known books, it is Darwin.

The Death of Charles Darwin

Charles Darwin died on 19 April 1882. He was 74. In July 1881, Darwin had written to Alfred Wallace, "What I shall do with my few remaining years of life I can hardly tell. I have everything to make me happy and contented, but life has become very wearisome to me."[59] Fun-loving student, explorer, naturalist, husband, father, best-selling author, public figure, and old man: Darwin had lived a full life. From shy schoolboy to the most prominent scientist of the nineteenth century: it had been a very ordinary and an extraordinary life.

For some, Darwin's life had to be recognized. On 21 April, a group of twenty Members of Parliament suggested to the dean of Westminster Abbey, George Granville Bradley, that Darwin ought to be buried in one of the two most important churches in Britain. Darwin's family members, who had intended to bury Darwin in a private ceremony, were persuaded that a large, public ceremony was a better option.

Darwin was buried on 26 April. Among the pallbearers were Thomas Huxley, James Russell Lowell, the United States' ambassador to Britain, Alfred Russel Wallace, Sir Joseph Hooker, and three members of the House of Lords. His grave is on the north aisle of the nave, a few feet away from the monument to Isaac Newton.

Why was Darwin, whose theory supposedly undermined religion in general and Christianity in particular, accorded such an honor? As one French commentator put it, "after Darwin" everything in science changed.[60] His cousin Francis Galton (1822–1911), better known as the founder of the eugenics movement, called Darwin "the Aristotle of our days."[61] Darwin's theory of descent by modification through natural selection, as explained in *The Origin of Species*, meant that the major questions and answers in biology were radically different in 1882 from those of 1809. As Darwin himself acknowledged in his typical self-deprecating manner, "With such moderate abilities as I possess, it is truly surprising that thus I should have influenced to a considerable extent the beliefs of scientific men on some important points."[62]

Notes

1. *The Descent of Man, and Selection in Relation to Sex* (London: John Murray, 1871), I: 68 and *The Expression of the Emotions in Man and Animals* (London: John Murray, 1872), 44–45, 120.

2. Gavin de Beer, *Charles Darwin: Evolution by Natural Selection* (London: Thomas Nelson and Sons, 1963); Adrian Desmond and James Moore, *Darwin* (London: Michael Joseph, 1991); and Janet Browne, *Charles Darwin*. Volume 1: *Voyaging* (London: Jonathan Cape, 1995), Volume 2: *The Power of Place* (London: Jonathan Cape, 2002).

3. Tom McIver's book *Anti-Evolution: A Reader's Guide to Writing Before and After Darwin* (Baltimore: Johns Hopkins University Press, 1992) lists more than a thousand books written in opposition to Darwin's ideas.

4. *Life and Letters of Charles Darwin*, I: 32.

5. Ibid., I: 31–32.

6. Ibid., I: 32.

7. Ibid., I: 36.

8. Ibid., I: 48.

9. Ibid., I: 46, 48.

10. Ibid., I: 50.

11. Browne, *Voyaging*, illustration between page 110 and page 111.

12. James Stephens, *Illustrations of British Entomology; or, A Synopsis of Indigenous Insects: Containing Their Generic and Specific Distinctions; with an Account of Their Metamorphoses, Times of Appearance, Localities, Food, and Economy, as Far as Practicable*, Volume II: Mandibulata (London: Baldwin and Cradock, 1829), 11, 49, 51, 70, 71, 87, 188, 191, 192, 194.

13. *Life and Letters of Charles Darwin*, I: 52.

14. Ibid., 55.

15. Letter dated 24 August 1831 in *The Correspondence of Charles Darwin*, eds. Frederick Burkhardt and Sydney Smith (Cambridge: Cambridge University Press, 1986), I: 128–129.

16. Peacock to Henslow, Letter from 6 or 13 August 1831 in *Correspondence of Charles Darwin*, I: 127–128. Jenyns classified the fish in Part IV of Darwin's *The Zoology of the Voyage of H.M.S. Beagle* (1842).

17. Letter dated 24 August 1831 in *Correspondence of Charles Darwin*, I: 128–129.

18. *Life and Letters of Charles Darwin*, I: 197.

19. Ibid., I: 197.

20. Ibid., I: 59.

21. Ibid.

22. Darwin, *The Zoology of the Voyage of the H.M.S. Beagle, Under the Command of Captain Fitzroy, R.N., During the Years 1832 to 1836* (London: Smith, Elder and Co., 1840), i.

23. De Beer, *Darwin*, 34.

24. *Life and Letters of Charles Darwin*, I: 61.

25. *Correspondence of Charles Darwin*, Volume I (1821–1836): 142.

26. See Lucile H. Brockway, *Science and Colonial Expansion: The Role of the British Royal Botanic Garden* (New York: Academic Press, 1979), 77–102, for a description of the role of naturalists in promoting Britain's imperial policies.

27. The majority of Darwin's observations in the entries dated 16 January to 4 April 1832 are geological. See *Journal of Researches in Geology and Natural History of the Various Countries Visited by* H.M.S Beagle*, under the Command of Captain Fitzroy, R.N. from 1832 to 1836* (London: Henry Colburn, 1839), 1–20.

28. *Life and Letters of Charles Darwin*, I: 63–64.

29. Ibid., I: 66.

30. Darwin, *Journal of Researches in Geology and Natural History*, xiii, 461.

31. Ibid., xiii, 489.

32. *Life and Letters of Charles Darwin*, I: 68.

33. "Second Note on Marriage" (possibly written in July 1838) in *Correspondence of Charles Darwin*, Volume II (1837–1843): 444. Darwin spelled "marry" incorrectly as "mary" in the second of the three uses.

34. See *The Structure and Distribution of Coral Reefs* (London: Smith, Elder and Co., 1842), Preface, iv and *The Origin of Species*, 1.

35. *Life and Letters of Charles Darwin*, I: 224–225.

36. *Journal of Researches in Geology and Natural History*, 403. Darwin was bitten on 26 March 1835.

37. See Ralph Colp, *To Be an Invalid: The Illnesses of Charles Darwin* (Chicago: University of Chicago Press, 1977), 109–144, for a summary of the various theories about Darwin's illnesses.

38. George M. Gould, *Biographic Clinics: The Origin of the Ill-Health of De Quincey, Carlyle, Darwin, Huxley and Browning* (Philadelphia: P. Blakiston's Son and Co., 1903), 88–106.

39. *Life and Letters of Charles Darwin*, I: 82.

40. Ibid., 83.

41. *Correspondence of Charles Darwin*, III (1844–1846): 2.

42. Darwin, *The Expression of the Emotions in Man and Animals*, 19.

43. *Life and Letters of Charles Darwin*, I: 93.

44. Hooker to Darwin, Letter dated 29 January 1844 and Darwin to Hooker, Letter dated 23 February 1844, *Correspondence of Charles Darwin*, III: 7, 10–12.

45. *Life and Letters of Charles Darwin*, I: 89.

46. See James H. Secord, *Victorian Sensation: The Extraordinary Publication, Reception, and Secret Authorship of Vestiges of the Natural History of Creation* (Chicago: University of Chicago Press, 2002), 9–40; and Robert Chambers, *Vestiges of the Natural History of Creation and Other Evolutionary Writings*, ed. James H. Secord (Chicago: University of Chicago Press, 1994), xxvi–xxxiii, for a summary of the furor.

47. *Life and Letters of Charles Darwin*, I: 88. "His essay" is the one Wallace sent to Darwin in June 1858.

48. Ibid., 84.

49. Ibid.

50. Ibid., II: 84, 85.

51. The existing manuscript is published as *Charles Darwin's Natural Selection: Being the Second Part of His Big Species Book Written from 1856 to 1858*, ed. R. C. Stauffer (Cambridge: Cambridge University Press, 1975). See pages 5–14 for background information on the manuscript.

52. Letter dated 18 June 1858, *Correspondence of Charles Darwin*, VII (1858–1859): 107.

53. Ibid.

54. Moore and Desmond, *Darwin*, 470.

55. Knight, "Introduction to Volume IX," *The Evolution Debate, 1813–1870* (London: Routledge, 2003), IX: vii.

56. Thomas Bell (1792–1880), the president of the Linnean Society, supposedly remarked that nothing significant had occurred in the field of biology in 1858 when summarizing the papers presented that year.

57. See Paul H. Barrett, ed., *The Collected Papers of Charles Darwin* (Chicago: University of Chicago Press, 1977), II: 31–281.

58. According to Darwin, the success of *The Origin of Species*, both the number of copies sold and the general acceptance of his ideas by scientists, persuaded him to write *The Descent of Man*. See *The Descent of Man, and Selection in Relation to Sex* (London: John Murray, 1871) I: 1, 2.

59. *Life and Letters of Charles Darwin*, III: 356.

60. Hubert Thomas in preface to *Discours sur Les Révolutions de La Surface du Globe* (Paris: Christian Bourgois Éditeur, 1985), 8.

61. Galton, *English Men of Science: Their Nature and Nurture* (London: Macmillan, 1874), 45.

62. *Life and Letters of Charles Darwin*, I: 107.

CHAPTER 3

THE ORIGIN OF SPECIES: THE BOOK AND ITS BACKGROUND

The Origins of *The Origin of Species*

The Debate about Origins before Darwin

On 12 November 1800, the French zoologist Georges Cuvier read a paper at a meeting of the Académie des sciences in which he stated that he knew of twenty-three species that were now extinct.[1] Today, such an announcement would produce a heated discussion about the way humans are affecting or destroying the environment. In the early nineteenth century, however, Cuvier's announcement reignited the debate about the fixity of species among scientists and philosophers in Europe and North America. Cuvier was no supporter of a theory of evolution, but his findings drew attention to a problem that scientists had been discussing for more than a century. Ever since naturalists in the seventeenth century realized that fossils were actually the remains of living plants or animals, there had been a debate about the precise nature of the creation and continuance of life on Earth. Leaving aside the question of whether the Christian God was the creator, naturalists and philosophers confronted a number of pressing questions. Had all species been created at the same time? In what form had species been created? Did all species look the same now as they had when first created? If there had been any change, what had caused it? Cuvier's research suggested that there was a problem with the orthodox theory about the origin of species.

Until the work of seventeenth- and eighteenth-century paleontologists and geologists became common knowledge, the fixity of species did seem to be an adequate explanation for the state of organic life on Earth. The idea that dogs had always been dogs or that apple trees had always grown from apple seeds made sense based on the available evidence. There were records dating back to the ancient Greeks and Romans that listed the species of plants and animals common at that time: those lists matched the flora and fauna of the seventeenth century. Other records from ancient civilizations, such as the Egyptians, contained drawings of recognizable species of cats, dogs, and birds. Obviously then, so the thinking went, the species had not changed over thousands of years.

Doubts about the fixity of species had a long history. Greek philosophers such as Anaximander of Miletus (ca. 610–ca. 546) and Empedocles (ca. 492–432) argued that animals mutated and became extinct. By the seventeenth century, the standard explanation for the extinction and mutation of animals was catastrophism. Cuvier actually coined the term in the nineteenth century to describe a cataclysmic or large-scale geological event, but the idea was not new. Some scientists thought there had been only one catastrophe: the flood mentioned in the biblical book of Genesis. Noah had saved a pair of each type of animal in the ark: the animals not saved died in the flood and became extinct. In his book *Recherches sur les ossements fossils de quadrupèdes: où l'on rétablit les caractères de plusieurs espèces d'animaux que les revolutions du globe paroissent avoir détruites* (1812), Cuvier argued that there had been several catastrophes in the Earth's history. The catastrophes accounted for the large number of fossils being found by amateur and professional geologists in the eighteenth and nineteenth centuries.[2]

Cuvier's explanation made sense, but it did not quell the debate about origins. The wealth of information found by professional and amateur scientists did not seem compatible with a theory of catastrophism whether there was one or several floods. Commenting on the recently settled continent of America, Sir Thomas Browne (1605–1682), a British physician, wondered in 1635 why the horse, a "necessary creature," did not exist there.[3] And in the next two centuries, naturalists discovered a number of animals—some useful or harmless, some not—in America that did not exist in Europe, Africa, and Asia. Catastrophism was not a satisfactory explanation for such particular and continent-specific development of various species.

In the late-nineteenth and early twentieth centuries, after the widespread dissemination of Darwin's ideas, some writers blamed seventeenth-century naturalists such as John Ray (1627–1705) for what they called the "doctrine" of the fixity of species. Vernon Faithfull Storr (1869–1940), a British theologian and philosopher, suggested that Ray had tried to do scientifically what John Milton had done poetically in *Paradise Lost*: describe creation in a way that illustrated and conformed to the literal text of the Bible. Aubrey Moore (1848–1890), another British theologian and philosopher, argued that the fixity of species was a theological, rather than a scientific, idea—although prominent scientists such as the Swede Carl Linnaeus (1707–1778) and Cuvier supported it.[4] John Ray had written about the fixity of the species in books such as *The Wisdom of God Manifested in the Works of the Creation* (1691), but Storr was incorrect when he suggested that Ray was the author of the doctrine. The idea predated Ray by many centuries. The fixity of species was simply one answer to a question posed by many people living before and after Charles Darwin: from where did all the species on the Earth originate?

William Paley and the Divine Watchmaker

Before the publication of *The Origin of Species* the most popular answer to the question of origins was the one provided by the British theologian William Paley (1743–1805). In his two books *A View of the Evidences of Christianity* (1794) and *Natural Theology: or, Evidences of the Existence and Attributes of the Deity, Collected from the Appearances of Nature* (1802), Paley explained what is called natural theology. Natural theology provided a unique answer to the questions about extinct species and the fixity of species. The answer was persuasive enough to convince most of the scientists of Darwin's time that any theory of evolution used to explain the origin of species must be wrong.

Paley's natural theology contained three major ideas. First, nature was a source of information about God and Christianity. Anybody, even someone without access to an organized religious institution, could learn about the god of Christianity. People did not need to read the Bible or know a set of doctrines: they just had to look at the organization, beauty, and complexity of nature. Second, studying nature would lead a person to accept the belief that God created the universe and is in control of it. People could become Christians simply by studying nature. Third, studying nature reveals that God's creation is ordered and logical. There are reasonable explanations for all the phenomena of nature.

Paley's objective in his two books was to convince his readers that Christianity made sense. According to Paley, Christianity was true because it was logical. The truths of the Bible as expressed in the doctrines of the Christian Church were confirmed by nature. The order in nature, natural theology, was another way to learn about Biblical doctrines, called revealed theology. And why was the connection between natural theology and revealed theology important? Because the problems with one could be solved by examining the other. If the fixity of the species did not make sense, a person could turn to the Bible (or the Church) and learn that God created all of nature. If a person was unsure about the existence of God, he could examine nature and know that there was a creator god. Using a watch found in a field as an analogy for the existence of the universe, Paley said, "The watch must have had a maker; there must have existed, at some time and at some place or other, an artificer or artificers who formed it for the purpose which we find it actually to answer"—telling the time.[5]

Paley's theory about nature and natural theology was not new. Since the seventeenth century, philosophers and theologians such as John Toland (1670–1722) and George Berkeley (1685–1753) had said the same. In the Age of Reason, the seventeenth- and eighteenth-century intellectual movement in Europe that stressed the importance of logic, thinkers emphasized that nature could be explained and scientific theories could be written about it. Isaac Newton's famous statement that God made a sensible universe is an example of this thinking. Paley's books were the most comprehensive and, judging by their popularity, easily understood explanation of the connection between nature and God.

Paley was not a deist. Unlike many of the philosophers during the Age of Reason who asserted that nature was logical, he did not believe that God created the universe and its laws and then left the universe to operate according to those laws. Deists did not think God was interested in or intervened in human activity: Paley did. To use Paley's metaphor, God did not simply wind up the watch: he adjusted the hands regularly. But Paley's view of nature was very mechanical. The machine of nature could be observed.

Like Paley, Darwin's view of biology was mechanical. The difference between *The Origin of Species* and *Natural Theology* was that Darwin did not invoke an entity outside of nature to make the machine of nature work. Darwin chose to explain extinction and the distribution of different species around the world by referring to the action of natural selection; Paley chose to refer to the creative action of the Christian God. Before 1859, Paley's solution was the only one available.

The Importance of Classification to Darwin's Work

Paley's natural theology relied on three assumptions. First, the world and the universe were not very old, not much more than six thousand years. Second, at least one catastrophe had occurred in Earth's history, hence the fossil deposits and evidence of extinct species. Third, the universe was orderly and complex. Thus, as Paley argued, only an intelligent being, the Christian God, could create a complicated organ such as the eye or summon up the destructive power that resulted in the formation of thousands of fossils.

One problem with Paley's view of nature was that it left little room for change. Paley's universe was a static universe. Such a view was feasible as long as there was no evidence of development in nature. Was nature changing? No, it was not, according to the orthodox scientific view in 1800. This is why Cuvier's research was so significant. Cuvier recognized that his discoveries of extinct species suggested something important about living species: they were changing. The research of his contemporaries Étienne Geoffroy Saint-Hilaire and Jean-Baptiste Lamarck confirmed what Cuvier was unwilling to state explicitly: mutation and evolution were occurring in present-day species.

In the late-eighteenth and early nineteenth centuries, there were two groups of people paying particular attention to mutation: naturalists interested in classifying species and breeders interested in producing new varieties of species. What these groups had in common was the ability to notice the large number of changes occurring in nature, although the naturalists were usually scientists, such as Lamarck, and the breeders were usually farmers, agriculturalists, or horticulturalists, such as the British politician Sir John Sebright (1767–1846). The multitudinous changes meant that naturalists looked for characteristics that demonstrated the familial relationship between different species, and breeders looked for opportunities to produce new, interesting, or useful varieties of species.

John Ray and Carl Linnaeus were two of the most important naturalists in the history of classification. Both men attempted to create a system that naturalists could use to identify quickly and easily whether a particular plant or animal was related to another different plant or animal. Ray followed the natural system of classification. He tried to find as many matching characteristics as possible. Linnaeus created a system based on sex organs; a flowering plant might be related to another plant because they had the same number and type of stamens, for example. These systems enabled scientists to explain clearly the relationships among species, particularly the differences.

In fact, the science of classification became so vital that virtually all of the well-known naturalists of the late-eighteenth and early nineteenth centuries attempted to do it. Lamarck established his reputation as one of the great scientists of his generation on the basis of his classification of the animal kingdom. A version of Lamarck's system is still used today.

These classifiers discovered three important facts by the beginning of the nineteenth century: there were an incredibly large number of species and varieties in the world, the number was increasing, and the number could be increased artificially. Furthermore, such was the fecundity of species and varieties that it was difficult at times to distinguish whether a plant or animal was a variety or a new species. Commenting on the propensity of a fellow botanist Charles Babington (1808–1895) to find new species, Hewett Cottrell Watson (1804–1881) supposedly remarked that there were "species, subspecies, and Bab-ies."[6]

Both breeders and naturalists began to speculate about the meaning of the diversity of organic life. Why were there so many species? Based on the scientific assumptions of the day, there was no obvious answer to this question. But were all species created at the same time? That question, however, did have an answer: "no." According to the British veterinary surgeon William Youatt (1776–1847) some breeders could "summon into life whatever form and mould [they pleased]."[7] If that was possible, then someone needed to propose a new theory about the origin of species. Humans, it seemed, were just as capable of changing nature as Paley's intelligent creator. These facts became important elements of Darwin's theory of descent by modification.

The Uniqueness of *The Origin of Species* and Darwin's Debts to Other Thinkers

Given the debates in the eighteenth and nineteenth centuries, Darwin did not write *The Origin of Species* in a vacuum. It may have been a "glorious book" with "a mass of close reasoning on curious facts and fresh phenomena," according to Joseph Hooker, but Darwin's theory of descent by modification was based solidly on the knowledge of his day.[8] For example, Thomas Malthus's theory about the shortage of food affecting the growth of the population gave Darwin the idea that different species had to compete for resources: Darwin called this "the struggle for existence." Charles Lyell's theory of uniformitarianism in geology—that the changes in the Earth take place gradually over eons—gave Darwin the idea that the transmutation of species must be a slow process that occurred over a long period of time. Darwin acknowledged the importance of Malthus and Lyell to his theory both in *The Origin of Species* and his other writings.[9] But equally clear in *The Origin of Species* is the debt

Darwin owed to specialists in classifying species, such as George Robert Waterhouse (1810–1888), zoologists such as Isidore Geoffroy Saint-Hilaire (1805–1861), botanists such as Hewett Cottrell Watson, and paleontologists such as Edward Forbes (1815–1854).

Nor was Darwin the first scientist to muse about the relationships among the species based on the new information found by geologists, paleontologists, zoologists, and botanists. Based on his research on classification, Lamarck decided that the transmutation of species had occurred. He was not certain about the process—he eventually decided that new characteristics appeared spontaneously in species and that these were transferred wholesale to the species' progeny—but Lamarck was certain about the event. Darwin's grandfather Erasmus became convinced that the diversity and complexity of nature proved that evolution occurred. He wrote down his ideas in the form of an extended poem, *The Temple of Nature* (1803). Étienne Geoffroy Saint-Hilaire, while studying abnormalities and deformities in species, began to argue for a "unity of form" that linked all species of the animal or plant kingdom. Similarities of form, homologies, such as the bone structure of a hand, claw, or flipper, suggested that all animals had developed from a common ancestor. The idea of a common ancestor is a key component of the theory of evolution.

Harriet Martineau (1802–1876), the novelist and social commentator, marveled at Darwin's "sagacity."[10] But she, too, recognized that Darwin had not worked in isolation from other naturalists and scientists. It was "the patient power by which [Darwin] has collected such a mass of facts, to transmute them by such sagacious treatment into such portentious knowledge," that impressed her.[11] Part of Darwin's genius was his ability to synthesize. The evidence for a theory of evolution may have been well known, but no one had put all the pieces together before 1859, not even Alfred Russel Wallace.

Could Darwin have created a major scientific theory without all the connections he had? Probably not. One group of connections was an inner circle of friends who Darwin used as a sounding board to try out his ideas. Lyell, Hooker, and Gray became his confidants and were the first people to know that Darwin was formulating a theory about origins. These friends acted as editors or reviewers. A second group of connections included acquaintances who stimulated Darwin's thinking. These men were mainly experts in particular fields, such as botany, with whom Darwin exchanged information. The research of these acquaintances helped to confirm Darwin's thinking about a topic, such as the hive-making instincts of bees, or led Darwin to think about a problem, such as the relationship between the finches of the Galapagos Islands. Could Darwin have written *The*

Origin of Species without his conversations and correspondence with men such as William Tegetmeier (1816–1912) and John Gould (1804–1881)? No, Darwin would not have had such intimate knowledge of bees and finches without these men.

There were two other groups of men just as vital to Darwin's thinking and writing. These connections are less well known today, but that fact does not diminish their importance. The first of these connections included Darwin's scientific colleagues. In meetings of the Geological Society of London, the Linnean Society, and the Zoological Society of London, Darwin met other men interested in the questions he was asking. Some of these men were conducting scientific research full time and professionally; others were amateurs in the sense that they had full-time careers in politics, for example. Sir John Lubbock (1834–1913), Darwin's friend and neighbor in Downe, was one of these amateurs. Their status as scientists was unimportant to Darwin: he read papers at these meetings of his scientific colleagues, and their comments and criticisms helped him to hone his ideas.

The fourth group of connections was the largest by far. Perhaps these men—and virtually all of them were male—can be best described as correspondents or consultants. Sometimes Darwin wrote letters to them and they replied. Sometimes he read their articles or books. Sometimes he found out about their work secondhand. Darwin did not meet all of these consultants. They were spread all around the world: in countries such as Australia, India, the United States, and Denmark. And some of them only lived in their books and articles: they had died before Darwin began his research. But Darwin referred to their work frequently: sometimes in passing, simply adding another name to a point he had already made; sometimes extensively, using the person's work to bolster a point he wanted to make.

A careful reading of *The Origin of Species* reveals just how indebted Darwin was to his consultants. For example, in the chapter on hybridism, Chapter VIII, Darwin mentions the German botanist Karl Friedrich von Gärtner (1772–1850) thirty times. Could Darwin have written this chapter without reference to Gärtner's work on plant hybrids? Perhaps, but the chapter would be quite different from the one Darwin actually wrote. To repeat Harriet Martineau's point, Darwin had consulted a wealth of material before he wrote *The Origin of Species*.

To say that Darwin consulted far and wide seems to prove the charge that Darwin attempted to refute: he was not an original thinker, he was simply a synthesizer. But to accuse Darwin of this is to miss another important feature of *The Origin of Species*: Darwin's own experiments. Darwin's theory of descent by modification is also indebted to Darwin himself. It was Darwin who checked on the structure of cells built by bumble bees after talking to his friend George Robert Waterhouse, who was an architect before he became a full-time naturalist. It was Darwin who created experiments to test how long seeds could remain in seawater and still germinate, even though he later admitted that the Belgian botanist Martin Martens (1797–1863) had done better experiments. It was Darwin who observed the habits of South American flycatchers and British titmice to learn more about animals' ability to adapt to their surroundings.[12]

If Darwin was a genius because he could synthesize the research of others, he was also a genius because he could see the larger picture. Darwin created a whole theory while others were suggesting or outlining parts of a theory of evolution. Darwin wrote out a theory of descent by modification and provided ample proof to substantiate his theory: others could not do this. *Vestiges of the Natural History of Creation* received a great deal of attention after its publication, but the ideas and the evidence convinced few people to accept a theory of evolution. Sir John Sebright, a renowned breeder, could write in 1809 that "the greatest number of females will ... fall to the share of the most vigorous males; and the strongest individuals of both sexes, by driving away the weakest, will enjoy the best food, and the most favourable situations, for themselves and for their offspring" but was not able to make this observation the basis of a theory of evolution.[13] Even Alfred Russel Wallace had not developed a complete theory of evolution in the essay he sent to Darwin in 1858. It was in *The Origin of Species* that the numerous facts that might support a theory of evolution were marshaled into a coherent argument. And Darwin was the person who did this.

The Organization of *The Origin of Species*

Basic Organization of *The Origin of Species*

Although the argument in *The Origin of Species* is not difficult to follow, the book itself has a large amount of detail. In one chapter, Darwin discusses the varieties of pigeon, in another chapter he comments on the distribution of species between the 25° and 35° latitudes. In the chapter on instinct, Darwin describes the habits of *Formica sanguinea*, a species of ant, and in a chapter on the relationships between organic beings Darwin comments on the difficulty of classifying the Malpighiaceae, a group of plants that includes the miniature holly.[14] It may be easy to explain the basic idea of evolution, descent by modification through natural selection, but the evidence Darwin used to support his theory was far from simple. Only experts in scientific fields ranging from botany to geology could read *The Origin of Species* without consulting a dictionary.

Darwin did not ignore the nonspecialist. Despite the mass of detail, Darwin organized *The Origin of Species* in a way that made it accessible to readers who knew little about science. For example, at the beginning of each chapter, following a convention used by several authors of scientific books, Darwin included an outline of the main points of the chapter. Readers who became lost in the botanical, zoological, or geological detail could return to beginning of the chapter and find their place in the overall argument again. In fact, it was possible to follow Darwin's argument in *The Origin of Species* simply by reading all the outlines at the beginning of each chapter in succession.[15]

Because Darwin wanted readers of *The Origin of Species* to follow his argument and not miss any of the important points he made, he concluded most chapters with a summary of the main points or significant conclusions. Only Chapter III, "Struggle for Existence," lacked a detailed summary (but it did have a concluding paragraph). Darwin included the summary of Chapter IX, "On the Imperfection of the Geological Record," with the summary of Chapter X, "On the Geological Succession of Organic Beings." He did the same for Chapters XI and XII, which were actually one long chapter on the geographical distribution of species. Chapter XIV was a recapitulation of the important points in the whole book; the summary of this chapter was a plea by Darwin for scientists to take his theory seriously. All the other chapters had a section entitled "Summary." Just like the chapter outlines, it was possible to follow Darwin's argument simply by reading each chapter's concluding summary. *The Origin of Species* could be "read" without reading the whole book.

Darwin's Editing: Changes in *The Origin of Species*

During his life, Darwin worked on and oversaw the publication of six British editions of *The Origin of Species*. These editions were published in 1859, 1860, 1861, 1866, 1869, and 1872. Darwin worried about his writing style: he believed it was neither clear nor interesting enough. Most of the changes between editions were attempts at better clarity. For example, the sixth edition was entitled *The Origin of Species* rather than *On the Origin of Species*.[16] Darwin may have felt more certain about his theory in 1872 than in 1859, but the new title was also less awkward.

Some of Darwin's editing was both substantive and significant. Perhaps the best-known change was Darwin's use of the phrase "the survival of the fittest." Although the idea is associated with Darwin and the theory of evolution, he did not use this phrase in the first edition. Commenting on the survival of some species in the "struggle for existence," Darwin writes, "This preservation of favourable variations and the rejection of injurious variations, I call Natural Selection."[17] After not being able to explain to some of his critics how and why natural selection worked, Darwin wrote in the fifth edition, "This preservation of favourable variations, and the destruction of injurious variations, I call Natural Selection, or the Survival of the Fittest."[18] And Darwin expanded the explanation still further in the sixth edition: "This preservation of favourable individual differences and variations, and the destruction of those which are injurious, I have called Natural Selection, or the Survival of the Fittest."[19]

The survival of the fittest was an idea Darwin borrowed from Herbert Spencer (1820–1903), a British sociologist, philosopher, and acquaintance of Darwin's. Although the idea seemed to explain why natural selection occurred, the survival of the fittest did not quell the objections to Darwin's theory about natural selection. The objections could be put in the form of a question: "Does natural selection really explain all of the complicated phenomena of nature?" To address these criticisms, Darwin added a new chapter entitled "Miscellaneous Objections to the Theory of Natural Selection" to the sixth edition.[20]

The main target of the chapter was the British zoologist and Catholic theologian, St. George Jackson Mivart (1827–1900). According to Darwin, in the book *On the Genesis of Species* (1871), Mivart "collected all the objections which have ever been advanced by myself and others against the theory of natural selection … and … illustrated them with admirable art and force."[21] Among his arguments, Mivart suggested that a series of sudden changes rather than slow, gradual change might better explain the development of species. Thus, Darwin's attempt to explain the missing parts in the sequence of fossil forms in Chapter IX, "On the Imperfection of the Geological Record," was the wrong approach: there were no gaps. Gradualism, uniformitarianism, and the idea that "nature does not make any jumps" were false foundations for Darwin's theory of evolution.[22] After consulting with Alfred Russel Wallace, among others, Darwin decided to devote a new chapter in *The Origin of Species* to Mivart's book.

As well as answering objections and improving the style of his writing, Darwin also oversaw the publication of *The Origin of Species* outside of Britain. There were seven editions published in the United States: three in 1860, and one each year in 1861, 1871, 1872, and 1883. (Typical of Darwin's propensity to tinker, the seventh edition was a revised version of the sixth English edition of 1872.) And there were translations into French, German, Italian, Swedish, Dutch, and Russian: the translators consulted with Darwin as the new British editions necessitated new foreign language editions. Editing *The Origin of Species* was the work of a lifetime.

Natural History and the Argument in *The Origin of Species*

The natural history in *The Origin of Species* was typical of scientific writing in the first half of the nineteenth century. Everyone interested in studying living organisms was also interested in describing them and tracing or discussing their origins. For example, it was not enough to know about the habits and physical characteristics of dogs; naturalists also wanted to know whether dogs had always behaved a particular way, whether one species of dog derived from another or was in some sense original and indigenous to an area, and the precise relationship between dogs and other animals such as wolves. And these studies were not limited to particular groups of animals or plants: naturalists also wrote about regions, countries, and even continents.

A survey of early nineteenth-century books on science shows the pervasiveness of natural history writing, writing that was literally historical as well as scientific. Charles Babington, a British botanist, wrote *Flora Bathioniensis: or, A Catalogue of the Plants Indigenous to the Vicinity of Bath* (1834). Georges Buffon (1707–1788), the French naturalist, wrote the nine-volume *Histoire naturelle des oiseaux* [The Natural History of Birds] with a group of four fellow scientists (1770–1783). Magnus Fries (1794–1878), the Swedish botanist, wrote *Sveriges Ätliga och Giftiga Svamper tecknade efter naturen* [Sweden's Edible and Poisonous Mushrooms Drawn as They Look in Nature], which was published in 1860. Louis Agassiz (1807–1883), the American zoologist, wrote the four-volume *Natural History of the United States* (1848–1854). Natural history writing was a worldwide and common preoccupation of scientists when Darwin wrote *The Origin of Species*.

If *The Origin of Species* had a theme apart from the one suggested by its title it was this: what do the latest discoveries in natural history suggest about the organization and development of the natural world? The British veterinary surgeon William Youatt

(1776–1847) wrote books on the natural history of horses, dogs, and pigs in 1834, 1845, and 1847, but he left untouched the question of a unifying theory connecting all species. That was the difficult task Darwin undertook in *The Origin of Species*.

Again, Darwin was not the first to consider a grand theory of nature. Leaving aside famous philosophical works dating back to Aristotle's *Physics*, in the nineteenth century, there was Chambers's *Vestiges of the Natural History of Creation*. There were also lesser-known and much less controversial works. Charles Hamilton Smith (1776–1859), author of several books in a series entitled The Naturalist's Library, wrote *The Natural History of the Human Species, its Typical Forms, Primaeval Distribution, Filiations, and Migrations* (1848). William Martin (1798–1864), another author of several natural history books, wrote *A General Introduction to the Natural History of Mammiferous Animals, with a Particular View of the Physical History of Man, and the More Closely Allied Genera of the Order of Quadrumana, or Monkeys* (1849). Both of these books were progressivist: they attempted to demonstrate that humans were at the top of the scale of organic beings.

Darwin took the opposite approach in *The Origin of Species*. The differences between species and the variations of species did not prove that one species was superior to another; rather, variation was evidence of the process of evolution at work. Variation was linked to common origins not necessarily to a scale of being.

The first points Darwin makes in the opening chapters of *The Origin of Species* are about the individual characteristics of animals and plants. Given the debate about origins, Darwin had to explain the differences between the species and their varieties. Were the differences permanent, part of a preestablished order, or was nature in a constant state of change? If there was continual change, how was this change produced? Was the change (that is, the mutation) passed on to other members of a species and could the mutation lead to transmutation?

By the end of the fifth of fourteen chapters, Darwin had answered these questions. The title of Chapter VI, "Difficulties on Theory," is the clue. In Chapter VI, Darwin dealt with the "crowd of difficulties" that he thought a reader of *The Origin of Species* would have.[23] Darwin's primary concern was to prove that mutation occurs in organic life and that this fact was significant to understanding the origin of species: he believed he had already accomplished this by the beginning of Chapter VI.

The structure of the argument Darwin used to prove his theory was significant. In Chapter I, "Variation Under Domestication,"

Darwin shows that mutation occurs in domestic animals: he begins with easily observable phenomena. In Chapter II, "Variation Under Nature," Darwin shows that it is difficult to distinguish between species and varieties in the wild: he continues by casting doubt on the fixity of species. In Chapter III, "Struggle for Existence," Darwin shows that the competition for food and other resources means that large numbers of organic beings cannot survive: he establishes a cause for extinction. In Chapter IV, "Natural Selection," Darwin shows that there is a natural process that enables some organic beings, some species, to survive and thrive: he explains the relationship between all species. In Chapter V, "Laws of Variation," Darwin explains some of the reasons for the mutation of species: he establishes a nonsupernatural reason for the existence of organic beings as they are presently constituted.

From Chapter VI onward, Darwin deals with the important issues raised by his argument. As Darwin notes, he could have dealt with a subject such as instinct in earlier chapters. Such a discussion, however, would have cluttered the main part of his argument with extra detail and made it difficult to follow. Also, as Darwin put it, "I have nothing to do with the origin of primary mental powers, any more than I have with that of life itself."[24] The purpose of *The Origin of Species* was to explain the diversity of species and varieties, not the origin of life. That is why the first five chapters of *The Origin of Species* were so critical. An extended discussion of the geographical distribution of species, as in Chapters XI and XII, might help to explain their origins but not necessarily the origin of life. Although the theory of descent by modification through natural selection had implications for an understanding of the origin of life, and Darwin knew this, the raison d'être for *The Origin of Species* was natural history. The causes of hybridism and the various methods of classification, discussed in Chapters VIII and XIII, respectively, were more important to Darwin than the specific time when life on Earth began. *The Origin of Species* is a natural history of all species.

The Future of *The Origin of Species*

Darwin never intended *The Origin of Species* to be his last statement on his theory of natural selection. Darwin calls *The Origin of Species* an "abstract" five times: he hints strongly that he intends to write a longer work.[25] The fuller exposition of his theory appeared in Darwin's other books. Every book he wrote after 1859 dealt with at least one aspect of natural selection or descent by modification.

Thus, in the last book published before his death, *The Formation of Vegetable Mould* (1881), Darwin argued that worms could make a significance difference to the topography of an area. How was this possible? It was possible through the cumulative effect of large numbers of worms ingesting and expelling earth over a long period of time.[26] In other words, the book supported the principle of uniformitarianism made famous by Charles Lyell and was more proof that small changes over generations could produce major change: a key principle of evolution.

In *The Origin of Species*, Darwin's concern was not evolution as such but descent by modification. The important contribution to science made by Darwin in *The Origin of Species* was to demonstrate that the "doctrine" of the fixity of species was not plausible scientifically: transmutation and speciation had occurred and were occurring. All species had descended from a common ancestor: they had not been created independently; they had not been created at the same time. Although he did not stress this point too heavily in *The Origin of Species*, Darwin also ruled out a designer or an intelligent being as creator. As Ernst Haeckel (1834–1919), one of Darwin's prominent supporters, put it, "The gist of Darwin's theory ... is this simple idea: *that the Struggle for Existence in Nature evolves new Species* without *design, just as the Will of man produces new Varieties in Cultivation with design*."[27]

One reason why Darwin's theory of evolution survived the scrutiny and criticism of scientists was its elegance. Darwin based his theory on information on which naturalists agreed, the variability of domesticated animals, and applied those principles to the larger and more difficult problem of the origin of species. Despite the detailed botanical, zoological, geological, and paleontological information, Darwin's "answer" was simple: all species have a common ancestor; transmutation occurs because continuing variation over a long period of time will cause an organism to change significantly.

Darwin claimed that his theory provided the best explanation of all the evidence in nature about origins.[28] This claim is accepted by most scientists today, but that was not the case in 1859. There was nothing inevitable about the survival of Darwin's theory. *The Origin of Species* could have ended up in the same intellectual backwater as *Vestiges of the Natural History of Creation*—little more than a curious piece of nineteenth-century writing about science. The history of the theory of evolution over the next seventy years is the story of the way in which Darwin's theory was adapted to the new discoveries made by scientists in the late-nineteenth and early twentieth centuries. In this period, Darwin's theory gained, lost, and regained its prominence and ultimately became the popular explanation for the origin of life on Earth.

Notes

1. The paper was titled "Extrait d'un ouvrage sur les espèces de quadrupèdes dont on a trouvé les ossemens dans l'intérieur de la terre, addressé aux savans et aux amateurs des Sciences" [Extract from a work on the species of quadrupeds of which the bones have been found in the interior of the earth, addressed to scientific experts and amateurs]. The Académie des sciences was the premier scientific society in France.

2. Georges Cuvier, ed., *Research on Fossilized Bones of Quadrupeds: And the Re-establishment of the Characteristics of Various Animal Species Which Global Revolutions Have Destroyed*, 4 vols. (Paris: Déterville, 1812).

3. See Loren Eiseley, *Darwin's Century: Evolution and the Men Who Discovered It* (Garden City, NY: Doubleday, 1958), 2–3.

4. Vernon Faithfull Storr, *Development and Divine Purpose* (London: Methuen and Co., 1906), 37; and Aubrey Moore, *Science and Faith* (London: Kegan Paul, Trench and Co., 1889), 177–180.

5. William Paley, *Natural Theology* (London: R. Faulder, 1802), 3–4.

6. D. E. Allen, "Babington, (Charles) Cardale (1808–1895)," *Oxford Dictionary of National Biography* (Oxford University Press, 2004), available at http://www.oxforddnb.com/view/article/970 (accessed 5 December 2005).

7. Quoted in *The Origin of Species*, 31.

8. Hooker to Darwin, Letter dated November 21, 1859, *Life and Letters of Charles Darwin*, II: 227.

9. Darwin, *The Origin of Species*, 63–64, 282; and "Autobiography," *Life and Letters of Charles Darwin*, I: 62, 83–84.

10. Quoted in Edna Healey, *Emma Darwin: The Inspirational Wife of a Genius* (London: Headline Book Publishing, 2002), 249.

11. Ibid.

12. *The Origin of Species*, 225–233, 358–360, 183–184.

13. John Sebright, *The Art of Improving the Breeds of Domestic Animals. In a Letter Addressed to the Right Hon. Sir Joseph Banks, K.B.* (London: John Harding, 1809), 15.

14. *The Origin of Species*, 20–29, 347, 219–224, 417.

15. Most of Darwin's books have summaries at the beginning of each chapter. Other famous works of nineteenth-century science, such as Lyell's *Principles of Geology*, used the same technique.

16. Morse Peckham's *The Origin of Species By Charles Darwin: A Variorum Text* (Philadelphia: University of Pennsylvania Press, 1959) lists all of the changes, sentence by sentence, between the first and sixth editions.

17. *The Origin of Species*, 1st edition, 81.

18. *On the Origin of Species by Means of Natural Selection, or the Preservation of Favoured Races in the Struggle for Life*, 5th edition (London: John Murray, 1869), 92.

19. *The Origin of Species by Means of Natural Selection, or the Preservation of Favoured Races in the Struggle for Life*, 6th edition (London: John Murray, 1872), 63.

20. *The Origin of Species*, 6th edition, 168–204.

21. Ibid., 176.

22. St. George Jackson Mivart, *On the Genesis of Species* (London: Macmillan, 1871), 97–112; compare with *The Origin of Species*, 6th edition, 202–204. Darwin used the phrase *Natura non facit saltum* (nature does not make any jumps) six times in the first edition of *The Origin of Species*. Each time he called the idea a "canon" or fundamental principle of natural history.

23. *The Origin of Species*, 1st edition, 171.

24. Ibid., 207.

25. Ibid., 1, 2, 4, 481.

26. *The Formation of Vegetable Mould* (London: John Murray, 1881), 3–7, 305–308.

27. Ernst Haeckel, *The Evolution of Man: A Popular Exposition of the Principal Points of Human Ontogeny and Phylogeny* (New York: D. Appleton and Co., 1879), I: 95. The italics are Haeckel's.

28. *The Origin of Species*, 459, 488–489.

CHAPTER 4

THE RECEPTION OF DARWIN'S THEORIES, 1859–1920

Reactions to *The Origin of Species*: Darwin's Concerns

Charles Darwin did not expect everyone who read *The Origin of Species* to accept his theory. In the last chapter of the book, he surmised that most "experienced naturalists" would reject his theory and only "a few naturalists, endowed with much flexibility of mind, and who have already begun to doubt on the immutability of species" would find his arguments convincing.[1] Darwin thought that "young and rising naturalists, who will be able to view both sides of the question with impartiality" would be able to convince other scientists (and the rest of the world) that his explanation of the origin of species made sense.[2]

The fact that Darwin stated his concern about the reaction of naturalists to *The Origin of Species* so explicitly is important. It may be tempting to talk about the theory of evolution and the reaction to *The Origin of Species* in terms of a clash between science and religion, but the reaction of Christians or church leaders was not Darwin's only concern. The confrontation between Bishop Samuel Wilberforce (1805–1873) and Thomas Huxley at the British Association for the Advancement of Science meeting in Oxford in 1860 and the Scopes Trial in Dayton, Tennessee, in 1925 are two famous examples of controversy sparked by Darwin's ideas, but they are not representative of the problems Darwin anticipated. A clash between the supporters of evolution and Christian opponents of evolution sounds dramatic and historically important, but it is not the whole story. Darwin realized that the first difficulty for his theory would be the reaction of his fellow naturalists. Darwin had to convince the community of scientists that his theory was better than the prevailing ones.

The story of the reaction to *The Origin of Species* is more complex and more mundane than the jury's guilty verdict in the Monkey Trial, as the Scopes Trial was popularly called. If there was a controversy, it first broke out among scientists. Did Darwin's science make sense? That was the first point of debate. Furthermore, the scientific community in 1859 and 1925 (and later) was not homogeneous. In the United States, one of Darwin's staunchest defenders, Asa Gray, was a committed Christian, and one of Darwin's most vocal opponents, Louis Agassiz, had little interest in Christianity. The major question about *The Origin of Species* in the years after 1859 was whether the weak points in Darwin's argument were so numerous and so scientifically important that the whole theory had to be dropped.[3]

Darwin's ideas and the theory of evolution were not singled out for attack. Most all-encompassing or controversial scientific theories were not and are not accepted immediately by a large number of scientists. It has taken even longer for the rest of society, people who are not amateur or professional scientists, to understand and accept new scientific theories. Two prominent examples of this phenomenon that surfaced before Darwin's time were the theories of a heliocentric universe and the circulatory system consisting of the heart, arteries, and veins. Both Copernicus and William Harvey (1578–1657) had their theories treated with skepticism and regarded as unscientific. Similarly, when Louis Agassiz proposed the theory of an Ice Age and Georges Lemaître (1894–1966) and Georgy Gamow (1904–1968) suggested the Big Bang theory for the beginning of the universe, their theories were not accepted immediately. Was Charles Darwin's theory the best explanation of the origin of species based on the available facts and evidence? This was the question scientists around the world asked themselves after 1859. Scientists "attacked" Darwin's ideas in *The Origin of Species* because no scientific theory since the fifteenth century, since the beginning of the Scientific Revolution, has been accepted without testing. Because Darwin's theory also affected the contemporary understanding of the origin of life, it was no surprise that *The Origin of Species* was both praised and vilified by people who were not scientists.

Given the way scientists work, the word "controversy" must be used with care when describing the reaction to *The Origin of Species*. Furthermore, it is important to remember the time period during which Darwin wrote the book. Mass communication was not as quick in 1859 as it would be in 1909 or 1959. Darwin died before the radio or telephone became means of disseminating information. The reaction to *The Origin of Species* built up slowly compared with what could have happened if the book had been published in the early twenty-first century. The first reactions were in letters written to Darwin. Second were reviews of the book published in journals and magazines and the reaction to those reviews, mainly by scientists. Third was the debate in the scientific community, particularly at official meetings of scientists. Fourth were the articles and books written in reaction to *The Origin of Species* or what scientists and other commentators had written about Darwin's theory. Last was the popular reaction to the book and Darwin's theory of evolution.

The various reactions to *The Origin of Species* did not occur in a vacuum. The discussion of Darwin's ideas occurred at the same time as other important debates and developments. The rights of women, the definition of democracy, the fairness and legality of slavery, and whether socialism was a legitimate form of government were all contentious issues in 1859. How society viewed these issues could be profoundly affected by a new belief that the species were mutable and humans were not the product of a special creation by an intelligent god. The reactions to *The Origin of Species* were varied and complex, because Darwin's ideas became part of a larger debate about the direction of science and the direction of nineteenth-century society.

Weaknesses in Darwin's Argument

From a nineteenth-century scientist's point of view, there were two major problems with Darwin's theory. The first of these concerned natural selection. Natural selection might be the process that resulted in mutation and, ultimately, transmutation, but Darwin did not explain clearly and convincingly why natural selection occurred. The second problem was the plausibility of descent by modification. Was it really possible for small, sometimes imperceptible, mutations in one species to produce a completely new species? In other words, those scientists who might concede that one species of flower could produce several new varieties that had never existed before were less willing to accept that a fish by mutation could become a reptile. The other criticisms of Darwin's theory derived from these two fundamental problems. Darwin and his supporters convinced the scientific community and the rest of society that these problems were not serious threats to a theory of evolution: this is what led to the widespread acceptance of Darwin's ideas. Evolution became the explanation for the origin of life because ignorance about the mechanism of natural selection and the supposed impact of numerous small mutations did not undermine Darwin's basic theory.

In the case of natural selection, scientists, as Alfred Russel Wallace stated forty years later, accepted Darwin's argument that mutation occurred in living organisms even if they disagreed with "the particular means" that Darwin suggested.[4] Without a knowledge of chromosomes and genes, Darwin had already made the mental leap necessary to recognize that all species are related. Dispensing with the idea of the fixity of species was already a significant contribution to the discipline of biology. But, no matter how brilliant his ability to analyze, Darwin could not move too far beyond his fellow scientists. Darwin was interested in the relationship between species and varieties: that was his forte. To study the relationship of species to varieties required expertise in morphology, embryology, and physiology: these sciences were based on analyzing characteristics visible to the naked eye, an external view of nature. Because Darwin was not interested in subcellular biology, there was little chance that he would investigate mutation at a microscopic level. However, the science of genetics and the key to explaining why natural selection occurred was in the nucleus of cells. By the end of the nineteenth century, many scientists ignored natural selection, the unexplainable process, and looked for other theories to explain why mutation occurred.[5]

As for the plausibility of descent by modification, the major criticism was that Darwin relied too heavily on the example of domesticated animals and plants. This was "a weakness in Darwin's work," wrote Alfred Russel Wallace; Darwin should have based his theory on the measurement of "variations of organisms in a state of nature."[6] Darwin began *The Origin of Species* with practical examples and derived a theory from them. Wallace and others preferred erecting a theoretical framework that could be tested empirically. Darwin's method was that of a nineteenth-century naturalist; Wallace's method came to dominate scientific experimentation in the late-nineteenth century. Although some scientists complained about Darwin's approach, his theory was accepted by scientists, and society, because it could be tested in a laboratory as well as in the "wild."

Alfred Russel Wallace claimed, correctly, that the criticisms of *The Origin of Species* led Darwin to downplay the effect of natural selection in later editions.[7] Darwin did adopt a more Lamarckian explanation for mutation in the fourth, fifth, and sixth editions. He conceded that some mutations did appear spontaneously and others were transferred wholesale from the parent to the progeny. Darwin's explanation of the cause of mutation became Neo-Lamarckian because he could not explain some of the gaps in his theory. For example, if there were numerous transitional forms between a species and a variety about to become a new species, why was there no evidence of these transitional forms in the geological record? In Chapter IX of the first edition of *The Origin of Species*, Darwin argued that the geological record itself was "extremely imperfect." Even if it was possible to know what the transitional forms between a parent species and a new one looked like—and Darwin did not think it was—such a large amount of time had elapsed since some of the transmutations occurred that the geological evidence had been destroyed.[8] This answer did not satisfy some naturalists, hence Darwin's use of Lamarck's idea.

Even if the imperfection of the geological record explained the missing transitional links, there were other, equally difficult, problems with a theory that relied on numerous small mutations. How could these mutations produce "large" abilities, such as the instinct in birds to lay their eggs in the nests of other birds? Or, if a plant that mutated could become a hybrid, how could small mutations overcome the sterility of plant hybrids? Using the examples of slave-making ants and the comb-building of bees, Darwin showed that apparently innate instincts were not, in fact, natural. By comparing the work of Karl Gärtner and Joseph Kölreuter (1733–1806) with his own experiments, Darwin demonstrated that sterility in plants was caused mainly by interbreeding not by hybridity.[9]

Darwin did provide answers to some of the criticisms he anticipated but, as his theory was so universal, so all-encompassing, his answers did not and could not satisfy every naturalist. His chapters on the geographical distribution of species suggested that the orthodox view of the fixity of species was untenable, but that did not mean naturalists were bound to accept Darwin's theory of descent by modification. Just because oceanic islands have many distinct or unique species did not mean naturalists had to accept that evolution had occurred.[10]

Seen in this context, the debates about *The Origin of Species*, Darwin's ideas, and Darwinism make sense. With regard to *The Origin of Species*, naturalists discussed whether the book was well argued. When discussing Darwin's ideas about transmutation and speciation, naturalists discussed whether descent by modification was a viable scientific theory. As for the theory of evolution, naturalists debated whether they should accept Darwin's theory of evolution—which Thomas Huxley called Darwinism—or some other theory. And mixed in with the scientific debates were the questions about the philosophical, religious, and social implications of Darwin's theory. Whether God created humans was a question raised by Darwin's work; but in the period from 1859 to 1925, even those naturalists who doubted the existence of an intelligent creator wondered whether Darwin's theory of evolution explained how humans came to inhabit the Earth.

Darwin on *The Origin of Species*

What did Darwin himself think of *The Origin of Species*? His letters written in 1859 and 1860 and his autobiography written sixteen years later reveal that Darwin recognized very soon after the book's publication that he had done something very important. He had made an invaluable contribution to science. Even though Darwin tinkered with the text, trying to make it aesthetically pleasing, easier to understand, and scientifically more foolproof, the intellectual and economic success of the book pleased him.

"It is no doubt the chief work of my life," wrote Darwin in his autobiography.[11] Darwin wrote other books—some of them pioneering works in geology, marine biology and classification, and plant tropism or the movement of plants as a result of external stimuli—but none of his other books were as important nor took up as much of his time as *The Origin of Species*. The fact that Darwin was the first to suggest a viable theory for the formation of coral reefs, that he was the first person to examine and describe the relationship of all the species of barnacles, or that he was one of the first to explain how certain plants move is frequently forgotten. But even if everyone did remember these books, Darwin himself recognized that they were not as significant as *The Origin of Species*. It was *The Origin of Species*, not *The Structure and Formation of Coral Reefs* (1842), that established Darwin as one of the greatest scientists of the last five hundred years.

And scientists did take *The Origin of Species* seriously. There was a struggle, a lively debate among scientists, over the ideas in the book. As Darwin noted, "the reviews were very numerous; for a time I collected all that appeared on the *Origin* and on my related books, and these amount (excluding newspaper reviews) to 265; but after a time I gave up the attempt in despair."[12] Scientists, professional and amateur, had something to say about *The Origin of Species*, hence the large number of reviews.

The book also sold well. *The Origin of Species* "was from the first highly successful," noted Darwin.[13] By 1876, sixteen thousand copies had been sold in Britain alone and, as Darwin commented, "considering how stiff a book it is, this is a large sale."[14] *The Origin of Species* was a book the public wanted to have. People read the book because they wanted to know about Darwin's theory, because they agreed or disagreed with Darwin, and because it was controversial; whatever the reason, the pertinent fact is that they read it. All of this success pleased Darwin.

Reviews of *The Origin of Species*

The first major review of *The Origin of Species* appeared in *The Times* of London on 26 December 1859, one month after the book was published. *The Times* was the most important newspaper in Britain; all the intelligentsia read it, including scientists, professional and amateur. Whatever the reviewer said in this newspaper would have a significant influence on the public and popular view of *The Origin of Species*. If *The Times* review was positive, *The Origin of Species* would be more likely to receive a fair hearing among scientists (unlike *Vestiges of the Natural History of Creation*).

The Times review was positive. Like many book reviews of that time, the reviewer's name was not appended to the review, but Darwin found out that Huxley had written most of it. Huxley had told Darwin on 23 November that "I am ready to go to the Stake if requisite in support of Chap. IX" ("On the Imperfection of the Geological Record").[15] Huxley's review emphasized the logic of one of Darwin's major assertions: it was difficult to distinguish varieties from species. Without stating explicitly that Darwin's theory was correct, Huxley reiterated another of Darwin's major contentions: all species had a common ancestor.[16] The review was a triumph for Darwin.

Huxley wrote reviews in two other influential British journals, the *Westminster Review* and *Macmillan's Magazine*: they, too, were positive.[17] Asa Gray, the renowned American botanist (who was also Darwin's friend), wrote in the *American Journal of Science and Arts* that Darwin's theory was "not atheistical."[18] Thomas Wollaston, the British entomologist, wrote in *Annals and Magazine of Natural History* that "although we have felt compelled to say thus much against the theory so ably pleaded for in Mr. Darwin's book, we repeat that, in a very limited sense indeed, there seems no reason why the theory might not be a sound one."[19] These reviewers acknowledged the strength of Darwin's scientific evidence for his theory, but they also recognized the implications for the traditional Christian view of creation.

Other reviewers were not so kind. Richard Owen, a major figure in the British scientific establishment, wrote a disparaging review in the *Edinburgh Review.* Owen described the "gems" in *The Origin of Species* as "few indeed and far apart ... leaving the determination of the origin of species very nearly where the author found it." The book was a "disappointment."[20] Like Owen, Samuel Wilberforce, the Bishop of Oxford and a member of the Zoological and Geological societies, argued that species and varieties were not as malleable as Darwin suggested nor could Darwin use time like a "magician's rod."[21] Just because Darwin imagined that hundreds of millions of years were needed to produce mutation and transmutation, it did not mean that either the Earth or the universe were actually that old.

Darwin had hoped the reviews would decide the fate of *The Origin of Species*—positively, of course. They did not. Readers might be told that the book was a major contribution to science or filled with unproven speculation, depending on which journal or magazine they read. The next stage of the debate about *The Origin of Species* would be more personal: scientists would discuss the book face to face.

Discussion of *The Origin of Species* by Scientists

The best-known debate about *The Origin of Species* occurred on 30 June 1860, in Oxford, at a meeting of the British Association for the Advancement of Science. The British Association, as the organization was popularly known, met annually. The meetings were an opportunity for scientists to discuss new research and new theories with their peers and in the presence of an interested audience.

Although the British Association meeting is remembered for the clash between Thomas Huxley and Bishop Samuel Wilberforce, this event was one of many discussions of Darwin's ideas. Members of the Linnean Society, the Zoological Society, and the Royal Society discussed *The Origin of Species.* Members of the Académie des sciences in France discussed the book. In fact, these discussions occurred around the world in places as far apart as India and the United States.

The key question at these discussion was this: had Darwin solved the mystery of the origin of species? Even scientists who believed that the Christian God had created each species individually thought that there had to be a scientific explanation for the diversity and distribution of varieties of species. Whatever the religious or philosophical implications of Darwin's descent by modification, it was worth asking whether the action of natural selection could explain the natural world as it existed.

The first major opportunity to "debate" this question in public occurred at the British Association meeting. In fact, this famous incident was not a debate in the sense that ideas were argued back and forth: the participants gave a series of speeches. Furthermore, the eyewitness accounts of the "debate" vary. Two of the protagonists, Huxley and Wilberforce, both left the meeting thinking that his position had triumphed.

Some of the details of the meeting are indisputable. The debate occurred at a session of the meeting dealing with botany and zoology. John William Draper (1811–1882), an American scientist who was the president of City University of New York, read a paper entitled "On the Intellectual Development of Europe, Considered with Reference to the Views of Mr. Darwin." (In 1874, Draper published one of the best-known nineteenth-century books describing the supposed clash between science and religion, *History of the Conflict between Religion and Science*: it was more a diatribe against religion and for the preeminence of science than a history.) Because there were more than seven hundred people packed into the room, including Oxford professors, Oxford students, and visiting scientists, the session had to be moved to a larger room. Draper's paper lasted more than an hour and, with the introductory speeches, the session had been going for two hours by the time Samuel Wilberforce stood up to reply to Draper. The room was stuffy. Wilberforce pontificated elegantly—his smooth speaking style had earned him the nickname "Soapy Sam"—but many of the scientists present thought he had been coached by Richard Owen, a known opponent of Darwin's theory. Wilberforce repeated most of the arguments he used in his as-yet-unpublished review of *The Origin of Species*. Then Wilberforce, probably in an attempt to lighten the mood of the audience, made a flippant comment asking whether Thomas Huxley had descended from an ape on his grandfather or grandmother's side. (Darwin had said nothing about man's descent from apes in *The Origin of Species*.) Huxley gave a impassioned response to Wilberforce, which included saying that he would rather have descended from apes than misuse the talents he had by injecting ridicule into a serious scientific debate. Although Huxley thought he had been convincing, most of the audience either could not hear what he said or were not persuaded by his arguments. More effective was the speech of Joseph Hooker who addressed Wilberforce's points one by one and pointed out that Wilberforce's arguments suggested that he had not read *The Origin of Species*. Among the other speakers was FitzRoy, now Admiral FitzRoy, who begged the audience to adhere to the account of creation in the Bible: he was shouted down.

At most, neither side won. The audience enjoyed themselves. (The undergraduates in the audience had come to see and be part of the spectacle.) The hot conditions resulted in at least one woman fainting, which added to the sense of drama. Perhaps the most important result of the British Association meeting was that the Darwinians, Huxley's name for the supporters of Darwin's theory of evolution, did not suffer a defeat. A draw meant more time to convince their fellow scientists and the rest of society that Darwin's explanation of the origin of species was the right one.

The combination of articles in journals and magazines and discussions among scientists was effective. Between 1859 and 1872, more than one hundred British periodicals had multiple articles discussing Darwin's ideas.[22] Within a decade, many scientists considered Darwin's explanation of the origin of species more plausible than the idea of a special creation or multiple creations by God. Furthermore, the progressivist element in Darwin's theory—that natural selection could effect greater complexity as well as more diversity—fit well into European and American cultural ideas about the progress in society. As one contemporary noted,

> Ten years later [than 1860] I encountered [Huxley] ... at the Exeter meeting of the Association. Again there was a bitter assault on Darwinism, this time by a Scottish doctor of divinity; with smiling serenity Huxley smote him hip and thigh, the audience, hostile or cold at Oxford, here ecstatically acquiescent. The decade had worked its changes.[23]

In fact, the period after 1870 would have been a complete triumph for Darwinism had it not been for two significant objections. In 1867, Fleeming Jenkin (1833–1885), a British engineer, asserted that the blending of male and female characteristics in sexual reproduction would mean that any beneficial mutation would reduce by half in each succeeding generation. (Jenkin, like all scientists of the nineteenth century including Darwin, did not know about the discrete genetic units involved in reproduction: this was not discovered until the twentieth century.) Three years later, in 1871, the physicist William Thomson (1821–1907) read a paper at the British Association meeting in which he suggested that the Earth was about 100 million years old, based on his calculation of the cooling of the Earth's crust. Thomson was one of the foremost mathematician/ physicists of the nineteenth century—he was ennobled as Lord Kelvin in 1892 and the Kelvin scale of temperature measurement was named after him—if his calculations suggested the Earth was much younger than the millions of years posited by Charles Lyell in *Principles of Geology*, then Thomson must be right. Unfortunately, Darwin had relied upon Lyell's calculations for the long periods of time needed for species to mutate from one form to another.

Darwin and his supporters had to react to Jenkin and Thomson's critiques. First, Darwin changed his argument about the transmission of single mutations. In the fifth edition of *The Origin of Species*, he suggested that single variations or mutations occurred but that they were much less likely to be preserved in the next generation. Second, Darwin used some of the evolutionary ideas of Jean-Baptiste Lamarck. He deemphasized the superior power of natural selection to cause and preserve mutations and emphasized the role of "speedier" evolutionary mechanisms, such as the use and disuse of organs and the wholesale transfer of new habits or characteristics from parent to progeny.

Darwin's adaptations of his theory solidified a split among scientists about the mechanism of evolution. The problem for scientists was not whether evolution occurred—it did—but how it occurred. Of the many explanations scientists theorized, three were the most popular. One group of scientists, usually called Neo-Darwinists, argued that natural selection was the sole mechanism of evolution. The best-known and most dogged defender of natural selection was the German biologist August Weismann (1834–1914), who proposed the germ plasm theory of heredity. The germ plasm was the basic reproductive unit of the parents that created the progeny, but the parents simply passed on the germ plasm to the next generation without changing it: any changes in the parents' structure caused by external conditions or use and disuse were not passed on to the progeny. The germ plasm could only be affected by natural selection. Other Neo-Darwinists, such as the British biologists George John Romanes (1848–1894) and Edward Bagnall Poulton (1856–1943), were less dogmatic but insisted that natural selection was the major driving force of evolution.

Another group of scientists, the Neo-Lamarckians, emphasized the idea that characteristics developed in response to external conditions, or through use and disuse, could be passed on to the next generation. Herbert Spencer was the most prominent Neo-Lamarckian in Britain; he had originally supported a theory of evolution that combined natural selection and the inheritance of acquired characteristics but changed in reaction to Weismann's emphasis on natural selection. Other scientists, such as the German zoologist Theodor Eimer (1843–1898) and the American paleontologists Edward Drinker Cope (1840–1897) and Alpheus Hyatt (1838–1902), supported Neo-Lamarckianism because the theory allowed them to argue that there was something inherent in each organism that drove it to evolve. For Cope, in particular, that internal mechanism was placed in each organism by God.

A third group of scientists, sometimes called saltationists but more often Mendelians, argued that evolution sometimes occurred in rapid spurts or could occur suddenly: slow and steady transformation was unnecessary. As early as 1859, in his letter congratulating Darwin on the brilliance of *The Origin of Species*, Thomas Huxley wrote, "You have loaded yourself with an unnecessary difficulty in adopting 'Natura non facit saltum' so unreservedly. I believe she does make *small* jumps"[24] In 1900, the rediscovery of Gregor Mendel's research on heredity by the botanists Carl Erich Correns (1864–1933), Erich Tschermak von Seysenegg (1871–1962), and Hugo de Vries seemed to reveal a new and more plausible explanation for evolution. The idea that discrete genetic units were passed on from one generation to another was, to the Mendelians, a more systematic and mathematically simple way of explaining inheritance. In 1901, de Vries published the first extended explanation of what he called "the mutation theory" in a book with the same title. His ideas, particularly the transmission of sudden mutations by genes, were supported and disseminated by the research of three men in particular: the British biologist William Bateson (1861–1926), who coined the term genetics; the American biologist Thomas Hunt Morgan (1866–1945), whose experiments on fruit flies (*Drosophila melanogaster*) established the theory that chromosomes are involved in heredity; and the Danish botanist Wilhelm Johannsen (1857–1927), whose distinction between genotype, the genetic constitution of an organism, and phenotype, the physical characteristics of an organism, are an important foundation of modern genetics.

The most important consequence of the discussions and disputes among scientists was that Darwin's theory about evolution was virtually ignored. Scientists sought alternative explanations for the reason why evolution occurred. They were debating the ideas in *The Origin of Species* very tangentially. Apart from one or two proponents, such as Alfred Wallace, Darwinism as Darwin understood it was a dead theory. Looking back on the period from 1880 to 1920, the British zoologist Julian Huxley (1887–1975), the grandson of Thomas Huxley, called it "the eclipse of Darwinism."[25]

Public Reaction to Darwin

The numerous disagreements among scientists about the mechanism of evolution had unfortunate timing. They occurred just as the public acceptance of the theory of evolution began to grow. Darwin's accomplishments as a scientist were recognized by a number of honors given to him in the years before and after his death: an honorary doctorate from Cambridge University; membership of the prestigious Académie des sciences of France; his statue in the Natural History Museum in London; a new medal, the Darwin Medal, created by the Royal Society to honor scientists doing research in similar areas to Darwin; and burial in Westminster Abbey. At the same time, scientists took Darwin's ideas about how and why evolution occurred less and less seriously.

In the public view, however, the theory of evolution became more and more "the truth." To most nonscientists, the evidence to support what they supposed were Darwin's theories became overwhelming. In 1863, Charles Lyell's *The Geological Evidences of the Antiquity of Man with Remarks on Theories of the Origin of Species* and Thomas Huxley's *Evidence as to Man's Place in Nature* were published. Both books did what Darwin had not done in *The Origin of Species*: applied the theory of descent by modification to human origins. (Darwin did this later in *The Descent of Man.*) Humans, like Darwin's pigeons in *The Origin of Species*, had a common ancestor. In 1862, *Macmillian's Magazine* serialized a children's story about evolution entitled "The Water Babies." The author was Charles Kingsley (1819–1875), an Anglican priest, poet, and amateur naturalist. In 1863, *The Water Babies* was published as a book and it became a best seller (and, later, a classic piece of British literature). In 1872, Walter Bagehot (1826–1877), one of best-known legal scholars and political commentators of the time, published *Physics and Politics, or Thoughts on the Application of the Principles of Natural Selection and Inheritance to Political Society*; by 1879, the book was a best seller with five editions. The public in Britain wanted to read about Darwin's idea, particularly the application of the theory of evolution to the problems and direction of society. The same was true in the rest of the world, particularly the Western world.

The public interest in evolution was stimulated by the supporters of Darwin's theories. Foremost among the supporters was Thomas Huxley. Darwin did very little to defend his ideas publicly. He wrote the occasional letter to natural history magazines and journals, but he was content to let advocates like Huxley be in the vanguard. Huxley's six lectures on evolution to working men of London, which he gave in 1862, and his series of lectures defending evolution during a tour of the United States in 1876 were typical of Huxley and atypical of Darwin.[26]

Although *The Origin of Species* was the starting point for these promotional efforts, like the debates among scientists occurring contemporaneously, the actual topic of discussion was evolution. This was especially true of the discussion, debates, and writing of Christian opponents of Darwin's ideas. Their concern was much less about the specific ideas in *The Origin of Species* and much more focused on the implications of the theory of evolution. They worried about Darwinism rather than Darwin. Darwinism was synonymous with evolution in the minds of Christian opponents: and evolution was the danger, or evil, that had to be challenged.[27]

According to William Jennings Bryan (1860–1925), the populist politician and three-time candidate for president of the United States, a naturalist scientific theory supported a materialist approach to life. Materialism, living life as though God did not exist or was not important, led to excessive capitalism, imperialism and a world war, and a society with no moral foundation. Other Christian opponents of Darwinism echoed these claims.

Was evolution a good (in the moral sense) theory? At the beginning of the twentieth century, the question of the effect on society of accepting a theory of evolution became a greater concern to Christian opponents of Darwinism. The impact of the theory on belief in the creation story in the Bible was troubling; however, looking at the state of the world, what these opponents saw as the collapse in society's morals was far worse. From 1920 onward, the social impact of the theory of evolution was as much a part of the twentieth-century debate about Darwin and *The Origin of Species* as were the disputes among scientists about the mechanism of evolution.

Notes

1. *The Origin of Species*, 481–482.

2. Ibid., 482.

3. Darwin recognized this in the chapters "Difficulties on Theory" and "Recapitulation and Conclusion." See *The Origin of Species*, 171–172, 459–466.

4. Alfred Russel Wallace, *Darwinism: An Exposition of the Theory of Natural Selection with Some of its Applications* (London: Macmillan, 1889), v.

5. In Darwin's defense, the German pathologist and biologist Rudolf Virchow (1821–1902) did not propose his theory that cells were the basic building blocks of every living organism until 1858. Cytology, the study of cells, was a very new science, dating from the 1840s.

6. Wallace, *Darwinism*, vi. Wallace did some of the measurements he suggested; see *Darwinism*, 47, 48, 51, 53, 55, 56, 58, 60–61, 67, 72–73.

7. Ibid., vi–viii.

8. *The Origin of Species*, 282–293.

9. See *The Origin of Species*, 219–242, 255–276, chapters entitled "Instinct" and "Hybridism."

10. *The Origin of Species*, 406–409.

11. *Life and Letters of Charles Darwin*, I: 86.

12. Ibid.

13. Ibid.

14. Ibid.

15. *Correspondence of Charles Darwin*, VIII: 390.

16. "Darwin on The Origin of Species," *The Times*, 26 December 1859, 8–9.

17. Thomas Huxley, "Time and Life: Mr Darwin's 'Origin of Species'," *Macmillan's Magazine* (December 1859): 142–148; and "Darwin on the Origin of Species," *Westminster Review* 17 (1860): 541–570.

18. "Review of Darwin's Theory on the Origin of Species by means Natural Selection," *American Journal of Science and Arts* 29 (March 1860): 180–183.

19. "Biographical Notice," *Annals and Magazine of Natural History* 5 (1860): 143 [132–143].

20. "Darwin on the Origin of Species," *Edinburgh Review* 111 (April 1860): 494, 495 [487–532].

21. Samuel Wilberforce, *Essays Contributed to the "Quarterly Review"* (London: John Murray, 1874), I: 63–68, 84–85.

22. Alvar Ellegård, *Darwin and the General Reader: The Reception of Darwin's Theory of Evolution in the British Periodical Press, 1859–1872* (Gothenberg: Elanders Boktryckeri Aktiebolag, 1958), 369–383.

23. W. Tuckwell, *Reminiscences of Oxford*, 2nd ed. (London: Smith, Elder and Co., 1970), 51, quoted in J. Vernon Jensen, *Thomas Henry Huxley: Communicating for Science* (Newark: University of Delaware Press, 1991), 51.

24. Letter dated 23 November 1859, *Correspondence of Charles Darwin*, VII: 391.

25. Julian Huxley, *Evolution: The Modern Synthesis* (New York: Harper and Brothers Publishers, 1943), 22–28.

26. Both lecture series were published as books. The first as *On Our Knowledge of the Causes of the Phenomena of Organic Nature* (1863). The second as *American Addresses, with a Lecture on the Study of Biology* (1877).

27. See James R. Moore, *The Post-Darwinian Controversies: A Study of the Protestant Struggle to Come to Terms with Darwin in Great Britain and America 1870–1900* (Cambridge: Cambridge University Press, 1979), 193–216.

CHAPTER 5

DARWIN, DARWINISM, AND EVOLUTION IN THE TWENTIETH CENTURY

Darwinism and Evolution at the Beginning of the Twentieth Century

Historians usually divide the nineteenth century from the twentieth in 1914 or 1918, the beginning or end of the First World War. This division is unhelpful in the history of the theory of evolution. Nothing epoch-making occurred in the reception of Darwin's ideas during the War years.

A more useful date is 1925 or one of the five years after it. On 10 July 1925, the Scopes Trial began and, in the words of one historian, so did "America's continuing debate over science and religion."[1] In 1927, legislators in nineteen states rejected antievolution bills. Two years later, the American astronomer Edwin Hubble (1889–1953) provided proof that the universe was very old and expanding. At the same time, as a result of the research done by scientists such as William Bateson and Thomas Hunt Morgan, the discipline of genetics began to become a specialized field in science.

These developments were significant for three reasons. First, the Scopes Trial and the attempts to pass antievolution bills indicated a desire by opponents of evolution to draw attention to the social impact of the theory. This new approach was added to the nineteenth-century tactic of defending the biblical account of creation. Second, the discovery by Hubble began the elimination of one of the major scientific objections to Darwin's theory of evolution: the relatively short age of the Earth. The assertion by William Thomson that the laws of physics suggested the Earth was not old enough to accommodate the millennia required for evolution to occur was finally demonstrated to be incorrect. Third, and even more significant, the science of genetics looked likely to provide the answer to the question that Darwin could not answer in *The Origin of Species*: how and why natural selection worked. Two of the major problems with the ideas Darwin developed in *The Origin of Species* began to recede. The period from 1930 onward was the beginning of a new era for the reception of *The Origin of Species*.

The Scopes Trial is evidence that the year 1930 did not mark the end of the debate about and opposition to the ideas in *The Origin of Species*. In fact, in the years after 1925, Christian opponents of evolution formed a new group whose approach to science was more like the majority of society in the twentieth century. Calling themselves creationists, these Christians used the newest findings in geology to develop ideas about the age of the Earth and the impact of the flood mentioned in the book of Genesis: they used modern science to defend the Bible.

The difference between 1930 and 1900 was the way in which scientists and the educated public perceived *The Origin of Species*. In 1900, it was possible that scientists might ignore, discount, or even reject Darwin's theories. That was not the case after 1930. Darwin's theory needed more refinement—not until the discovery of the structure of DNA and RNA in the 1950s would scientists be able to explain how genes worked and the connection between genes and mutation—but scientists still accepted the majority of Darwin's theory as he wrote it in *The Origin of Species*. The linking of genetics, statistical analysis of the growth of populations, and the research of naturalists in the 1930s and 1940s led to what scientists called "the grand synthesis" in the 1950s. The action of natural selection and why it occurred could be explained by the mutation of genes. This agreement on the mechanism of evolution was called Neo-Darwinism. The ideas of *The Origin of Species* now had a permanent place in Western and world thought.

The Scopes Trial and Renewed Opposition to Evolution

In 1940, the British theologian Vernon Faithfull Storr wrote:

The panic caused by the publication in 1859 of *The Origin of Species* appears to us today almost unbelievable. The doctrine of evolution was regarded as materialistic and atheistic in tendency.

> It challenged in the first place, the authority of the Bible, with its divinely inspired narrative of Creation in Genesis. It degraded human nature by its suggestion that man had an animal ancestry.[2]

Storr's comment helps to explain why the Scopes Trial of 1925 was so compelling. In 1859, some Christians thought the theory of evolution was a direct challenge to the veracity of the Bible. Most Christians at that time believed the words in the Bible were literally true. If Genesis 2:1–2 said that God created "the heavens and earth" in six days, then that was what had occurred. However, by 1900, many Christians in Europe were no longer reading or interpreting the Bible so literally; as this was the case, the theory of evolution was less threatening. Not so in the United States: the rise of Christian fundamentalism ensured that the debate about evolution—whether the theory explained the origin of life correctly—would continue.

Christian fundamentalists desired a return to what they called the fundamental truths of Christianity. They thought too many Christians were willing to abandon such doctrines as the inerrancy of the Bible, that it contained no mistakes, or that the world was created in six days. According to fundamentalists, anyone who held beliefs such as evolution helped to weaken American society by destroying its moral foundation. When the American Civil Liberties Union found a teacher, John Scopes (1900–1970), willing to test the ban in Tennessee on teaching evolution in school, William Jennings Bryan eagerly accepted the opportunity to be a prosecuting lawyer.

The context of the Scopes Trial is important to note. Neither Darwin nor *The Origin of Species* was on trial in Dayton, Tennessee, that year: evolution was. Bryan stated in a lecture three years earlier,

> I believe there is ... a menace to fundamental morality. The hypothesis to which the name of Darwin has been given—the hypothesis that links man to the lower forms of life and make him a lineal descendant of the brute—is obscuring God and weakening all the virtues that rest upon the religious tie between God and man.[3]

Bryan was reacting against what he considered the consequences of accepting the theory of evolution.

In one sense, the trial was a farce. Bryan was not a fundamentalist even though he was a vocal opponent of evolution and a proponent of making America more Christian. John Scopes admitted he had broken the law, but he probably had never taught evolution in a Dayton school. The trial only occurred in Dayton because the town elders wanted some publicity (and money from tourists) for their hamlet.

The conviction of Scopes after eight days of high drama—including the lead defense lawyer, Clarence Darrow (1857–1938), making William Jennings Bryan take the stand—only stimulated the fundamentalist attack on evolution. The most significant consequence of the trial was the lobbying for the suppression of references to evolution in textbooks, particularly in southern states. As scientists moved toward a consensus about evolution "American schools taught less evolution in 1960 than they had in 1920."[4]

Fundamentalists had also been ridiculed in the media during the Scopes Trial. Labeled as backward and ignorant, fundamentalists sought more appealing ways to oppose evolution. The most common of these was to use scientific information to support the biblical account of creation. Men such as George McCready Price (1870–1963) and Dudley Joseph Whitney (1883–1964) argued that there was scientific evidence to prove that a worldwide and catastrophic flood had caused the fossil deposits geologists discovered and that the height of the layers of rock formations proved that the Earth was not very old, probably no more than 10,000 years.

Wanting to stand for something, the new group of opponents of evolution called themselves creationists rather than antievolutionists. Not all of them were fundamentalists: neither was their opposition to evolution the same. Some argued that the Earth was about 6,000 years old, a "Young Earth." Others argued that the days of creation in Genesis were actually ages—how long was another point of dispute—and that the Earth was "Old." Some believed science and modern ideas were dangerous and morally debilitating; others thought science could be used for the good of humankind, provided the scientists had a Christian frame of reference.

Scientific Creationism and Creation Science, while remaining a significant fact of American life and culture, declined in national prominence in the 1960s. As scientists found more evidence to substantiate the theory of evolution, it became harder to win popular support for antievolutionary ideas. In 1982, the District Court decision in *McLean v. Arkansas*, which ruled out that state's desire to have equal treatment for the teaching of Creation Science and "Evolution Science," was critical. The presiding judge William R. Overton deemed Creation Science a religious doctrine: public school teachers could not teach it as an alternative to evolution.

Another attempt to link scientific evidence with a critique of evolution, the Intelligent Design Movement, faced the same hurdle as Scientific Creationism. Using an approach similar to William Paley, proponents of Intelligent Design argued that the complexity of organic life meant that it had to be the product of a designer. The eye, for example, could not work as an eye unless the retina, pupil, and cornea evolved at the same time; such an occurrence was unlikely and mechanisms such as sight were "irreducibly complex," that is, they had basic components that could not work without the other components. Furthermore, the theoretical and experimental problems with the theory of evolution meant that scientists should search for an alternative theory. Because the proponents of Intelligent Design were unwilling to state who the designer was, this movement, which began in the late 1980s, has been labeled an inferior version of Creationism.

The opposition by some Christians to evolution has been to the larger theory rather than to Darwin or *The Origin of Species*. The varieties of opinion among scientists about the precise nature of evolution—some taking a position closer to Darwin's theory, others further away—has been of little interest to these mainly Protestant, mainly fundamentalist, and mainly American opponents of evolution. Darwin is the symbol of evolution. Opponents of evolution objected to the ideas in *The Origin of Species* only because Darwin was the "father of evolution."

The Neo-Darwinist Synthesis and Beyond

Commenting on the future of Darwinism and the efforts of scientists to work out the precise mechanism of evolution, William Bateson wrote, in 1913,

> That species have come into existence by an evolutionary process no one seriously doubts; but few who are familiar with the facts that genetic research has revealed are now inclined to speculate as to the manner by which the process has been accomplished. Our knowledge of the nature and properties of living things is far too meagre to justify any such attempts. Suggestions of course can be made: though, however, these ideas may have a stimulating value in the lecture room, they look weak and thin when set out in print. The work which may one day give them a body has yet to be done.[5]

Less than thirty years later the situation had changed. In 1942, Julian Huxley wrote, "Biology at the present time is embarking upon a phase of synthesis ... nowhere is this movement toward unification more likely to be valuable than in this many-sided topic of evolution; and already we are seeing the first-fruits in the re-animation of Darwinism."[6] By 1970, the "work" Bateson wrote about had been done. In 1977, the American paleontologist Stephen Jay Gould (1941–2002) wrote, "Our understanding of genetic mutation suggests that Darwin was right in maintaining that variation is not predirected in favorable ways. Evolution is a mixture of chance and necessity—chance at the level of variation, necessity in the working of selection."[7] What historians of science call the Neo-Darwinist synthesis had occurred.

Three major trends contributed to the reemergence of Darwin's theories as a major component of the explanation for evolution. The first of these was population genetics, the study of the spread of species based on mathematics. The American scientist Sewall Wright (1889–1988) and the British scientists Ronald Aylmer Fisher (1890–1962) and J. B. S. Haldane (1892–1964) are the best-known proponents of this approach to evolution. In his book *The Genetical Theory of Natural Selection* (1930), Fisher suggested that genes spread through a population as discrete units; the more adaptive a gene became the faster it would increase through a population. As genes were the source of mutation, a "good" gene, one that adapted the best, would produce increasingly useful mutations. Haldane demonstrated that the spread of a "good" gene could occur much more rapidly than Fisher thought. He drew attention to examples such as the peppered moth. Between 1850 and 1900, the darker form of the moth began to dominate the species because it could hide from predators in the soot, which was a common feature of cities in Britain. Wright demonstrated that the interaction of genes was much more complex than Fisher and Haldane suggested. Multiple genes might affect one characteristic in an organism. Thus, the mutation in one gene could produce a large range of variations in a species because of its interaction with other genes. Through natural selection, the most adaptive of these variations would survive—just as Darwin had predicted.

Fisher, Haldane, and Wright's work was highly theoretical. The second major trend was the "translation" of the theories of population geneticists into experiments and laws that naturalists could use in their research. The American zoologist Theodosius Dobzhansky (1900–1975) was the most important contributor to this trend. In *Genetics and the Origin of Species* (1937), Dobzhansky explained that the application of the laws of genetics to small populations showed how a mutation could occur and spread. Like Darwin, he argued that what occurred on a microlevel could occur on a macrolevel. Mutation ultimately led to transmutation or speciation.

Other scientists had been working on the connection between genetics and evolution. The Russian population geneticist Sergei

S. Chetverikov (1880–1959) showed that recessive genes could produce even more variation in a population. His colleague Aleksandr S.
Serebrovsky (1892–1948) coined the term "gene pool" to explain the
large number of genes available to an organism or population facing
any particular situation during its life. The American biologist Ernst
Mayr (1904–2005) united the ideas of early twentieth-century naturalists and population geneticists. In *Systematics and the Origin of
Species* (1942), Mayr argued that species were groups of organisms
that could only breed among themselves. Geographic location, particularly in isolated areas, could lead to the genes in related individuals drifting apart as the individuals adapted to their environment:
new species would evolve by natural selection.

The third trend involved the research of paleontologists. The
American George Gaylord Simpson (1902–1984) was one of the first
paleontologists to apply population genetics to the discipline. In
Tempo and Mode in Evolution (1942), Simpson argued that the fossil
record was uneven and irregular. Sometimes evolution occurred
quickly, too quickly for the extinct species to leave a fossil record;
sometimes evolution occurred so slowly that it was impossible to
detect. In either case, Darwin was correct: there would be gaps in
the geological record.

One of the most important points made by scientists involved
in the modern version of Darwinism, Neo-Darwinism, was that Darwin's main contention in *The Origin of Species* was correct. Studying
variation on an easily observed level was the key to understanding
evolution. What Darwin called "Variation under Domestication" and
"Variation under Nature" was like observing microevolution. As Darwin rightly asserted, the continuing accumulation of microevolution
led to something much larger—transmutation or macroevolution.

The "grand synthesis" or "modern synthesis" would have been
enough to solidify Darwin's reputation as a pioneering scientist. The
discovery of very old hominid, "human-like," fossils and experiments
by chemists that focused on the origins of life confirmed that Darwin
was one of the greatest scientists since 1500.

In 1924, Raymond Dart (1893–1988), an Australian paleontologist teaching at the University of Witerwatersrand in South Africa,
obtained a skull that he recognized as belonging to a hominid, a primate that stood erect and walked on two legs. Dart nicknamed the
fossil "Taung baby" after the area in which it was found. He classified
the fossil *Australopithecus africanus* (or "southern ape from Africa")
in an article published in 1925.[8] Dart claimed the fossil was an inter-
mediary between apes and humans. Although most scientists at the
time discounted Dart's claim, the discovery of more australopithecine

fossils by Robert Broom (1866–1951) in the 1930s and 1940s confirmed Dart's hypothesis.

In 1959, the husband and wife anthropologists Louis Leakey (1903–1972) and Mary Leakey (1913–1996) discovered a fossil of a hominid in the Olduvai Gorge of Northern Tanzania. The *Zinjanthropus bosei* ("East African man") fossil was dated at more than 1.75 million years old. (It is now classified *Australopithecus bosei*.) It was the oldest human fossil found up to that date and helped to stimulate numerous expeditions to East Africa to search for more fossils. In 1974, a team led by the American paleontologist Donald Johanson (1943–) found "Lucy," an australopithecine fossil more than 3.2 million years old. In 1978, a team led by Mary Leakey found the oldest footprints made by hominids, dating back 3.5 million years. These discoveries and others confirmed Darwin's hypothesis in *The Descent of Man* that the earliest ancestors of humans originated in Africa.[9]

At the same time as Robert Broom was making his discoveries, the Russian biochemist Alexander Oparin (1894–1980) began formulating theories about the beginning of all life. He argued that there was no difference between the evolution of inorganic and organic life: both occurred by slow processes based on chemical reactions. Oparin explained his theory of chemical evolution in *The Origin of Life* (1936). He claimed that the Earth was nearly four billion years old. Methane, ammonia, hydrogen, and water vapor were the materials in the atmosphere that interacted to begin life. More important for the Darwinian explanation of evolution, Oparin argued that natural selection was the cause of some molecules surviving: these molecules evolved to become amino acids, the building blocks of proteins and life itself.

Paleontologists proved that Darwin was correct to assign many millennia for evolution (including human evolution) to have occurred. Molecular biologists demonstrated that evolution went far beyond the origin of species and organic life. Both groups of scientists confirmed Darwin's theory about evolution as he expressed it in examples such as the "tree of life": evolution is a slow process that takes billions of years and does not occur in a straight line from simple to complex organisms.

Darwin's Legacy

"Evolution—The Greatest Show on Earth—The Only Game in Town!" So read the words on a T-shirt sent to the evolutionary biologist Richard Dawkins.[10] According to John Selby Spong, the

Episcopal bishop of Newark between 1976 and 2000, "we are living in a post-Darwinian world."[11] Both men were drawing attention to the profound significance of Darwin's theory. Although descent by modification would not be the foundation of the theory of evolution without the work of many scientists, the man who proposed the idea must receive the appropriate credit. In the twentieth century, the connection between genetics and evolution would not be complete without the work of Rosalind Franklin (1920–1958), Francis Crick (1916–2004), and James Watson (1928–) on the structure of DNA. Measuring the age of the Earth in billions rather than a few million years would not have been possible without the research on light and relativity by Albert Einstein (1879–1955) and Henri Poincaré (1854–1912). The whole community of scientists, not just biologists or naturalists, was responsible for working out the details of the theory of evolution in the twentieth century. No individual can claim preeminence for his or her contribution. All were vital. However, Darwin deserves a position of prominence among these scientists because it was his work that stimulated so much of the scientific research and writing on evolution in the twentieth century.

Darwin's legacy was that his ideas in *The Origin of Species* were still being debated and applied. Sometimes these discussions resulted in developments that would be repudiated later in the century—the Eugenics Movement, for example. For some in the twentieth century, Darwin's ideas could not be reconciled with their beliefs, and they continued to oppose evolution. In other developments, scientists seemed to be finding ways for humans to better understand themselves and their surroundings. The work of ecologists, sociobiologists, and evolutionary psychologists led to a recognition that humankind should recognize itself as part of nature rather than the lord of nature. As the many reactions to his work demonstrated, Darwin and *The Origin of Species* were among the major topics of debate in the twentieth century.

Notes

1. Edward J. Larson, *Summer for the Gods: The Scopes Trial and America's Continuing Debate over Science and Religion* (New York: Basic Books, 1997), 3–8.

2. Vernon Faithfull Storr, *Freedom and Tradition: A Study of Liberal Evangelicalism* (London: Nisbet and Co. Ltd., 1940), 1230–1231.

3. William Jennings Bryan, *In His Image* (New York: Fleming H. Revell Company, 1922), 88.

4. Jeffrey P. Moran, *The Scopes Trial: A Brief History with Documents* (Boston: Bedford/St. Martin's, 2002), 53.

5. William Bateson, *Problems of Genetics* (New Haven, CT: Yale University Press, 1913), vii.

6. Huxley, *Evolution: The Modern Synthesis*, 13.

7. Gould, *Ever Since Darwin: Reflections in Natural History* (New York: W. W. Norton, 1977), 12.

8. Raymond Dart, "*Australopithecus africanus*: The Man-Ape of South Africa," *Nature* 105 (February 1925): 195–199.

9. Darwin, *The Descent of Man*, I: 199.

10. Richard Dawkins, *The Blind Watchmaker: Why the Evidence of Evolution Reveals a Universe without Design* (New York: W. W. Norton, Inc., 1986; reprint, W. W. Norton, 1996), xi.

11. John Selby Spong, Interview with Penny Nelson, *Forum*, KQED Radio, 22 October 2001.

CHAPTER 6

Conclusion: Darwin, Darwinism, and Beyond

Evolution: The Popularizing of an Idea

In recent years evolution has been a popular theme among film-makers. At the end of the film *X2: X-Men United*, one of the characters, Jean Grey, says, "Mutation, it is the key to our evolution. It is how we have evolved from a single-celled organism into the dominant species on the planet. This process is slow, normally taking thousands and thousands of years. But every few hundred millennia evolution leaps forward." Evolution is the key to understanding the world as it exists, according to Agent Smith, a computer program, in the film *The Matrix*. Smith also tells Morpheus, a human, that he has had difficulty classifying the humans because they do not act like true mammals. Smith believes humans are more like viruses because of their propensity to multiply and consume everything without coming to an equilibrium with the environment. And in the film *Men in Black* a giant cockroach tells Agent Jay, a human, "Compared to you, I'm at the top of the evolutionary ladder!"[1]

Apart from the fact that evolution may be the flavor of the month for certain film-makers, the use of the theory in blockbuster films suggests that evolution is now embedded in popular culture. No matter the objections of opponents, religious or philosophical, evolution is an essential component of the Western, and world, psyche. To name a city after a person is an honor; to name a shopping mall after a person suggests that the person is more than a symbol of greatness. Naming a city in the Northern Territory of Australia "Darwin" recognizes the importance of Darwin's work on coral reefs. Placing a statue of Darwin in the Natural History Museum in London acknowledges the importance of Darwin's work for the biological sciences. But what does The Darwin Shopping Centre in Shrewsbury, the town of Darwin's birth, recognize: the commonness of Darwin, perhaps?

Darwin definitely sells. The number of books dealing with the life, ideas, and impact of Darwin is so voluminous that more than one commentator has called these analyses "the Darwin industry." Talking about Darwin or seeming to talk about Darwin draws attention to the speaker. For example, the book *Darwinian Dominion: Animal Welfare and Human Interests* (1999) is actually about animal rights but putting "Darwinian" in the title makes the book seem more appealing. Social Darwinism and the dominance of one species over another, ideas addressed in *Darwinian Dominion*, are more accurately associated with Herbert Spencer and Francis Galton. Charles Darwin was not a Social Darwinist. Darwin's theory, however, has had such an impact on everything from zoology to ethics that "Darwinian" is a beginning point for a discussion of what is good or bad about society.

The debates about Creationism or Intelligent Design or Saltationism or Punctuated Equilibrium may have less to do with Darwin or the theory of evolution and much more to do with understanding or explaining the place of humankind in the world and the universe.[2] Humans may seem superior to all other species, but Darwin suggests in *The Origin of Species*, and states explicitly in *The Descent of Man*, that humankind is not that much different or better than the other animals on the planet. Darwin's theories confirm that the special place of humankind is only in its skills. Compared with the long periods of time in which the Earth evolved, and the vast size of the universe, humankind is quite small.

The Continuing Significance of Charles Darwin and *The Origin of Species*

What would Darwin have thought about the continuing use and misuse of his name and his ideas? He would have been pleased and displeased. Commenting on the time when he heard that Adam Sedgwick thought he would become a leading scientist, Darwin said

> I clambered over the mountains of Ascension [Island] with a bounding step, and made the volcanic rocks resound under my geological hammer. All this shows how ambitious I was; but I think that I can say with truth that in after years, though I cared in the highest degree for the approbation of such men as Lyell and Hooker, who were my friends, I did not care much about

the general public. I do not mean to say that a favourable review or a large sale of my books did not please me greatly, but the pleasure was a fleeting one, and I am sure that I have never turned one inch out of my course to gain fame."[3]

Darwin was ambitious. At the end of his life, he recognized that he had made an important contribution to science, but he would have been surprised at how pervasive his ideas would become.

Clarence Ayres, who wrote a biography of Thomas Huxley, drew attention to the growing importance of Darwin and his ideas in the 1930s:

The last half of the nineteenth century witnessed the growth of a great myth. In 1851 Huxley placed Darwin "far below" Owen and Forbes "in learning, originality and grasp of mind." *The Origin of Species* appeared and put him at once in a class with von Baer. After this the myth grew fast. By the time of Darwin's death Huxley was comparing him to Lamarck and Buffon, though he was "disposed to think" that they would "run him hard in both genius and fertility." But three years later Darwin had been canonized and Huxley anointed: Darwin's statue had been set up in the National Museum at South Kensington and Huxley as President of the Royal Society was presenting it to H.R.H. the Prince of Wales. The circle of Darwin's greatness has now widened to embrace the sixteenth century. His name "runs no more risk of oblivion than does that of Copernicus, or that of Harvey."[4]

Sixty years later Daniel Dennett would add that "we still have not come to terms with its [the revolution begun by Darwin's ideas] mind-boggling implications."[5]

Today, Darwinism is as much a philosophy as a scientific theory. Evolution is the universally accepted scientific explanation for the origin of life on Earth; evolution is also a theory that expresses the universal hope and expectation for human progress.

In the preface to his book *Species and Varieties: Their Origin by Mutation* (1905), the pioneering geneticist Hugo de Vries tried to explain the scientific significance of Darwin's work by comparing it with his own and Jean-Baptiste Lamarck's:

The origin of species is a natural phenomenon.
—Lamarck
The origin of species is an object of inquiry.
—Darwin
The origin of species is an object of experimental investigation.
—De Vries

Given the impact of Darwin's theory, De Vries could have added another line: The origin of species is the subject of philosophical investigation.

Science beyond Darwin

The naturalistic approach to knowledge has had a significant impact on the development of human society. Investigating natural phenomena without reference to the supernatural has led to advances in science and technology that were inconceivable before the Modern Age. What person in Medieval Europe or Early Ming China would have thought it possible for humans to travel faster than the speed of sound or to walk on the moon?

The ideas in *The Origin of Species* were an important component of the naturalistic revolution in the biological sciences: artificial insemination, Pre-implantation Genetic Diagnosis (PGD), cloning, the mapping of the human genome, genetically modified crops, and the use of stem cells—none of these developments would be possible without the foundation of the evolutionary theory of the origin of life.

Furthermore, the naturalistic revolution in the sciences, particularly biology, shows no sign of abating. The quest to find which genes make a person more susceptible to cancer, for example, seems far too important to discontinue. Knowing about the origins of life has prompted the human race's desire to cure, fix, or ameliorate the problems and difficulties of life. Humans living before Darwin and before 1500 wanted to prolong life or make it more comfortable, but the scientific tools available since the publication of *The Origin of Species* are far greater.

The more important question concerning the theory of evolution may be what should humankind do with the power it seems to have over nature (rather than whether or not the theory of evolution is true). The potential problems are moral rather than scientific. Much seems possible. Even if the impossible is achievable, however, does humankind want to aim that high? It may be possible to produce "designer babies" using PGD techniques, but is that a good idea? (Most people today find the ideas associated with the eugenics movement of the early twentieth century repulsive: making "designer babies" seems eerily similar.) Is it ethically sound to genetically modify food even if the process seems safe? Would humankind diminish or fundamentally alter its humanity if the advances derived from knowledge about the origins of life were used in these particular ways? What exactly is the place of humankind in the world and the universe? People asked the latter question after the publication of *The Origin of Species*. Darwin's book challenged the orthodox view of the importance of humankind. The reaction to *The Origin of Species*, and other books that suggested humankind was not a special creation, was part of a late-nineteenth century debate about the uniqueness and responsibility of humans. The debate continues more than one hundred years later.

Not all the advances based on the theory of evolution are so worryingly negative. Thanks to Darwin and a plethora of nineteenth- and twentieth-century scientists, a great deal more is known about the natural world. Concepts such as biodiversity, conservation, and environmentalism have their origins in the work of scientists such as Darwin. Knowing about the great number and diversity of species had led to a concern about protecting those species. Knowing about the relationship between ecosystems and the distribution of species has led to a concern about the effect humans have on their environment. Darwin loved nature. (After reading his books it is impossible to think about pigeons, barnacles, and worms as mundane and insignificant creatures.) He would have been pleased by the number of scientists and nonscientists alike who now believe it is important to live in harmony with the rest of the natural world rather than dominate it.

A Final Assessment

Reflecting on his work, Darwin said the following:

> I have almost always been treated honestly by my reviewers, passing over those without scientific knowledge as not worthy of notice. My views have often been grossly misrepresented, bitterly opposed and ridiculed, but this has been generally done as, I believe, in good faith. On the whole I do not doubt that my works have been over and over again greatly overpraised.[6]

While there are debates in the parts of the United States about whether to teach the theory of evolution—the opponents of evolution forgetting that the most tested and proven scientific ideas are still called theories—it is worth noting that Darwin was not bothered by people who disagreed with him. The opponents who annoyed him were those who had not taken the trouble to read and understand the science underpinning his ideas. A person could study natural history and come to a different conclusion from Darwin about the origin of species: the important act was the studying.

As scientists in the late-nineteenth and early twentieth century found, there were several ways to explain the origin of species. Darwin's name is intimately associated with the theory of evolution, but he was one of many scientists working on the problem. Darwin had brilliant insights about the relationship between organic life in the natural world, but he could not have formulated his theory of descent by modification through natural selection without the pioneering work of scientists such as Charles Lyell, Isidore Geoffroy Saint-Hilaire, and Joseph Kölreuter. No matter the brilliance of the theory, Darwin's ideas would not have spread without the aid of scientists such as Thomas Huxley, Asa Gray, and Ernst Haeckel. Darwin was not a "lone wolf." Neither were he and Alfred Russel Wallace "lone wolves." The scientific community of the nineteenth century deserves credit for the theory of evolution, too.[7]

Furthermore, the ordinariness of Darwin is a reminder not to "overpraise" his accomplishment. "A novel, according to my taste, does not come into the first class unless it contains some person whom one can thoroughly love, and if a pretty woman all the better," Darwin wrote.[8] These are not the sentiments of person removed from the humdrum activity of human existence. Darwin was human: a great scientist but human nonetheless. Above all, science is a human activity. Scientists make mistakes because they are human; the weaknesses of Darwin's theory, his inability to explain how exactly natural selection operated, for example, occurred because he was human. One person cannot know everything.

What then is the most accurate assessment of Darwin's work? Is it fair to call *The Origin of Species* "an intellectual time bomb"?[9] It is fair to say that "more than any other thinker—even Freud or Marx—this affable old-world naturalist from the minor Shropshire gentry has transformed the way we see ourselves on the planet"?[10] Someone in the nineteenth century, perhaps Alfred Russel Wallace, would have found a way to write a convincing scientific explanation of the theory of evolution had there been no Charles Darwin. To make this point only emphasizes the significance of the theory of evolution. But it was not Lamarck, or Buffon, or Chambers, or Wallace, who formulated the theory: it was Darwin.

Notes

1. *X2: X-Men United*, directed by Bryan Singer (Twentieth-Century Fox, 2003); *The Matrix*, directed by Larry and Andy Wachowski (Warner Bros., 1999); and *Men in Black*, directed by Barry Sonnenfeld (Columbia TriStar, 1997).

2. Punctuated Equilibrium is another theory about the progress of evolution. Evolution occurs rapidly at some points in time, argue scientists such as Stephen Jay Gould.

3. *Life and Letters of Charles Darwin*, I: 66–67.

4. Clarence Ayres, *Huxley* (New York: W. W. Norton, Inc., 1932), 73–74. Karl von Baer (1792–1876) was a Russian embryologist, anatomist, and ethnologist who discovered that humans developed from eggs.

5. Daniel Dennett, *Darwin's Dangerous Idea*, 19.

6. *Life and Letters of Charles Darwin*, I: 89.

7. See Martin Fichman, *Evolutionary Theory and Victorian Culture* (New York: Humanity Books, 2002), particularly pages 13–50, 97–122.

8. *Life and Letters of Charles Darwin*, I: 101.

9. Peter Brent, *Charles Darwin* (London: Heinemann, 1981), 5.

10. Desmond and Moore, *Darwin*, xxi.

Charles Darwin, age 31.

Charles Darwin at approximately age 45.

Charles Darwin at approximately age 65, ca. 1874. (Courtesy of the Armstrong Browning Library, Baylor University, Waco, Texas)

Charles Darwin, 1881.

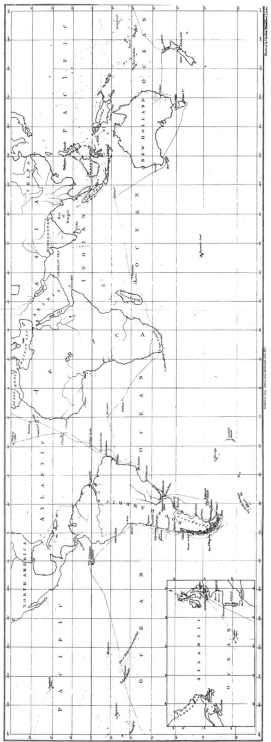

GENERAL CHART shewing the PRINCIPAL TRACKS of H.M.S. BEAGLE _ 1831 - 6.

The Voyage of the *Beagle*: a map of Darwin's journey taken from Captain FitzRoy's book on the voyage (1839).

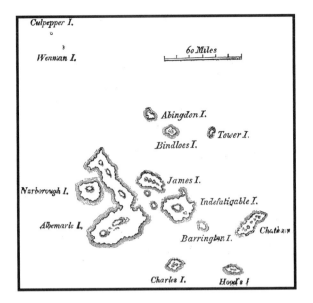

The Galapagos Islands, visited during Darwin's *Beagle* voyage. The map is in Darwin's published journal of the voyage. (Courtesy of the Armstrong Browning Library, Baylor University, Waco, Texas)

"Natural Selection": cartoon of Darwin, published in *Vanity Fair*, 1871.

"Not a brawler": cartoon of Bishop Samuel Wilberforce, published in *Vanity Fair*, 1869.

"A great Med'cine-Man among the Inqui-ring Redskins": cartoon of Thomas Huxley, published in *Vanity Fair*, 1871

ON

THE ORIGIN OF SPECIES

BY MEANS OF NATURAL SELECTION,

OR THE

PRESERVATION OF FAVOURED RACES IN THE STRUGGLE FOR LIFE.

By CHARLES DARWIN, M.A.,

FELLOW OF THE ROYAL, GEOLOGICAL, LINNÆAN, ETC., SOCIETIES;
AUTHOR OF 'JOURNAL OF RESEARCHES DURING H. M. S. BEAGLE'S VOYAGE
ROUND THE WORLD.'

LONDON:

JOHN MURRAY, ALBEMARLE STREET.

1859.

The right of Translation is reserved.

The title page of *The Origin of Species.*

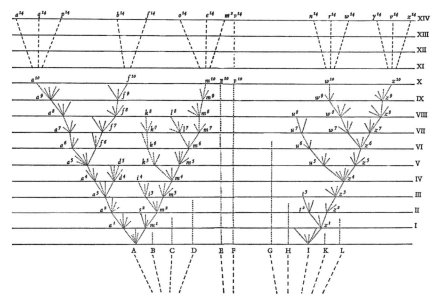

Darwin's "Tree of Life," from *The Origin of Species.*

PEDIGREE OF MAN.

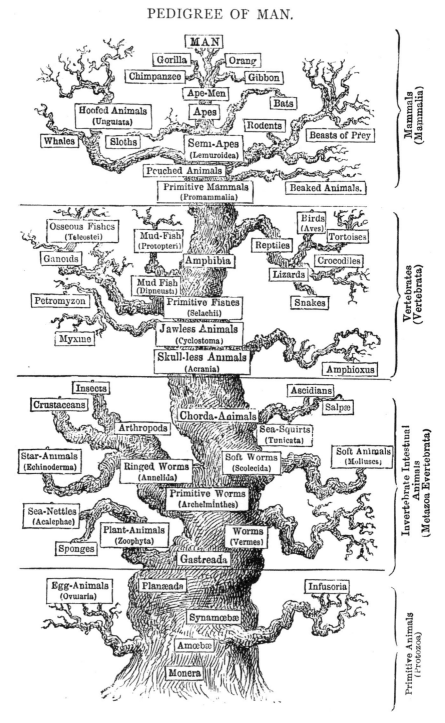

The Genealogical Tree of Humanity by Ernst Haeckel.

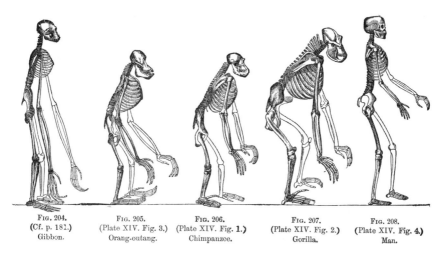

FIG. 204.	FIG. 205.	FIG. 206.	FIG. 207.	FIG. 208.
(Cf. p. 181.)	(Plate XIV. Fig. 3.)	(Plate XIV. Fig. 1.)	(Plate XIV. Fig. 2.)	(Plate XIV. Fig. 4.)
Gibbon.	Orang-outang.	Chimpanzee.	Gorilla.	Man.

Skeleton of a Man and the Four Anthropoid Apes by Waterhouse Hawkins, used in Thomas Huxley's *Man's Place in Nature*.

MONKEYANA.

"Monkeyana": a play on the Wedgwood's antislavery motto, "Am I Not a Man and a Brother?" Cartoon in *Punch*, 1881. (Courtesy of the Armstrong Browning Library, Baylor University, Waco, Texas)

"Man is But a Worm": this cartoon shows the origin of man from a worm to Darwin. (Courtesy of the Armstrong Browning Library, Baylor University, Waco, Texas)

BIOGRAPHIES: PERSONALITIES IMPORTANT TO DARWIN AND DARWINISM

Emma Darwin (2 May 1808–1 October 1896)

Emma Darwin was the daughter of Josiah Wedgwood II, the pottery magnate, and Charles Darwin's wife. Emma was also Darwin's cousin: Josiah Wedgwood was Darwin's favorite uncle whom he affectionately called Uncle Jos.

Emma was probably the most important nonscientist in Darwin's life. Darwin married her because he valued and desired female companionship and she was a best friend as well as a spouse. Darwin sought her judgment on his scientific work—she read and commented on the manuscript of his unpublished work on natural selection and the manuscript for *The Origin of Species*—as well as on domestic decisions such as buying Down House. Emma was an orthodox Christian by Victorian standards; one reason Darwin did not discuss the origins of humans in *The Origin of Species* was respect for Emma's belief that God created humankind (as stated in the Bible).

Emma and Charles Darwin were a little unusual for the Victorian period because theirs was a relationship of equals. (It helped that they had known each other since childhood.) For example, in 1844, Darwin gave Emma the task of finding someone to edit and expand his manuscript on the origin of species if he died prematurely.

Emma provided stability in Darwin's life. She insisted that Darwin take care of his health, convincing him to take holidays or seek specialist help when he became too ill. Emma read to Darwin on most evenings so that he could continue to enjoy nonscientific books without the strain of more reading. Emma also played the piano to Darwin to help him relax. Most important, Emma managed the household (which included children and servants) so that Darwin was able to concentrate on his scientific work.

After Darwin died in 1882, Emma continued to live in Down House until her own death in 1896. With the visits of children and grandchildren she continued to be what she had been since her marriage to Charles in 1839: the fulcrum of the Darwin family.

Isidore Geoffroy Saint-Hilaire (16 December 1805–10 November 1861)

Isidore Geoffroy Saint-Hilaire was one of several world-renowned French scientists of the first half of the nineteenth century, along with Georges Cuvier (1769–1832), Henri Milne-Edwards (1800–1885), and Alphonse De Candolle (1806–1893). Geoffroy Saint-Hilaire's work on monstrosities, major deformities in animals, was a critical component of Darwin's theory of mutation. Geoffroy Saint-Hilaire argued that monstrosities were more common that naturalists had recognized previously. Darwin used this idea to argue that the number of species was not fixed: varieties of species, including those with monstrosities, were evolving into new species.

Geoffroy Saint-Hilaire was born into a scientific family. His father Étienne (1772–1844) was a prominent zoologist. Isidore followed his father into zoology and even Isidore's research on deformities in organisms was a continuation of work begun by his father. Also like his father, he became professor of zoology at the Muséum d'Histoire naturelle [Natural History Museum] in Paris (1841–1850).

The importance of Geoffroy Saint-Hilaire's seminal work on anomalies and abnormalities in the structure of organisms was recognized during his life. He was elected to the prestigious Académie des sciences [Academy of Science] in 1833. He was director of the Ménagerie de Jardin des Plantes [Zoo of the Botanical Garden] in Paris (1841–1861) and professor of zoology at the Sorbonne (1851–1861), the foremost university in France.

Geoffroy Saint-Hilaire coined the term teratology, the study of major abnormalities in organic beings. He wrote several important works on the subject. The best-known work was his four-volume *Histoire générale et particulière des anomalies de l'organisation chez l'homme et les animaux: ouvrage comprenant des recherches sur les caractères, la classification, l'influence physiologique et pathologique, les rapports généraux, les lois et les causes des monstruosités, des variétés et vices de conformation ou Traité de tératologie* [General and Particular History of the Organizational Anomalies in Humans and Animals: A Work consisting of Research on the Nature, Classification, Physiological and Pathological Influence, General Relationships, Laws and Causes of these Monstrosities, the Diversity and Corruption of Structure, or Treatise on Teratology] (1823–1837).

Asa Gray (18 November 1810–30 January 1898)

Asa Gray was an important confidant of Darwin's while he developed his theory of evolution by natural selection. Gray was one of the first three people with whom Darwin shared his theory. Darwin sent Gray an outline of the theory as an enclosure in a letter dated September 5, 1857; a copy of this letter was used by Charles Lyell and Joseph Hooker to prove that Darwin had been working on a theory about natural selection before Alfred Russel Wallace. And it was Gray who provided Darwin with an important piece of evidence to support a theory of evolution: the close affinity between the flora of North America and Japan.

After the publication of *The Origin of Species,* Gray was the most prominent endorser of Darwin's theory in the United States. Gray argued that Darwinism was compatible with Christian theology in *Natural Selection not Inconsistent with Natural Theology. A Free Examination of Darwin's Treatise on the Origin of Species, and of its American Reviewers* (1861), a reprint of three articles published in the journal *Atlantic Monthly* in 1860, and *Darwiniana: Essays and Reviews Pertaining to Darwinism* (1876).

Gray was the leading American botanist of the nineteenth century. Gray and Darwin's mutual interest in the geographical distribution of plants had led to their initial correspondence. Gray's work with his mentor John Torrey (1796–1873) on the classification of species by affinity helped to establish botany as a systematic scientific discipline in the United States. *A Flora of North America: Containing Abridged Descriptions of all Known Indigenous and Naturalized Plants Growing North of Mexico; Arranged according to the Natural System* (1838–1843) was Gray's best-known book on the subject and was published in numerous editions during and after Gray's life.

Gray also wrote several textbooks on botany that became the standard reference works in this field, including *The Botanical Textbook: for Schools, Colleges, and Private Students* (1845) and *The Elements of Botany for Beginners and for Schools* (1887).

The significance of Gray's work was recognized in the United States and Europe. He was the Fisher Professor of Natural History at Harvard University between 1842 and 1888 (where he established the Gray Herbarium in 1864). He was president of the American Academy of Arts and Sciences between 1863 and 1873 and president of the American Association for the Advancement of Science in 1872. He was also an honorary member of the Linnean and Royal Societies as well as the academies of science of Paris, Berlin, and Stockholm.

Sir Joseph Dalton Hooker (30 June 1817– 10 December 1911)

Sir Joseph Dalton Hooker was one of Darwin's closest friends. Darwin asked Hooker to comment on his work more than any other person; only Charles Lyell and Thomas Huxley were as close. But Hooker was an important scientist notwithstanding his connection to Darwin. Through his writing and his position as assistant director and director of the botanical gardens at Kew, London (1855–1885), he helped to establish botany as an academic discipline in Britain. (Kew Gardens was and still is one of the largest botanical gardens in Britain.)

Like Darwin, Hooker made a name for himself by participating in a voyage in which scientific research was a major task. Hooker sailed on HMS *Erebus* between 1839 and 1843. Unlike Darwin, however, he was not independently wealthy and took the position of assistant surgeon to pay his fare. The six-volume book *The Botany of the Antarctic Voyage of H.M. Discovery Ships* Erebus *and* Terror, *in the Years 1839–1843, Under the Command of Captain Sir James Clark Ross, K.t., R.N., F.R.S. & L.S., etc.*, published between 1844 and 1860, sealed his reputation as a significant scientist. Hooker's main research in botany was on the geographical distribution of plants. He was interested in describing all the flora in a particular area and working out the relationship between these flora and others at similar latitude or longitude. *Flora Indica: Being a Systematic Account of the Plants of British India, Together with Observations on the Structure and Affinities of Their Natural Orders and Genera* (1855) coauthored with Thomas Thomson (1817–1878) and *Handbook of the New Zealand Flora: A*

Systematic Description of the Native Plants of New Zealand and the Chatham, Kermadec's, Lord Auckland's, Campbell's, and Macquarrie's Islands (1864) were based on this type of research.

Hooker also wanted to make it easier for future botanists to engage in systematic research. He wrote popular books such as *The Student's Flora of the British Islands* (1870) and *Botany* (1876) for this purpose.

Hooker was one of the first to read Darwin's manuscript of 1844, which outlined the theory of descent by modification. Hooker, with Charles Lyell, organized the presentation of Darwin and Alfred Russel Wallace's papers on natural selection to the Linnean Society in 1858: this action established the fact that Darwin wrote his theory before Wallace. It was Hooker who urged Darwin to write the book that became *The Origin of Species* and, even though he had reservations about it, Hooker was one of the prominent promoters of Darwin's theory.

Hooker was one of Britain's preeminent botanists in the nineteenth century: he received numerous scientific and public honors in his lifetime. The Royal Society awarded him the Royal, Copley, and Darwin medals (1854, 1887, and 1892). He was knighted in 1877 and given the rarely awarded Order of Merit in 1907 for distinguished service to science. When he died, his widow was offered the opportunity to have Hooker buried next to Darwin in Westminster Abbey (which she declined).

Friedrich Wilhelm Heinrich Alexander Humboldt (14 September 1769–6 May 1859)

Friedrich Wilhelm Heinrich Alexander Humboldt was the preeminent naturalist-explorer of his generation. Even if the voyages of the British explorer James Cook to the Pacific and Australasia (1768–1771, 1772–1775, 1776–1779), the French expedition to Egypt led by Napoleon (1798–1801), and Darwin's *Beagle* voyage are included, Humboldt's five-year expedition in Latin America with the French botanist Aimé Bonpland (1773–1858) still deserves the title of one of the most significant scientific journeys of the eighteenth and nineteenth centuries. The discovery of thousands of new plant species, the exploration of the Orinoco River and its connection to the Amazon River, the research on the Earth's magnetic field, and the discovery of rocks created by volcanoes (igneous rocks) revolutionized the study of botany, geography, meteorology, and geology.

Humboldt's travels and research inspired numerous other naturalists and scientists. Foremost among these was Charles Darwin. It was after he read a translation of Humboldt's three-volume *Relation*

historique du voyage aux régions équinoxiales du nouveau continent
[Personal Narrative of Travels to the Equinoctial Regions of the New
World] (1814–1825) that Darwin decided he wanted to become a famous naturalist. It was Humboldt's discovery of numerous new species in South America that gave Darwin a vital piece of evidence that
the species were not fixed and were continually diversifying.

Humboldt had shown an interest in science as a child—he collected and labeled plants, insects, and shells—and decided to become
a naturalist and explorer in his late teens. By the age of 21, he had already published a description of the mineral deposits on the Rhine
river (*Mineralogische Beobachtungen über einige Basalte am Rhein* [Min-
eralogical Observations of Certain Basalts on the Rhine], 1790).
While working as an inspector of mines, he wrote books on the sub-
terraneous flora of the Freiberg area (*Florae Fribergensis specimen
plantas cryptogamicus praesertim subterraneas exhibens* [Examples of
the Flora of Freiburg, Especially Displaying Cryptogamic Under-
ground Plants], 1793) and the conduction of impulses through nerves
(*Versuche über die gereizte Muskel-und Nervenfaser nebst Versuchen über
den chemischen Prozess des Lebens in der Thier-und Pflanzenwelt*
[Experiments on Stimulated Muscle and Nerve Fibers together with
Experiments on the Chemical Process of Life in the Animal and Plant
World], 1797), which established his reputation as a good naturalist.

The death of his mother in 1796 and the inheritance he
received enabled Humboldt to do what he really desired: travel and
explore. He and Aimé Bonpland planned an ambitious exploration of
Spanish America, which they began in 1799. The five-year journey
was a great success. The Leonids, a periodic meteor shower, and
electric eels are two of the many extraordinary discoveries made by
Humboldt and Bonpland. One work based on the voyage, *Voyage aux
régions équinoctiales du Nouveau Continent, fait en 1799–1804* [Voyage
in the Equinoctial Regions of the New World, during the years
1799–1804] (1807–1839), consists of thirty volumes.

Humboldt's contribution to science did not end with the voyage
to Spanish America. He wrote a seminal book on meteorology, *Des
lignes isothermes et de la distribution de la châleur sur le globe* [Isother-
mal Lines and the Distribution of Heat around the Earth] (1817);
traveled and explored more than nine thousand miles in the Asian
part of the Russian Empire in 1829; and wrote, but did not complete,
a book attempting to unify all scientific knowledge, *Kosmos: Entwurf
einer physischen Weltbeschreibung* [Cosmos: An Outline of the Physical
Description of the Universe] (1845–1847, 1850–1858, 1862).

In *The Origin of Species*, Darwin calls Humboldt "illustrious"
(*The Origin of Species*, 374). Humboldt's fame and reputation

declined rapidly after his death. It was superseded by men such as Darwin, Charles Lyell, and Louis Agassiz. Fortunately, Humboldt's name is not forgotten. Counties in California, Iowa, and Nevada bear his name. The same is true of the Monumento Nacional Alejandro de Humboldt, a national monument in Venezuela. Humboldt was one of the greatest promoters of scientific research in the nineteenth century: it is appropriate that such a polymath has an area of the Moon, Mare Humboldtianum, named after him.

Thomas Henry Huxley (4 May 1825–29 June 1895)

Thomas Henry Huxley was the most vocal defender of Darwin's theory of evolution in the British scientific community in the last half of the nineteenth century. Darwin asked Huxley to be his agent, his spokesman, in public disputes about *The Origin of Species*. Huxley performed this task so well that he is known as "Darwin's bulldog."

Huxley was one of the first scientists to support Darwin's theory openly. (Darwin had sent Huxley one of the prepublication copies.) In the last chapter of *The Origin of Species,* Darwin expressed the hope that younger naturalists would be more receptive of his theory: Huxley was one of these naturalists. He wrote positive reviews of *The Origin of Species* in *The Times* (London) in 1859 and in the *Westminster Review* in 1860. He defended the theory of evolution when Bishop Samuel Wilberforce attacked it at a meeting of the British Association for the Advancement of Science in 1860. He wrote *Evidence as to Man's Place in Nature* (1863), which argued that human evolution was a part of the evolution of all organisms. He coined the term "Darwinism:" a word signifying Darwin's explanation of the origin of species. He was a founder of the X Club (in 1864), a group of men dedicated to the defense of scientific inquiry such as Darwin's. He gave numerous lectures explaining and defending Darwinism in Britain and the United States in the 1860s and 1870s.

Huxley was not solely a defender of Darwin. He also was a preeminent British zoologist, anatomist, paleontologist, and scientific educator. His family was not wealthy and it was not part of the British establishment like Darwin's—his father was a mathematics teacher at a small school in Ealing, West London. Huxley's humble background explains why he valued the democratizing effect of education. Throughout his career, Huxley opposed the control of knowledge by elites, whether in the Church of England or the moneyed classes. He promoted science and education for everyone, particularly the working class and even including women. The books *Lessons in Elementary*

Physiology (1866) and *Physiography: An Introduction to the Study of Nature* (1877) are examples of this populist approach to science.

Huxley first made a name for himself by the publication of research based on a four-year voyage on H.M.S. *Rattlesnake*. His paper "On the Anatomy and the Affinities of the Family of the Medusae" (1849) sent to the Royal Society earned him election as a fellow of the Society in 1850. The Royal Society awarded him its Royal Medal in 1852 for his research on sea anemones and related organisms. His book *The Oceanic Hydrozoa: A Description of the Calycophoridæ and Physophoridæ Observed during the Voyage of H.M.S. "Rattlesnake," in the Years 1846–1850. With a General Introduction* (1859) confirmed his status as notable naturalist. This recognition was the beginning of a distinguished career in which Huxley wrote more than four hundred books and articles.

Huxley's scientific curiosity and dislike of the establishment led him to defend agnosticism. He coined the term; for Huxley, it meant the willingness to question all traditional or generally accepted ideas. Books such as *Hume* (1878) and *Science and the Christian Tradition* (1894) were written from this skeptical point of view. A man who believed everything could be sacred but nothing was inherently so was the ideal person to defend Darwin's theory of evolution.

Joseph Gottlieb Kölreuter (27 April 1733– 11 November 1806)

Joseph Gottlieb Kölreuter was a German botanist whose research on plant hybrids formed a critical component of Darwin's argument in *The Origin of Species*. Kölreuter argued that plant hybrids, the offspring of two different plants, were not always sterile. Darwin used this idea to suggest that varieties of a species that mutated did not lose their ability to pollinate or be pollinated: these varieties could continue to produce plants that were increasingly different from the original species through successive generations. This idea was a key point in Chapter VIII of *The Origin of Species*, Hybridism.

Like several other well-known naturalists of the era, Kölreuter began his career in medicine. His father was a pharmacist and Kölreuter was inclined to followed a similar career path. He studied medicine at the universities of Tübingen and Strasbourg from 1748 onward and received his degree from Tübingen in 1755. In 1756, he obtained a position, probably as a curator of the natural history collection, at the Academy of Sciences in St. Petersburg, Russia, which he held until 1761. While at St. Petersburg, Kölreuter began to do experiments on the pollination of flowers. He tried, successfully, to work out the mechanics of fertilization and self-fertilization. His research led him to confirm the theory of earlier botanists, such as Rudolph Jacob Camerarius (1665–1721), that plants had sexual organs: he was the first botanist to prove this experimentally. He published his findings in four reports entitled *Vorläufige Nachrict von einigen das Geschlecht der Pflanzen betreffenden Versuchen und Beobachtungen* [Preliminary Report about Several Experiments and Observations Concerning the Sexuality of Plants] (1761); *Fortsetzung der Vorläufigen Nachrict von einigen das Geschlecht der Pflanzen betreffenden Versuchen und Beobachtungen* [Continuation of the Preliminary Report about Several Experiments and Observations Concerning the Sexuality of Plants] (1763), *Zweyte Fortsetzung der Vorläufigen ...* [Second Continuation of the Preliminary Report about Several Experiments and Observations Concerning the Sexuality of Plants] (1764), and *Dritte Fortsetzung der Vorläufigen ...* [Third Continuation of the Preliminary Report about Several Experiments and Observations Concerning the Sexuality of Plants] (1766).

Kölreuter was the first botanist to do extensive experiments on plant hybridization, the study of interbreeding, and plant pollination. His experiments revealed the critical role insects play in pollination of plants and the basic principles of plant crossing or interbreeding. Before Mendel, he came the closest to working out a theory of genetics. Furthermore, he recognized that his theories about plant hybridization had implications for the ongoing debate about the origin of species. (Kölreuter concluded that the new mutations produced by hybridization were not new species.) Kölreuter's work makes him one of the most important figures in the history of plant biology.

Although Kölreuter was one of the foremost authorities on the sexuality of plants and hybridization fifty years after his death, the importance of his work was not recognized during his life. He was director of court gardens of the German prince the Margrave of Baden (1763–1786), but he was dismissed from his position and probably discontinued his experiments. He was professor of natural history at Karlsruhe (1763–1806) but never achieved financial stability nor found the opportunity to publish a comprehensive survey of his research.

Jean-Baptiste-Pierre-Antoine de Monet de Lamarck (1 August 1744–28 December 1829)

Jean-Baptiste-Pierre-Antoine de Monet de Lamarck was a pioneering French scientist, particularly in zoology, and the foremost proponent of the transmutation of species before Darwin. He coined the term "invertebrates"; wrote *Flore françoise* (1778), which became the standard work on French plants for fifty years; made the suggestions that resulted in the Jardin de Roi [Royal Botanical Garden] in Paris being reorganized into the Muséum national d'Histoire naturelle [National Museum of Natural History], which is the natural history museum today; and the word "Lamarckian," an explanation of heredity and evolution, was coined for his ideas. Despite his accomplishments, Lamarck had no formal training in science or experimental methods: he was one of the last of the great "amateur" scientists.

After several attempts at other careers such as soldier and banker, Lamarck began to study botany seriously. He even managed to take a course from the prominent botanist Bernard de Jussieu (1699–1777), professor of zoology at the Jardin de Roi. Over a ten-year period Lamarck collected all the information that he could find about French plants and wrote the book *Flore françoise, ou description succincte de toutes les plantes qui croissent naturellement en France, disposée selon une nouvelle méthode d'analyse à laquelle on a joint la citation de leurs vertus les moins équivoques en médecine, et de leur utilité dans les arts* [French Flora, or A Succinct Description of all the Plants which Grow Naturally in France, Organized by a New Method of Analysis to which is Added a List of their Better Ascertained Virtues in Medicine and their Use in the Arts] (1778). This book and the patronage of the naturalist George Louis Leclerc, Comté de Buffon (1707–1788) enabled Lamarck to begin his career in science. He was elected to the prestigious Academié des sciences in 1779 and obtained a post as an assistant botanist at the Jardin de Roi in 1781.

In 1793, Lamarck was offered a professorship in zoology at the newly organized Muséum national d'Histoire naturelle. His area of expertise was insects, worms, and microscopic animals. Lamarck knew nothing about these organisms but used the position to begin a prolific period of research and writing. In a twenty-year period he wrote nine major works, including *Système des animaux sans vertèbres* [System of Invertebrate Animals] (1801); *Philosophie zoologique, ou exposition des considérations relatives à l'histoire naturelle des animaux* [Zoological Philosophy, or An Exposition of the Considerations Relative to the Natural History of Animals] (1809); and *Extrait du cours de zoologie du Muséum d'histoire naturelle sur les animaux sans vertèbres; présentant la distribution et la classification de ces animaux, les caractères des principales divisions, et une simple liste des genres; a l'usage de ceux qui suivent ce cours* [Extract of the Zoological Classes of Invertebrates at the Natural History Museum; Documenting the Distribution and Classification of these Animals, the Characteristics of Principle Divisions, and a Simple List of Genres; for the Use of

Students of the Classes] (1812). In these books, he created a classification system for invertebrates, reorganized the classification of the animal kingdom, and postulated a theory of evolution.

Lamarck's laws of transformation were responsible for the lack of recognition that his theories received during his lifetime. Lamarck argued that species progressed or evolved. Use or disuse made some structures of an organism larger or smaller and these changes were passed on to the next generation. Lamarck's colleague Georges Cuvier was completely opposed to this idea and worked hard to discredit Lamarck. Unfortunately for Lamarck, Cuvier had much more support in the Academy and Lamarck never acquired the fame or financial stability his research deserved. Lamarck went blind in 1818 and died a pauper eleven years later.

Sir Charles Lyell (14 November 1797– 22 February 1875)

Sir Charles Lyell was Darwin's friend and mentor. Lyell's theory of uniformitarianism was a foundational principle of Darwin's theory of descent by modification. (Darwin applied Lyell's theory of the slow and steady development of the Earth's strata outlined in *Principles of Geology* to organic life.) Lyell was one of the few people Darwin told about his belief in transmutation before 1859. Lyell, with Joseph Hooker, urged Darwin to write out his theory about the origin of species in the early 1850s; and Lyell and Hooker arranged for the reading of Darwin and Alfred Russel Wallace's papers on natural selection at the meeting of the Linnean Society on July 1, 1858, which eventually led to Darwin writing *The Origin of Species*.

Although he became the premier British geologist of the nineteenth century, geology was a second career for Lyell. He became a qualified lawyer in 1822. However, as had been the case when he was a student at Oxford University, natural history, particularly geology, interested Lyell more than the law. Between 1821 and 1825 Lyell did a series of tours in southern England, southern Scotland, and northern France, studying the geology of both areas and meeting important figures in the field such as Georges Cuvier (1769–1832) and Constant Prévost (1787–1856). He was particularly interested in the larger questions of geology, such as the reasons why geological strata were arranged as they were. A paper published in 1826 entitled "On the Freshwater Strata of Hordwell Cliff, Beacon Cliff, and Barton Cliff, Hampshire" exemplified the traits that made Lyell famous: clear writing in a style easily understood by nonspecialists, an emphasis on the importance of careful observation, and a desire to elucidate general principles in science.

Lyell's best-known work was *Principles of Geology, Being an Attempt to Explain the Former Changes of the Earth's Surface, by Reference to Causes Now in Operation*, a three-volume work (1830, 1832, 1833). In the first volume, Lyell wrote a history of the study of geology and explained why present geological events, such as erupting volcanoes, could explain the history of the Earth. (This was one of the books Darwin took with him on his *Beagle* voyage.) In the second volume, he discussed the relationship between living organisms and their environment. Lyell argued that extinct species were replaced by new ones: the process occurred gradually and existing species did not mutate into new species. In the third volume, Lyell provided evidence for his theory of uniformitarianism and divided the newest geological period, the Tertiary Period, into four epochs: Eocene, Miocene, Older Pliocene, and Newer Pliocene. *Principles of Geology* was a bestseller, going through twelve editions before Lyell died. Through the book, Lyell helped to establish geology as a science (free from the use of the supernatural to explain events).

For most of his life, Lyell did not believe in the evolution of humankind's moral capacity. Despite his association with Darwin, Lyell did not support a theory of organic evolution unequivocally until the late 1860s. Lyell had to rewrite his popular books, *The Principles of Geology, Elements of Geology, or the Ancient Changes of the Earth, and its Inhabitants, as illustrated by its Geological Monuments* (1838) and *The Geological Evidences of the Antiquity of Man* (1863), to reflect this change.

Lyell received numerous honors during his life. He was elected a fellow of the Royal Society in 1826 and received the Society's highest honor, the Copley Medal, in 1858. The Geological Society gave him its highest honor, the Wollaston Medal, in 1866. He was a scientific advisor to the government and this role earned him a knighthood (1848) and a baronetcy (1864).

John Murray (16 April 1808–2 April 1892)

John Murray was the head of the company that published *The Origin of Species*. The financial success of the book and the cordial relationship between publisher and author resulted in Murray publishing all but one of the books Darwin wrote after 1859.

Murray was the third John Murray to head the company. His grandfather started a trading business in 1768, which eventually became the publishing company John Murray. John Murray III took over the company in 1843. He turned it into a financially stable and thriving business.

There were two major reasons for the company's success under Murray. The first was the publishing success of Murray's Handbooks for Travellers. While traveling around England and Scotland in 1827 and 1828, Murray noticed a dearth of good guidebooks for both countries: he decided to write his own. He traveled all over Europe between 1829 and 1843 taking extensive notes and writing travel guides. The sales of these handbooks generated a regular and lucrative source of income for the company. The second reason was Murray's ability to recognize manuscripts that would become bestsellers. Apart from *The Origin of Species*, Murray published *Missionary Travels and Researches in South Africa; Including a Sketch of Sixteen Years' Residence in the Interior of Africa, and a Journey from the Cape of Good Hope to Loanda on the West Coast; thence across the Continent, down to the River Zambesi, to the Eastern Ocean* (1857), the account of the Scottish explorer and missionary David Livingstone, and *Lux Mundi* (1889), the controversial group of essays written by Anglicans who integrated new ideas such as evolution into the Church of England's doctrines.

Darwin chose Murray as his publisher for *The Origin of Species* because of Murray's good reputation, wide scholarly interests, and useful connections. In science, Murray was a keen amateur geologist and mineralogist. Murray even wrote a book on geology, *Skepticism in Geology* (1877). Murray had several famous friends, including the four-time British prime minister William Gladstone (1809–1898); George Grote (1794–1871), the historian who had written what most contemporary critics considered the definitive history of Greece; and Arthur Stanley (1815–1881), the Dean of Westminster Abbey (1864–1881). Murray even made the acquaintance of Queen Victoria. In 1862, he published a volume of speeches by Victoria's husband Prince Albert. The company who had the initial contract was not able to publish the book by the anniversary of Albert's death: Murray did and the Queen was grateful. Most important, Murray was unafraid of the controversy generated by the books he published and treated his authors well; for example, he gave Darwin complete control over the content and writing style of his books.

Sir Richard Owen (20 July 1804–18 December 1892)

Sir Richard Owen was remembered, in the years after his death, for two so-called accomplishments: his opposition to Darwin's theory of descent by modification and coining the word dinosaur. These are not a fair reflection of his contribution to science.

In the mid-nineteenth century, Owen was the best-known and preeminent British scientist. He was a respected figure in the world-wide scientific community. His work as assistant curator and curator at the Hunterian Museum in London (1827–1856), classifying the specimens in the collection and producing catalogs, was a major contribution to the science of comparative anatomy. His reconstructions of extinct species from fossil bones made him a renowned paleontologist who was consulted by naturalists from all over the world. His research on the anatomy of primates, particularly higher apes, helped to establish the close relationship between humans and apes. Government ministers consulted Owen on scientific questions because of his wide range of knowledge. He was a popular lecturer who even taught Queen Victoria's children science lessons.

Owen's greatest contribution to the public understanding of science is the Natural History Museum of London. In 1856, Owen became superintendent of the Natural History Departments of the British Museum. (He held the position until 1883.) Owen recognized immediately that the burgeoning collection of specimens needed its own building as well as independence from the British Museum's emphasis on archeological exhibits and the national library. His lobbying was one of the main reasons the government approved the idea. The Museum opened in 1881 and Owen was its first director.

Owen received numerous honors for his work. He was elected to the Royal Society in 1834; he received the Royal and Copley medals from the Society for his research on Australian marsupials and monotremes (such as anteaters) in 1846 and 1851, respectively. He received the Wollaston Medal from the Geological Society for his classification of the fossil mammals in Darwin's *Zoology of the Voyage of the Beagle*. He was a corresponding or foreign member of every major scientific society outside of Britain; the French even made him a member of the Legion of Honor in 1855. In 1888, he (and Joseph Hooker) received the first Linnean Medal of the Linnean Society for his lifelong contributions to science. He was rightly called the English Cuvier.

His adherence to ideas similar to those of the French anatomist Georges Cuvier and a seemingly vindictive personality are the reasons why Owen's reputation has suffered. Like Cuvier, Owen held to the idea of functional similarity in anatomy. For example, wings served a similar function whether they were on birds, bats, or beetles. Owen extended this idea to include homology, a term he coined. Some structures in animals performed similar tasks even though they were different: the hand in humans and the fins in sea lions. Knowing homology and function enabled an anatomist to recreate the structure of extinct species. On one occasion, using a fossil bone from New Zealand, Owen predicted correctly that paleontologists would find that extinct flightless birds had lived on the islands.

Both Owen and Cuvier objected to evolution. They believed the similarities in different species were part of a larger plan created by God. Owen wrote a review of *The Origin of Species* in the *Edinburgh Review* in 1860 that attacked Darwin's scientific expertise. When Owen refused to accept Thomas Huxley's incontrovertible evidence that human and ape brains were similar, his defense of tradition seemed unscientific. The man who had written *A History of British Fossil Mammals, and Birds* (1846) and *On the Archetype and Homologies of the Vertebrate Skeleton* (1848) seemed too wedded to the science of the previous century.

Alfred Russel Wallace (8 January 1823–7 November 1913)

Alfred Russel Wallace developed a theory of evolution independently of Darwin. Wallace began to articulate his theory in 1855, eighteen years after Darwin had started to write down his ideas about the transmutation of species. Even though he was not first, Wallace deserves some credit as a codiscoverer of evolution: it was his essay on transmutation, "On the Tendency of Varieties to Depart Indefinitely from the Original Type," published in 1858, that spurred Darwin to write *The Origin of Species*. Furthermore, Wallace had been thinking about the relationship between the geographical distribution of species and their environment since 1848.

Wallace and Darwin developed a very friendly relationship. The two men wrote to each other regularly after 1858. It is clear from their letters that the two men liked and respected each other. Wallace also became one of the most vocal defenders of Darwin's theory of evolution: descent by modification through natural selection. Other scientists, including Darwin's close friend and dogged defender Thomas Huxley, wanted to downplay the primary role of natural selection, but not Wallace. Noting his deference to Darwin, his defense of Darwin's ideas in books such as *Darwinism: An Exposition of the Theory of Natural Selection with Some of its Applications* (1889), and his cordial relationship with Darwin, Wallace was sometimes called Darwin's Moon.

Wallace was much more than a naturalist who was a friend and inferior colleague of Darwin's. *A Narrative of Travels on the Amazon and Rio Negro, with an Account of the Native Tribes, and Observations on the Climate, Geology, and Natural History of the Amazon Valley* (1853), a description of the four years he spent in South America, established his reputation as a good naturalist. His research in Indonesia, described in *The Malay Archipelago: The Land of the Orang-Utan, and the Bird of Paradise. A Narrative of Travel with Studies of Man and Nature* (1869), during which he traveled more than 14,000 miles and collected more than 120,000 specimens, established his reputation as one of the premier British naturalists of the nineteenth century. His writings on ethnography, zoogeography, geology, and astronomy in books such as *The Geographical Distribution of Animals with a Study of the Relations of Living and Extinct Faunas as Elucidating the Past Changes of the Earth's Surface* (1876) and *Man's Place in the Universe: A Study of the Results of Scientific Research in Relation to the Unity or Plurality of Worlds* (1903) earned him the nickname The Grand Old Man of Science.

Wallace was more than a great scientist. He was also a leading figure in the spiritualist movement. He lectured on the subject in Britain and the United States and wrote a book of essays, *On Miracles and Modern Spiritualism* (1875). He was a well-known social critic, writing books such as *Social Environment and Moral Progress* (1913) and *The Revolt of Democracy* (1913). He supported land nationalization so that the proceeds could benefit the poor; he opposed vaccination because he did not believe the policy actually prevented disease in children and was thus a waste of valuable public resources.

Wallace's interest in numerous causes—he called them "heresies"—may have prevented him from receiving the full recognition he deserved during his lifetime. He did not have a full-time professional job in science (which meant he struggled financially until he obtained a government pension from 1881 onward). He was not made a fellow of the Royal Society until 1893 (although he received the first Darwin Medal of the Society in 1890). Medallions bearing his name were placed in the Natural History Museum of London and Westminster Abbey, but he did not receive the attention accorded to Darwin. Wallace thought of himself as a common man who defended the common man: his achievements suggest that Wallace was anything but common.

PEOPLE MENTIONED IN THE ORIGIN OF SPECIES

At the end of each entry, there are two page numbers (for example, 12/75). The first number refers to page references in the first edition of *The Origin of Species*; the second number refers to page references in the Penguin Classics edition. When it is not stated, the person's nationality is English.

Agassiz, Jean Louis Rodolphe [Louis] (1807–1873): American zoologist, paleontologist, and geologist
References in *The Origin*: 139/179, 302/309, 305/312, 310/315–316, 338/337 (twice), 366/359, 418/403, 439/419, 449/427

Archiac, Etienne Jules Adolphe Desmier de Saint-Simon (1802–1868): French army officer (until 1830), geologist, paleontologist, and historian of geology
Reference in *The Origin*: 325/327

Audubon, John James La Forest (1785–1851): American ornithologist and illustrator
References in *The Origin*: 185/216, 212/238, 387/377

Babington, Charles Cardale (1808–1895): Botanist and archeologist
Reference in *The Origin*: 48/104

Bakewell, Robert (1725–1795): Sheep and cattle breeder
References in *The Origin*: 35/93, 36/94 (twice)

Barrande, Joachim (1799–1883): French-born Bohemian paleontologist and stratigrapher
References in *The Origin*: 307/313 (twice), 310/315–316, 313/318, 317/321, 325/327 (twice), 328/330, 330/331

Beaumont, Jean Baptiste Armand Louis Léonce Elie de (1798–1874): French mining engineer and geologist
Reference in *The Origin*: 317/321

Bentham, George (1800–1884): Botanist
References in *The Origin*: 48/104, 419/404

Berkeley, Miles Joseph (1803–1889): Naturalist and Church of England priest
Reference in *The Origin*: 358/354

Birch, Samuel (1813–1885): Egyptologist and archeologist
Reference in *The Origin*: 27/87

Blyth, Edward (1810–1873): Zoologist and ornithologist
References in *The Origin*: 18/80, 163/198, 253/271, 254/271

Borrow, George Henry (1803–1881): Traveler and writer; listed incorrectly as "Barrow" in some editions of *The Origin*
Reference in *The Origin*: 35/93

Bory de Saint-Vincent, Jean-Baptiste-Geneviève-Marcellin (1778–1846): French army officer and naturalist
Reference in *The Origin*: 392–393/381

Bosquet, Joseph Augustin Hubert de (1814–1880): Dutch pharmacist, stratigrapher, and paleontologist
Reference in *The Origin*: 304/311

Brewer, Thomas Mayo (1814–1880): American ornithologist and publisher
Reference in *The Origin*: 217/242

Bronn, Heinrich Georg (1800–1862): German geologist and paleontologist
References in *The Origin*: 293/302, 312–313/317

Brown, Robert (1773–1858): Scottish botanist
References in *The Origin*: 415/400, 416/401

Buckland, William (1784–1856): Geologist and Church of England priest
Reference in *The Origin*: 329/330

Buckley, John (died ca. 1787): Sheep breeder
Reference in *The Origin*: 36/94

Buckman, James (1814–1884): Naturalist and horticulturist
Reference in *The Origin*: 10/74

Burgess, Joseph (died ca. 1807): British sheep breeder
Reference in *The Origin*: 36/94

Cassini, Alexandre Henri Gabriel (1781–1832): Also known as Henri Cassini, Vicomte de Cassini; French botanist
Reference in *The Origin*: 145/184

Cautley, Proby Thomas (1802–1871): Paleontologist, army officer, and government official
Reference in *The Origin*: 340/339

Chambers, Robert (1802–1871): Scottish publisher, author, and naturalist
Reference in *The Origin*: 3/67

Clausen, Peter (1804–1855?): Danish naturalist and army officer
Reference in *The Origin*: 339/338

Clift, William (1775–1849): Naturalist and museum curator
Reference in *The Origin*: 339/338

Collins (probably John) (died ca. 1820): Sheep and cattle breeder
Reference in *The Origin*: 35/93

Cuvier, Frédéric (1773–1838): French zoologist and anatomist; brother of Georges Cuvier
Reference in *The Origin*: 208/235

Cuvier, Georges (1769–1832): French zoologist, naturalist, historian of science, and politician; brother of Frédéric Cuvier
References in *The Origin*: 206/233, 303/310, 310/315–316, 329/331, 440/420

Dana, James Dwight (1813–1895): American geologist
References in *The Origin*: 139/179, 372/364–365, 376/367–368

Dawson, John William (1820–1899): Canadian naturalist and geologist
Reference in *The Origin*: 296/304–305

d'Azara, Félix (1746–1811 or 1821): Spanish army officer, administrator, explorer, geographer, and naturalist
Reference in *The Origin*: 72/124

de Candolle, Alphonse (1806–1893): Swiss botanist and politician; son of Augustin-Pyramus de Candolle
References in *The Origin*: 53/108, 115/158, 146/185, 175/208, 360/355, 379/370, 386/376, 387/377, 389/379, 392/381, 402/389, 406/392

de Candolle, Augustin-Pyramus (1778–1841): Swiss botanist and politician; father of Alphonse de Candolle
References in *The Origin*: 62/115, 146/185, 430/412

d'Orbigny, Alcide Charles Victor Dessalines (1802–1857): French paleontologist
Reference in *The Origin*: 297/305–306

Downing, Andrew Jackson (1815–1852): American horticulturist
Reference in *The Origin*: 85/134

Earl, George Samuel Windsor (1813–1865): Explorer, naturalist, and colonial administrator
Reference in *The Origin*: 395/383

Edwards, W. W. (unknown): Probably a nineteenth-century horse-racing expert
Reference in *The Origin*: 164/199

Elliot, Walter (1803–1887): Civil servant and archeologist
Reference in *The Origin*: 20/82

Eyton, Thomas (1809–1880): Naturalist
Reference in *The Origin*: 253/270–271

Fabre, Jean Henri Casimir (1823–1915): French entomologist and author of books on science
Reference in *The Origin*: 218/243

Falconer, Hugh (1808–1865): Scottish-born physician, botanist, and paleontologist
References in *The Origin*: 65/118, 310/315–316, 313/318, 334/335, 340/339, 378/369

Forbes, Edward (1815–1854): Naturalist and geologist
References in *The Origin*: 132/174, 174–175/208, 287/298, 290–291/300, 292/301, 307/313, 310/315–316, 316/320, 357/352–353, 358/353, 366/360, 372–373/365, 389/378, 409/395

Fries, Elias Magnus (1794–1878): Swedish botanist
References in *The Origin*: 57/111, 57/112

Gardner, George (1812–1849): Scottish botanist
Reference in *The Origin*: 374/366

Gärtner, Karl Friedrich von (1772–1850): German botanist
References in *The Origin*: 49–50/105, 98/144, 246–247/265–266 (seven times), 248/266–267 (twice), 249–250/267–268 (four times), 252/269, 255/272, 257/273–274, 258/274, 259/275, 262/277, 268/282, 270/283–284 (twice), 270/284, 272/285, 272/285–286 (twice), 273–274/286 (twice), 274/287 (twice)

Geoffroy Saint-Hilaire, Étienne (1772–1844): French zoologist, paleontologist, anatomist, and embryologist
References in *The Origin*: 147/185, 434/415

Geoffroy Saint-Hilaire, Isidore (1805–1861): French zoologist
References in *The Origin*: 8/72, 11/74, 144/183, 149/187, 155/192

Girou de Buzareingues, Louis-François-Charles (1773–1856): French agriculturist
Reference in *The Origin*: 270/284

Godwin-Austen, Robert Alfred Cloyne (1808–1884): Geologist
Reference in *The Origin*: 299/307

Goethe, Johann Wolfgang von (1749–1832): German poet and naturalist
References in *The Origin*: 147/185 (twice)

Gmelin, Johann Georg (1709–1755): German chemist and botanist
Reference in *The Origin*: 365/359

Gould, Augustus Addison (1805–1866): American physician and conchologist
Reference in *The Origin*: 397/385

Gould, John (1804–1881): Ornithologist, artist, and taxidermist
References in *The Origin*: 132/174, 133/174, 398/385, 404/391

Gray, Asa (1810–1898): American botanist
References in *The Origin*: 100/146, 115/158, 163/199, 165/200, 176/209, 218/242, 365/359, 371–372/364

Harcourt, Edward William Vernon (1825–1891): Politician and naturalist; called Mr. E. V. Harcourt by Darwin
Reference in *The Origin*: 391/380

Hartung, Georg (1822?–1891): German geologist
Reference in *The Origin*: 363/358

Heer, Oswald von (1809–1883): Swiss botanist, entomologist, and paleontologist
Reference in *The Origin*: 107/151

Herbert, William (1778–1847): Naturalist, politician, linguist, classical scholar, and Church of England priest; Dean of Manchester 1840–1847
References in *The Origin*: 62/115, 249–250/267–268, 250/268, 250–251/ 268, 251/269

Heron, Robert (1765–1864): Politician and a collector of unusual animals
Reference in *The Origin*: 89/137

Heusinger von Waldegg, Johann Friedrich Christian Karl (1792–1883): Also known as Karl Friedrich Heusinger von Waldegg; German physician and pioneer in comparative pathology
Reference in *The Origin*: 12/75

Hooker, Joseph Dalton (1817–1911): Botanist
References in *The Origin*: 2/65, 3/66, 53/108 (twice), 100/146 (twice), 140/180, 145/184, 373/365, 374/366, 375/367 (three times), 376/368, 378/369 (twice), 379/370, 381/371, 387/377, 391–392/381, 398/385, 399/386, 399/387, 429/411

Horner, Leonard (1785–1864): Scottish educationist, social reformer, and geologist; father-in-law of Charles Lyell
Reference in *The Origin*: 18/80

Huber, François (1750–1830): Swiss entomologist; father of Pierre Huber
References in *The Origin*: 230/252, 230/253, 231/253

Huber, Jean Pierre (1777–1840): Swiss entomologist; son of François Huber
References in *The Origin*: 207–208/234, 208/235, 219/243, 219/244 (three times), 220/244, 221/245, 225/248, 226/249

Humboldt, Friedrich Wilhelm Heinrich Alexander (1769–1859): Known as Alexander Humboldt or Alexander von Humboldt; Prussian/German explorer, geographer, and naturalist
Reference in *The Origin*: 374/366–367

Hunter, John (1728–1793): Scottish-born surgeon and anatomist
Reference in *The Origin*: 150/188

Hutton, Thomas (1807–1874): Naturalist and captain in the Bengal army
Reference in *The Origin*: 253/271

Huxley, Thomas Henry (1825–1895): Zoologist, physiologist, and science educator
References in *The Origin*: 101/146, 338/337, 438/419, 442/422

Johnston, Alexander Keith (1804–1871): Scottish cartographer, geographer, and publisher
Reference in *The Origin*: 359/355

Jones, John Matthew (1828–1888): British-born Canadian zoologist
Reference in *The Origin*: 391/380

Jussieu, Adrien-Henri-Laurent de (1797–1853): French botanist
Reference in *The Origin*: 418/402

Kirby, William (1759–1850): Entomologist and Church of England clergyman
Reference in *The Origin*: 135/176

Knight, Thomas Andrew (1759–1838): Horticulturist
References in *The Origin*: 7/71, 96/143

Kölreuter, Joseph Gottlieb (1733–1806): German botanist
References in *The Origin*: 98/144, 246/265, 246–247/265, 247/265, 248/266, 250/268, 258/274 (twice), 271/284, 274/286–287, 451/429

Lamarck, Jean-Baptiste de Monet (1744–1829): French zoologist
References in *The Origin*: 242/262, 427/409–410

Lepsius, Karl Richard (1810–1884): German Egyptologist
Reference in *The Origin*: 27/87

Linnaeus, Carl (Carl von Linné) (1707–1778): Swedish naturalist; created the classification categories for animals and plants and the binomial system of naming species
References in *The Origin*: 64/117, 413/399, 417/402, 427/410

Livingstone, David (1813–1873): Scottish explorer and missionary
Reference in *The Origin*: 34/92

Lubbock, John Avebury (1834–1913): Banker, politician, anthropologist, botanist, and entomologist; a neighbor of Darwin's in Downe
References in *The Origin*: 46/102, 241/261

Lucas, Prosper (1805–1885): French physician
References in *The Origin*: 12/75, 275/288

Lund, Peter Wilhelm (1801–1880): Danish naturalist and speleologist
Reference in *The Origin*: 339/338

Lyell, Sir Charles (1797–1875): Scottish-born geologist
References in *The Origin*: 2/65 (twice), 62/115, 95/142, 282/293, 283–284/294–295, 289/298–299, 289/299, 292/301, 296/304–305, 304/310–311, 307/313, 310/315–316, 310/316 (twice), 312/317, 313/318, 323/326, 328/330, 356/352, 363/357, 363/358, 381/372, 382/372, 385–386/376, 402–403/389, 481/453

Macleay, William Sharp (1792–1865): English-born diplomat and Australian naturalist
Reference in *The Origin*: 427/409–410

Malthus, Thomas (1766–1834): Political economist and Church of England priest
References in *The Origin*: 5/68, 63/117

Marshall, William (1745–1818): Agriculturist, horticulturist, and writer
References in *The Origin*: 41/98, 423/407

Martens, Martin (1797–1863): Belgian physician, chemist, and botanist
Reference in *The Origin*: 355/360

Martin, William Charles Linneaus (1798–1864): Author of natural history books
Reference in *The Origin*: 165/200

Matteucci, Carlo (1811–1868): Called Matteuchi by Darwin; Italian physicist and animal physiologist
Reference in *The Origin*: 193/222

Miller, Hugh (1802–1856): Scottish quarryman, geologist, poet, and ecclesiastical journalist
Reference in *The Origin*: 283/294

Miller, William Hallowes (1801–1880): Welsh-born mineralogist and crystallographer
Reference in *The Origin*: 226–227/249–250

Milne-Edwards, Henri (1801–1885): French zoologist and physiologist
References in *The Origin*: 115–116/158, 194/223, 418/403, 433/414

Moquin-Tandon, Christian Horace Bénédict Alfred (1804–1863): French botanist and naturalist
Reference in *The Origin*: 132/174

Morton, George Douglas (1761–1827): Naturalist; 16th Earl of Morton; incorrectly named Lord Moreton in the first edition
Reference in *The Origin*: 165/200

Müller, Johan Friedrich Theodor (1822–1897): Also known as Fritz Müller; German naturalist
References in *The Origin*: 10/73, 375/367

Murchison, Sir Roderick Impey (1792–1871): Scottish-born geologist and geographer
References in *The Origin*: 289/299, 307/313, 310/315–316, 317/321

Murray, Sir Charles Augustus (1806–1895): Diplomat
Reference in *The Origin*: 20/82

Newman, Henry Wenman (1788–1865): Army officer
Reference in *The Origin*: 74/125 (twice)

Noble, Charles (unknown): Nineteenth-century botanist
Reference in *The Origin*: 251–252/269

Owen, Richard (1804–1892): Comparative anatomist and paleontologist
References in *The Origin*: 134/175–176, 149/187, 150/188, 191/221, 192–193/222, 310/315–316, 319/322, 329/331 (twice), 339/338 (twice), 414/400, 416/401, 435/416, 437/417, 437/418, 442/421–422, 452/430

Paley, William (1743–1805): Theologian and Church of England priest
Reference in *The Origin*: 201/229

Pallas, Pyotr Simon (1741–1811): German naturalist and geographer
References in *The Origin*: 163/198, 253/271

Pictet de la Rive, François Jules (1809–1872): Swiss zoologist and paleontologist
References in *The Origin*: 302/309, 305/311, 305/312, 313/318, 316/320, 335/335, 335/335–336, 338/337

Pierce, James (unknown): Nineteenth-century American explorer, geographer, and geologist
Reference in *The Origin*: 91/139

Pliny the Elder (23–79): Latin name—Caius Plinius Secundus; Roman scholar, naturalist, and encyclopedist
References in *The Origin*: 28/87, 34/92, 37/95

Poole, Skeffington (born 1803): Army officer
References in *The Origin*: 163/198, 164/199 (twice), 165–166/200

Prestwich, Sir Joseph (1812–1896): Geologist
Reference in *The Origin*: 328/330

Ramond, Louis François Elisabeth (1753–1829): Baron Ramond de Carbonnières; French botanist
Reference in *The Origin*: 368/361

Ramsay, Sir Andrew Crombie (1814–1891): Scottish-born geologist
References in *The Origin*: 284/295, 285/296 (twice), 286/296

Rengger, Johann Rudolph (1795–1832): Swiss physician and naturalist
Reference in *The Origin*: 72/124

Richard, Achille (1794–1852): French botanist
Reference in *The Origin*: 417/402

Richardson, Sir John (1787–1865): Scottish navy surgeon, Arctic explorer, and naturalist
References in *The Origin*: 180/212, 376/368

Rollin, Charles (1661–1741): French historian and educationist
Reference in *The Origin*: 165/200

Sagaret, Augustin (1815–1884): French botanist
References in *The Origin*: 262/277, 270/284

Saint-Hilaire, Augustin François César Prouvençal de (1779–1853): Also known as Auguste de Saint-Hilaire; French botanist and naturalist
Reference in *The Origin*: 418/402

Schiödte, Jörgen Matthias Christian (1815–1884): Danish naturalist
References in *The Origin*: 138/178, 138/179

Schlegel, Hermann (1804–1884): German naturalist and ornithologist
Reference in *The Origin*: 144/183

Sebright, John Saunders (1767–1846): Politician, animal breeder, and agriculturist
References in *The Origin*: 20/81, 31/90

Sedgwick, Adam (1785–1873): Geologist and Church of England priest
References in *The Origin*: 302/309, 310/315–316

Silliman, Benjamin, Jr. (1816–1885): American chemist
Reference in *The Origin*: 137/178

Smith, Charles Hamilton (1776–1859): Also called Charles Smith, Jr.; Army officer and naturalist
Reference in *The Origin*: 164–165/199–200

Smith, Frederick (1805–1879): Entomologist
References in *The Origin*: 219–220/244, 220/244, 220/245, 222/246, 239/260, 239–240/260, 240/261

Smith, Joshua Toulmin (1816–1869): Lawyer, geologist, and publicist
Reference in *The Origin*: 283/294

Somerville, John Southey (1765–1819): 15th Lord Somerville; farmer and agriculturist
Reference in *The Origin*: 31/90

Spencer, John Charles (1782–1845): Viscount Althorp, 3rd Earl Spencer; politician and agriculturist
Reference in *The Origin*: 35/94

Sprengel, Christian Konrad (1750–1816): Darwin called him C. C. Sprengel; German botanist and Lutheran priest
References in *The Origin*: 98/144, 99/145, 145–146/184–185

Steenstrup, Johannes Japetus Smith (1813–1897): Also known as Japetus Steenstrup; Danish zoologist
Reference in *The Origin*: 424/407

St. John, Charles William George (1809–1856): Naturalist and sportsman
Reference in *The Origin*: 91/139

Tausch, Ignaz Friedrich (1793–1848): Austrian botanist
Reference in *The Origin*: 146/185

Tegetmeier, William Bernhard (1816–1912): Naturalist, journalist, pigeon-fancier, and poultry expert
References in *The Origin*: 228/250–251, 233–234/255

Temminck, Coenraad Jacob (1778–1858): Dutch ornithologist
Reference in *The Origin*: 419/403

Thouin, André (1747–1824): French botanist
Reference in *The Origin*: 262/277

Thwaites, George Henry Kendrick (1811–1882): Botanist and government official
Reference in *The Origin*: 140/180

Tomes, Robert Fisher (1823–?): Farmer, zoologist, and animal collector
Reference in *The Origin*: 394/383

Valenciennes, Achille (1794–1865): French zoologist
Reference in *The Origin*: 384–385/375

Van Mons, Jean Baptiste (1765–1842): Belgian chemist and horticulturist
Reference in *The Origin*: 29/88

Verneuil, Philippe Edouard Poulletier de (1805–1873): French geologist and paleontologist
Reference in *The Origin*: 325/327

Wallace, Alfred Russel (1823–1913): Welsh-born naturalist, explorer, and anthropologist; independent of Darwin, developed the theory of natural selection
References in *The Origin*: 1/65, 2/65, 355/351, 395/383

Waterhouse, George Robert (1810–1888): Entomologist and zoologist
References in *The Origin*: 116/159, 150/188, 151/189, 225/248, 429–430/412, 430/412 (twice)

Watson, Hewett Cottrell (1804–1881): Botanist and phrenologist
References in *The Origin*: 48/104, 53/108, 58/112 (three times),140/180, 176/209, 363/357–358, 367–368/361, 376/368

Westwood, John Obadiah (1805–1893): Entomologist and paleographer
References in *The Origin*: 57/111, 157/194, 415/401

Wollaston, Thomas Vernon (1822–1878): Entomologist and conchologist
References in *The Origin*: 48–49/105, 52/107, 132/174, 135/176, 135–136/176–177, 136/177 (twice), 176/209, 389/379, 402/389

Woodward, Samuel Pickworth (1821–1865): Naturalist and paleontologist
References in *The Origin*: 293/302, 316/320, 339/338

Youatt, William (1776–1847): Veterinary surgeon and author of books on domesticated animals
References in *The Origin*: 31/90, 36/94 (twice), 454/431

Primary Documents Relating to Darwin and Darwinism

Document 1: Vestiges of the Natural History of Creation

In *Vestiges of the Natural History of Creation* (1844), the author argued that a theory of evolution was the only way to explain the origin of life on earth. The book was controversial for three reasons. First, it was the first extended argument in favor of evolution written by a British author and published in prose form. (Erasmus Darwin, Darwin's grandfather, had written long poetic works such as *The Temple of Nature* (1803) discussing evolution.) Second, the author supported evolution in nature because he or she believed society would evolve or progress: to British readers this argument was too similar to the revolutionary ideas about an egalitarian society being discussed in France. Third, the author was anonymous—there was even a rumor that Prince Albert had written the book.

In this excerpt, at the beginning of a chapter entitled "Hypothesis of the Development of the Vegetable and Animal Kingdoms," the author suggested that all animal life came from a common ancestor. Darwin would discuss this idea in *The Origin of Species* and *The Descent of Man*.

The author was posthumously revealed as the Scottish author and publisher Robert Chambers (1802–1871). Chambers was an avid amateur geologist, but he was better known for writing and publishing histories of Scotland and guides to Scottish poetry.

> It has been already intimated, as a general fact, that there is an obvious gradation amongst the families of both the vegetable

and animal kingdoms, from the simple lichen and animalcule respectively up to the highest order of dicotyledonous trees and the mammalia. Confining our attention, in the meantime, to the animal kingdom—it does not appear that this gradation passes along one line, on which every form of animal life can be, as it were, strung; there may be branching or double lines at some places; or the whole may be in a circle composed of minor circles, as has been recently suggested. But still it is incontestable that there are general appearances of a scale beginning with the simple and advancing to the complicated. The animal kingdom was divided by Cuvier into four sub-kingdoms, or divisions, and these exhibit an unequivocal gradation in the order in which they are here enumerated:—Radiata (polypes, etc.;) mollusca, (pulpy animals;) articulata, (jointed animals;) vertebrata, (animals with internal skeleton.) The gradation can, in like manner, be clearly traced in the *classes* into which the sub-kingdoms are sub-divided, as, for instance, when we take those of the vertebrata in this order—reptiles, fishes, birds, mammals.

While the external forms of all these various animals are so different, it is very remarkable that the whole are, after all, variations of a fundamental plan, which can be traced as a basis throughout the whole, the variations being merely modifications of that plan to suit the particular conditions in which each particular animal has been designed to live. Starting from the primeval germ, which, as we have seen, is the representative of a particular order of full-grown animals, we find all others to be merely advances from that type, with the extension of endowments and modification of forms which are required in each particular case; each form, also, retaining a strong affinity to that which precedes it, and tending to impress its own features on that which succeeds. This unity of structure, as it is called, becomes the more remarkable, when we observe that the organs, while preserving a resemblance, are often put to different uses. For example: the ribs become, in the serpent, organs of locomotion, and the snout is extended, in the elephant, into a prehensile instrument.

Source: Robert Chambers, *Vestiges of the Natural History of Creation* (London: John Churchill, 1844), 191–193.

Document 2: Paley's Natural Theology

In his best-known book, *Natural Theology or, Evidences of the Existence and Attributes of the Deity, Collected from the Appearances of Nature* (1802), William Paley argued that the organization and sophistication of nature demonstrated that it was created by a designer. According to Paley, that designer must be God. Just as the existence of a watch implied that there was a watchmaker so nature suggested the existence of a creator God. Paley's arguments became the main ones used by theologians and Christians in Darwin's time to explain the relationship between the origin of life and the laws of nature. Theologians and philosophers had derived doctrines such as the existence of God from nature, hence the term natural theology, for more than a hundred years. Paley's explanation became the standard exposition of natural theology.

In the first two excerpts, Paley argues that it is illogical to talk about physical laws without conceding that a being must have created those laws. In the third excerpt, Alonzo Potter (1800–1865), professor of moral and intellectual philosophy at Union College, New York, and a future bishop of Pennsylvania, explains why studying nature is one way to learn about God. Potter's commentary at the beginning of an American edition of *Natural Theology* published in 1855 shows that Paley's approach to natural theology had gained widespread acceptance and popularity within fifty years of his death.

Written by William Paley

In crossing a heath, suppose I pitched my foot against a *stone*, and were asked how the stone came to be there, I might possibly answer, that, for anything I knew to the contrary, it had lain there for ever ; nor would it, perhaps, be very easy to show the absurdity of this answer. But suppose I had found a *watch* upon the ground, and it should be inquired how the watch happened to be in that place, I should hardly think of the answer which I had before given, that, for anything I knew, the watch might have always been there. Yet why should not this answer serve for the watch as well as for the stone? why is it not as admissible in the second case as in the first? For this reason, and for no other, viz., that, when we come to inspect the watch, we perceive (what we could not discover in the stone) that its several parts are framed and put together for a purpose, *e.g.*, that they are so formed and adjusted as to produce motion, and that motion so regulated as to point out the hour of the day; that, if the different parts had been differently shaped from what they are, of a different size from what they are, or placed after any other manner, or in any other order than that in which they are placed, either no motion at all would have been carried on in the machine, or none which would have answered the use that is now served by it.

Written by William Paley

And [a person who picked it up would] not [be] less surprised to be informed that the watch in his hand was nothing more than the result of the laws of *metallic* nature. It is a perversion of language to assign any law as the efficient operative cause of anything. A law presupposes an agent; for it is only the mode according to which an agent proceeds: it implies a power; for it is the order according to which that power acts. Without this agent, without this power, which are both distinct from itself, the *law* does nothing, is nothing. The expression, "the law of metallic nature" may sound strange and harsh to a philosophic ear; but it seems quite as justifiable as some others which are more familiar to him, such as "the law of vegetable nature," "the law of animal nature," or, indeed, as "the law of nature" in general, when assigned as the cause of phenomena, in exclusion of agency and power, or when it is substituted into the place of these.

Written by Alonzo Potter

Another reason which ought to recommend the study of Natural Religion is to be found in the present state of science. Our age is distinguished for its growing acquaintance with the great laws which regulate the operations of the physical world, and for the successful application of these laws to useful purposes, in the arts of life. Occupied with these discoveries and applications, it is not unnatural, that men should sometimes lose sight of the higher and more inspiring lessons which such laws are fitted to suggest. When, by patient observation and induction, we succeed in grouping a vast number of apparently incongruous facts under one simple principle, it is evident that the view of this principle *ought* to raise our thoughts to that Presiding Intelligence which has thus spread harmony over all his ways, and connected, by indissoluble bonds, bodies and changes the most remote and dissimilar. And when, from the contemplation of the law, we turn to the uses to which it may be applied, it is equally clear that, instead of resting upon some single use, such as the construction of a machine, or the perfecting of a process in the arts, we should endeavour to embrace those larger purposes which are all the while accomplishing, throughout the natural world, without the intervention of artisan or philosopher. As these various purposes rise into view, and we see how all things are made to work together for the promotion of happiness or virtue, ought such reflections to be attended with no adoring thoughts of Him who originally ordered and now sustains a system so fraught with blessing? But here science is often and sadly at fault. When she reaches the eminence where visions of something higher than sequences and generalizations are ready to break upon her, suddenly she becomes mute. Often, indeed, she dwells with such zeal upon the *constancy* of these laws, upon the stability of worlds and systems, that she would seem to intimate (if not directly teach) that here is an order of things resulting, not from will and wisdom, but from necessity. Nature is substituted for God, and an unalterable succession for the ever-present agency of the Creator and Ruler of the universe. Thus has science been robbed of half its glory; its views have been narrowed and often obscured; and truths which ought to have roused a world to the admiration of Eternal Power and Goodness, have been employed to lull the soul into a practical atheism.

Source: William Paley, *Natural Theology: or Evidences of the Existence and Attributes of the Deity. Collected from the Appearances of Nature* (London: R. Faulder, 1802), 1–2, 7–8; and Henry Brougham and Charles Bell, *Paley's Natural Theology: with Illustrative Notes, etc.* (New York: Harper and Brothers, Publishers, 1855), I: 24–25.

Document 3: Lyell on the Age of the Earth and Uniformitarianism

An important foundation of Darwin's theory of natural selection was the idea that the Earth was very old, millions of years as opposed to thousands: one book that helped Darwin to formulate this idea was Charles Lyell's three-volume *Principles of Geology* (1830–1833). Lyell argued that geological change such as the creation of mountains occurred very slowly and uniformly over millions of years. For Darwin, this long period of time was sufficient for some species to change into another species.

In this excerpt from his book, Lyell explains why it is difficult, if not impossible, to argue that geological formations such as mountain ranges could have developed in a short period of time (as other geologists at the time suggested).

He who should study the monuments of the natural world under the influence of a similar infatuation, must draw a no less exaggerated picture of the energy and violence of causes, and must experience the same insurmountable difficulty in reconciling the former and present state of nature. If we could behold in one view all the volcanic cones thrown up in Iceland, Italy, Sicily, and other parts of Europe, during the last five thousand years, and could see the lavas which have flowed during the same period; the dislocations, subsidences and elevations caused by earthquakes; the lands added to various deltas, or devoured by the sea, together with the effects of devastation by floods, and imagine that all these events had happened in one year, we must form most exalted ideas of the activity of the agents, and the suddenness of the revolutions. Were an equal amount of change to pass before our eyes in the next year, could we avoid the conclusion that some great crisis of nature was at hand? If geologists, therefore, have misinterpreted the signs of a succession of events, so as to conclude that centuries were implied where the characters imported thousands of years, and thousands of years where the language of nature signified millions, they could not, if they reasoned logically from such false premises, come to any other conclusion, than that the system of the natural world had undergone a complete revolution.

We should be warranted in ascribing the erection of the great pyramid to superhuman power, if we were convinced that it was raised in one day; and if we imagine, in the same manner, a mountain chain to have been elevated, during an equally small fraction of the time which was really occupied in upheaving it, we might then be justified in inferring, that the subterranean movements were once far more energetic than in out own times. We know that one earthquake may raise the coast of Chili for a hundred miles to the average height of about five feet. A repetition of two thousand shocks of equal violence might produce a mountain chain one hundred miles long, and ten thousand feet high. Now, should one only of these convulsions happen in a century, it would be consistent with the order of events experienced by the Chilians from the earliest times; but if the whole of them were to occur in the next hundred years, the entire district must be depopulated, scarcely any animals or plants could survive, and the surface would be one confused heap of ruin and desolation.

One consequence of undervaluing greatly the quantity of past time is the apparent coincidence which it occasions of events necessarily disconnected, or which are so unusual, that it would be inconsistent with all calculation of chances to suppose them to happen at one and the same time. When the unlooked for association of such rare phenomena is witnessed in the present course of nature, it scarcely ever fails to excite a suspicion of the preternatural in those minds which are not firmly convinced of the uniform agency of secondary causes;—as if the death of some individual in whose fate they are interested, happens to be accompanied by the appearance of a luminous meteor, or a comet, or the shock of an earthquake. It would be only necessary to multiply such coincidences indefinitely, and the mind of every philosopher would be disturbed. Now it would be difficult to exaggerate the number of physical events, many of them most rare and unconnected in their nature, which were imagined by the Woodwardian hypothesis to have happened in the course of a few months; and numerous other examples might be found of popular geological theories, which require us to imagine that a long succession of events happened in a brief and almost momentary period.

Source: Charles Lyell, *Principles of Geology, Being an Attempt to Explain the Former Changes of the Earth's Surface, by Reference to Causes Now in Operation* (London: John Murray, 1830), I: 79–80.

Document 4: Lamarck on Classification

In the history of evolution, the French zoologist Jean-Baptiste Lamarck is remembered best for his theories that were rejected by scientists in favor of Darwin's. The theories of spontaneous generation and the inheritance of acquired characteristics are associated with Lamarck. The first theory is an explanation of the way organic life began and the second is an explanation of the way mutations are passed on from parent to progeny. In fact, these theories are actually Neo-Lamarckian: they are modifications of Lamarck's theories made by scientists in the late-nineteenth century.

If Lamarck's explanation of the process of evolution was wrong, his work on the classification of organic life was critical in the development of the theory of evolution. Lamarck established some important rules for zoologists and botanists to use in their attempts to classify animal and plant life. In *Zoological Philosophy* (1794), Lamarck argued that it was impossible to understand the relationships between various plant or animal species without a proper approach to classification and that errors in the thinking of botanists and zoologists—on questions such as the immutability of the species—occurred because these scientists did not classify correctly. (Darwin made a similar argument in Chapter XIII of *The Origin of Species*, "Mutual Affinities of Organic Beings: Morphology: Embryology: Rudimentary Organs.") Taking the argument a stage further, Lamarck suggested that, if the species were not fixed, they must evolve from the simplest organisms to the most complex.

> I have already observed that the true aim of a classification of animals should not be merely the possession of a list of classes, genera and species, but also the provision of the greatest facilities for the study of nature and for obtaining a knowledge of her procedure, methods and laws.
>
> I do not hesitate to say, however, that our general classifications of animals up to the present have been in the inverse order from that followed by nature when bringing her living productions successively into existence; thus, when we proceed from the most complex to the simplest in the usual way, we increase the difficulty of acquiring a knowledge of the progress in complexity of organisation; and we also find it less easy to

grasp both the causes of the progress and of the interruptions in it.

When once we have recognised that a thing is useful and indeed indispensable for the end in view and that it is free from drawbacks, we should hasten to carry it into execution although it is contrary to custom.

This is the case with regard to the way in which a general classification of animals should be drawn up.

We shall see that it is not a matter of indifference from which end we begin this general classification of animals, and that the beginning of the order is not a mere matter of choice.

The existing custom of placing at the head of the animal kingdom the most perfect animals, and of terminating this kingdom with the most imperfect and simplest in organisation, is due, on the one hand, to that natural prejudice towards giving the preference to the objects which strike us most or in which we are most pleased or interested; and, on the other hand, to the preference for passing from the better known to what is less known.

When the study of natural history began to occupy attention these reasons were no doubt very plausible; but they must now yield to the needs of science and especially to those facilitating the progress of natural knowledge.

With regard to the numerous and varied animals which nature has produced, if we cannot flatter ourselves that we possess an exact knowledge of the real order which she followed in bringing them successively into existence, it is nevertheless true that the order which I am about to set forth is probably very near it: reason and all our acquired knowledge testify in favour of this probability.

If indeed it is true that all living bodies are productions of nature, we are driven to the belief that she can only have produced them one after another and not all in a moment. Now if she shaped them one after another, there are grounds for thinking that she began exclusively with the simplest, and only produced at the very end the most complex organisations both of the animal and vegetable kingdoms.

To assist us to a judgment as to whether the idea of species has any real foundations, let us revert to the principles already set forth; they show:

(1) That all the organised bodies of our earth are true productions of nature, wrought successively throughout long periods of time.

(2) That in her procedure, nature began and still begins by fashioning the simplest of organised bodies, and that it is these alone which she fashions immediately, that is to say, only the rudiments of organisation indicated in the term *spontaneous generation.*

(3) That, since the rudiments of the animal and plant were fashioned in suitable places and conditions, the properties of a commencing life and established organic movement necessarily caused a gradual development of the organs, and in course of time produced diversity in them as in the limbs.

(4) That the property of growth is inherent in every part of the organised body, from the earliest manifestations of life; and then gave rise to different kinds of multiplication and reproduction, so that the increase of complexity of organisation, and of the shape and variety of the parts, has been preserved.

(5) That with the help of time, of conditions that necessarily were favourable, of the changes successively undergone by every part of the earth's surface, and, finally, of the power of new conditions and habits to modify the organs of living bodies, all those which now exist have imperceptibly been fashioned such as we see them.

(6) That, finally, in this state of affairs every living body underwent greater or smaller changes in its organisation and its parts; so that what we call species were imperceptibly fashioned among them one after another and have only a relative constancy, and are not as old as nature.

Source: Jean-Baptiste Lamarck, *Zoological Philosophy: An Exposition with Regard to the Natural History of Animals*, trans. Hugh Eliot (London: Macmillan, 1914; first published 1809), 128–129, 40.

Document 5: Darwin on the Genesis of *The Origin of Species*

In this extract from his autobiography, Darwin describes his "eureka moment." Darwin explains how he succeeded where naturalists such as Lamarck or Buffon failed. The difficulty for naturalists was to explain how variation in species occurred. By the end of the eighteenth century, it was obvious that many varieties of the same species were very different from each other. How and why did these mutations occur was one of the problems naturalists had not solved before Darwin published *The Origin of Species*.

Darwin also describes the method of study that led him to develop the theory of natural selection. Three points Darwin made are particularly worth noting: the importance of Malthus's *Essay on the Principle of Population* (1798) on his thinking, the connection between artificial and natural selection, and one of the reasons why he took so long to write *The Origin of Species*. The solution to the problem of mutation was simple, but it took a great deal of research to find the evidence and make sense of it. Darwin, being both systematic and cautious, was not willing to publish his theory until he was certain that it was correct. His excitement when he had his "eureka moment" shows the personal investment Darwin had put into his research.

After my return to England it appeared to me that by following the example of Lyell in Geology, and by collecting all facts which bore in any way on the variation of animals and plants under domestication and nature, some light might perhaps be thrown on the whole subject. My first note-book was opened in July 1837. I worked on true Baconian principles, and without any theory collected facts on a wholesale scale, more especially with respect to domesticated productions, by printed enquiries, by conversation with skilful [sic] breeders and gardeners, and by extensive reading. When I see the list of books of all kinds which I read and abstracted, including whole series of Journals and Transactions, I am surprised at my industry. I soon perceived that selection was the keystone of man's success in making useful races of animals and plants. But how selection could be applied to organisms living in a state of nature remained for some time a mystery to me.

In October 1838, that is, fifteen months after I had begun my systematic enquiry, I happened to read for amusement 'Malthus on Population,' and being well prepared to appreciate the struggle for existence which everywhere goes on from long-continued observation of the habits of animals and plants, it at once struck me that under these circumstances favourable variations would tend to be preserved, and unfavourable ones to be destroyed. The result of this would be the formation of new species. Here then I had at last got a theory by which to work; but I was so anxious to avoid prejudice, that I determined not for some time to write even the briefest sketch of it. In June 1842 I first allowed myself the satisfaction of writing a very brief abstract of my theory in pencil in 35 pages; and this was enlarged during the summer of 1844 into one of 230 pages, which I had fairly copied out and still possess.

But at that time I overlooked one problem of great importance; and it is astonishing to me, except on the principle of Columbus and his egg,[1] how I could have overlooked it and its solution. This problem is the tendency in organic beings descended from the same stock to diverge in character as they become modified. That they have diverged greatly is obvious from the manner in which species of all kinds can be classed under genera, genera under families, families under sub-orders and so forth; and I can remember the very spot in the road, whilst in my carriage, when to my joy the solution occurred to me; and this was long after I had come to Down. The solution, as I believe, is that the modified offspring of all dominant and increasing forms tend to become adapted to many and highly diversified places in the economy of nature.

Source: Francis Darwin, ed., *The Life and Letters of Charles Darwin, Including an Autobiographical Chapter* (London: John Murray, 1887), I: 83–84.

Document 6: Darwin to Gray, September 1857

On 5 September 1857, Darwin wrote Asa Gray a letter about the origin of species. Gray had written a letter to Darwin the previous month in which Gray stated that his research on plants caused him to have doubts about the fixity of species. Darwin took the opportunity presented by Gray's revelation to describe his theory that could explain why certain species seemed to be changing. Appended to the letter was a summary of Darwin's theory of speciation—the idea that one species could become the progenitor of two or more new species. The essay Darwin sent to Gray was as good a summary of *The Origin of Species* as Darwin wrote before the book was published.

After Darwin received Alfred Wallace's essay entitled "On the Tendency of Varieties to Depart Indefinitely from the Original Type" in June 1858, he was uncertain about what he should do. Charles Lyell and Joseph Hooker suggested including the letter and summary that Darwin sent to Gray along with essays by Wallace and Darwin about speciation to help prove that Darwin had been working on the theory before Wallace.

The following extract is a copy of the essay that Darwin sent to Gray. Darwin corrected the version of essay he had written, and Lyell and Hooker sent that copy to the secretary of the Linnean Society, John Joseph Bennett (1801–1876). The major difference between the two essays was the postscript that Darwin took out of the copy sent to the Linnean Society.

The essay itself is a fascinating preview of *The Origin of Species*. The material that would form important components of Darwin's theory—artificial selection by breeders, the importance of geological time, the cumulative work of natural selection, the struggle for life, geographical distribution of species, and the importance of classification— is clearly evident. The examples of the mistletoe and the elephant that appeared in Chapter III, "Struggle for Existence," are in the essay. The problem Darwin had with his use of the term natural selection is also apparent: on one occasion natural is capitalized and on another it is not. Last, Darwin's self-deprecating manner is obvious: he predicts that Gray will find his theory "all rubbish."

I. It is wonderful what the principle of Selection by Man, that is the picking out of individuals with any desired quality, and breeding from them, and again picking out, can do. Even Breeders have been astonished at their own results. They can act on differences inappreciable to an uneducated eye. Selection has been *methodically* followed in *Europe* for only the last half century. But it has occasionally, and even in some degree methodically, been followed in the most ancient times. There must have been, also, a kind of unconscious selection from the most ancient times, namely in the preservation of the individual animals (without any thought of their offspring) most useful to each race of man in his particular circumstances. The "roguing" as nurserymen call the destroying of varieties, which depart from their type, is a kind of selection. I am convinced that intentional and occasional selection has been the main agent in making our domestic races. But, however, this may be, its great power of modification has been indisputably shown in late times. Selection acts only by the accumulation of very slight or greater variations, caused by external conditions, or by the mere fact that in generation the child is not absolutely similar to its parent. Man by this power of accumulating variations adapts living beings to his wants—he *may be said* to make the wool of one sheep good for carpets and another for cloth &c.—

II. Now suppose there was a being, who did not judge by mere external appearance, but could study the whole internal organization—who never was capricious—who should go on selecting for one end during millions of generations, who will say what he might effect! In nature we have some *slight* variations, occasionally in all parts: and I think it can be shown that a change in the conditions of existence is the main cause of the child not exactly resembling its parents; and in nature geology shows us what changes have taken place, and are taking place. We have almost unlimited time: no one but a practical geologist can fully appreciate this: think of the Glacial period, during the whole of which the same species of shells at least have existed; there must have been during this period millions on millions of generations.

III. I think it can be shown that there is such an unerring power at work, or *Natural Selection* (the title of my Book), which selects exclusively for the good of each organic being. The elder De Candolle, W. Herbert, and Lyell have written strongly on the struggle for life; but even they have not written strongly enough. Reflect that every being (even the Elephant) breeds at such a rate, that in a few years, or at most a few centuries or thousands of years, the surface of the earth would not hold the progeny of any one species. I have found it hard constantly to bear in mind that the increase of every single species is checked during some part of its life, or during some shortly recurrent generation. Only a few of those annually born can live to propagate their kind. What a trifling difference must often determine which shall survive and which perish!

IV. Now take the case of a country undergoing some change; this will tend to cause some of its inhabitants to vary slightly; not but what I believe most beings vary at all times enough for selection to act on. Some of its inhabitants will be exterminated, and the remainder will be exposed to the mutual action of a different set of inhabitants, which I believe to be more important to the life of each being than mere climate. Considering the infinitely various ways, beings have to obtain food by struggling with other beings, to escape danger at various times of life, to have their eggs or seeds disseminated &c. &c, I cannot doubt that during millions of generations individuals of a species will be born with some slight variation profitable to some part of its economy; such will have a better chance of surviving, propagating, this variation, which again will be slowly increased by the accumulative action of Natural selection; and the variety thus formed will either coexist with, or more commonly will exterminate its parent form. An organic being like the woodpecker or mistletoe may thus come to be adapted to a score of contingencies; natural selection, accumulating those slight variations in all parts of its structure which are in any way useful to it, during any part of its life.

V. Multiform difficulties will occur to everyone on this theory. Most can I think be satisfactorily answered.—"Natura non facit saltum" answers some of the most obvious.—The slowness of change, and only a very few undergoing change at any one time answers others. The extreme imperfections of our geological records answers others.

VI. One other principle, which may be called the principle of divergence plays, I believe, an important part in the origin of species. The same spot will support more life if occupied by very diverse forms; we see this in the many generic forms in a square yard of turf (I have counted twenty species belonging to eighteen genera), or in the plants and insects, on any little uniform islet, belonging almost to as genera and families as to species. We can understand this with the higher animals whose habits we best understand. We know that it has been experimentally shown that a plot of land will yield a greater weight, if cropped with several species of grasses than with two or three species. Now every single organic being, by propagating so rapidly, may be said to be striving its utmost to increase in numbers. So it will be with the offspring of any species after it has broken into varieties or sub-species or true species. And it follows, I think, from the foregoing facts that the varying offspring of each species will try (only a few will succeed) to seize on as many and as diverse places in the economy of nature, as possible. Each new variety or species, when formed will generally take the places of and so exterminate its less well-fitted parent. This, I believe, to be the origin of the classification or arrangement of all organic beings at all times. These always *seem* to branch and sub-branch like a tree from a common trunk; the flourishing twigs destroying the less vigorous—the dead and lost branches rudely representing extinct genera and families.

This sketch is *most* imperfect; but in so short a space I cannot make it better. Your imagination must fill up many wide blanks. Without some reflection it will appear all rubbish; perhaps it will appear so after reflection.

C. D.

P.S.—This little abstract touches only on the accumulative power of natural selection, which I look at as by far the most important element in the production of new forms. The laws governing the incipient or primordial variation (unimportant except as to groundwork for selection to act on, in which respect it is all important) I shall discuss under several heads, but I can come, as you may well believe, only to very partial & imperfect conclusions.

Source: Francis Darwin, ed., *The Life and Letters of Charles Darwin, Including an Autobiographical Chapter* (London: John Murray, 1887), I: 122–125.

Document 7: Darwin on Writing *The Origin of Species*

Although Darwin had begun sketching his ideas about natural selection in written form since 1842, he did not begin to write a book on the subject until 1856. In the 1850s, his friends Charles Lyell and Joseph Hooker urged Darwin to publish his theory as soon as possible: Lyell and Hooker were worried that another naturalist might preempt Darwin. The popular success of *Vestiges of the Natural History of Creation* demonstrated that many people were thinking about and interested in evolution. By June 1858, Darwin had written eleven chapters but not completed his (untitled) book about natural selection.

Darwin's shock at receiving Alfred Russel Wallace's essay on natural selection—Wallace would eventually entitle the essay "On the Tendency of Species to Form Varieties"—prompted Darwin to write a series of letters to Lyell. Darwin was distraught: he could hardly believe that he had been preempted. Wallace's essay was the catalyst that galvanized Darwin to write the book that became *The Origin of Species.*

Charles Darwin to Charles Lyell (written from Down House, 18 June 1858)

My Dear Lyell,

Some year or so ago you recommended me to read a paper by Wallace in the *Annals* [*and Magazine of Natural History*], which had interested you, and, as I was writing to him, I knew this would please him much, so I told him. He has to-day sent me the enclosed, and asked me to forward it to you. It seems to me well worth reading. Your words have come true with a vengeance—that I should be forestalled. You said this, when I explained to you here very briefly my views of Natural Selection depending on the struggle for existence. I never saw a more striking coincidence; if Wallace had my MS. sketch written out in 1842, he could not have made a better short abstract! Even his terms now stand as heads of my chapters. Please return me the MS., which he does not say he wishes me to publish, but I shall of course, at once write and offer to send to any journal. So all my originality, whatever it may amount to, will be smashed, though my book, if it will ever have any value, will not be deteriorated; as all the labour consists in the application of the theory.

I hope you will approve of Wallace's sketch, that I may tell him what you say.

My dear Lyell, yours most truly,

C. Darwin

Charles Darwin to Charles Lyell (written from Down House, 25 June 1858)

My Dear Lyell,

I am very sorry to trouble you, busy as you are, in so merely personal an affair; but if you will give me your deliberate opinion, you will do me as great a service as ever man did, for I have entire confidence in your judgment and honour....

There is nothing in Wallace's sketch which is not written out much fuller in my sketch, copied out in 1844, and read by Hooker some dozen years ago. About a year ago I sent a short sketch, of which I have a copy, of my views (owing to correspondence on several points) to Asa Gray, so that I could most truly say and prove that I take nothing from Wallace. I should be extremely glad now to publish a sketch of my general views in about a dozen pages or so; but I cannot persuade myself that I can do so honourably. Wallace says nothing about publication, and I enclose his letter. But as I had not intended to publish any sketch, can I do so honourably, because Wallace has sent me an outline of his doctrine? I would far rather burn my whole book, than that he or any other man should think that I had behaved in a paltry spirit. Do you not think his having sent me this sketch ties my hands? ...

If I could honourably publish, I would state that I was induced now to publish a sketch (and I should be very glad to be permitted to say, to follow your advice long ago given) from Wallace having sent me an outline of my general conclusions. We differ only [in] that I was led to my views from what artificial selection has done for domestic animals. I would send Wallace a copy of my letter to Asa Gray, to show him that I had not stolen his doctrine. But I cannot tell whether to publish now would not be base and paltry. This was my first impression, and I should have certainly acted on it had it not been for your letter.

This is a trumpery affair to trouble you with, but you cannot tell how much obliged I should be for your advice.

By the way, would you object to send this and your answer to Hooker to be forwarded to me, for then I shall have the opinion of my two best and kindest friends. This letter is miserably written, and I write it now, that I may for a time banish the whole subject; and I am worn out with musing. ...

My good dear friend forgive me. This is a trumpery letter, influenced by trumpery feelings.

Yours most truly,

C. Darwin

I will never trouble you or Hooker on the subject again.

Source: Francis Darwin, ed., *The Life and Letters of Charles Darwin, Including an Autobiographical Chapter* (London: John Murray, 1887), I: 116–118.

Document 8: *The Origin of Species:* Darwin's Revolutionary Idea

After the publication of the first edition of *The Origin of Species*, Darwin decided to add a short essay that he finally entitled "An Historical Sketch of the Progress of Opinion on the Origin of Species, Previously to the Publication of the First Edition of This Work." (Darwin added the sketch to the first American edition and the third British edition of *The Origin of Species*.) He did this to answer two groups of critics. One group claimed that Darwin's theory was unique, radical, and, because no one had proposed the theory previously, unscientific. A second group claimed that Darwin was simply repeating ideas that had already been suggested by other naturalists:

Darwin did not deserve any admiration for doing this, particularly because these ideas had been dismissed by prominent naturalists.

In the opening paragraph of the historical sketch, Darwin explains succinctly his revolutionary idea and the difference between it and orthodox thinking about the origin of species.

> I will here give a brief sketch of the progress of opinion on the Origin of Species. Until recently the great majority of naturalists believed that species were immutable productions, and had been separately created. This view has been ably maintained by many authors. Some few naturalists, on the other hand, have believed that species undergo modification, and that the existing forms of life are the descendants by true generation of pre-existing forms.

Source: *The Origin of Species by Means of Natural Selection, or the Preservation of Favoured Races in the Struggle for Life*, 6th edition (London: John Murray, 1872), xii.

Document 9: *The Origin of Species*: Artificial Selection

The main components of Darwin's theory about the origin of species and the evolution of organic life are in the first five chapters of *The Origin of Species*. (Darwin did not address the origin of life explicitly in the first edition of *The Origin of Species*.) Each of the chapters after the first contains an idea that is built on the ideas in the previous chapter.

As the prevailing theory among naturalists was that the species were fixed, Darwin dealt with this first. In the first chapter of *The Origin of Species*, Darwin proposed two important ideas: first, that the demarcation of species was not as definitive as some naturalists suggested; second, that humans were able to make significant alterations in species by choosing particular animals to breed or plants to cross. If different naturalists could not agree whether a particular plant was a species or a variety of a species, and if humans could breed animals so different from the original parents that an unknowing observer would not think the parents and the progeny were related, then the species were not fixed or immutable, Darwin argued.

In this excerpt, Darwin explains the power of selection. Later in the chapter, Darwin uses the term "unconscious" to describe selection that results in unintended changes in a species. Conversely, conscious selection or artificial selection is the deliberate action taken by humans to create varieties of animals and plants by breeding. If the process is continued over a long period of time, humans can create new species. Thus, Darwin argued, the wide variety of domestic animals and plants demonstrates that selection is the most powerful force in producing change in the natural world.

One of the most remarkable features in our domesticated races is that we see in them adaptation, not indeed to the animal's or plant's own good, but to man's use or fancy. Some variations useful to him have probably arisen suddenly, or by one step; many botanists, for instance, believe that the fuller's teazle, with its hooks, which cannot be rivalled by any mechanical contrivance, is only a variety of the wild Dipsacus;[2] and this amount of change may have suddenly arisen in a seedling. So it has probably been with the turnspit dog;[3] and this is known to have been the case with ancon sheep.[4] But when we compare the dray-horse and race-horse, the dromedary and camel, the various breeds of sheep fitted either for cultivated land or mountain pasture, with the wool of one breed good for one purpose, and that of another breed for another purpose; when we compare the many breeds of dogs, each good for man in very different ways; when we compare the game-cock, so pertinacious in battle, with other breeds so little quarrelsome, with "everlasting layers" which never desire to sit, and with the bantam so small and elegant; when we compare the host of agricultural, culinary, orchard, and flower-garden races of plants, most useful to man at different seasons and for different purposes, or so beautiful in his eyes, we must, I think, look further than to mere variability. We cannot suppose that all the breeds were suddenly produced as perfect and as useful as we now see them; indeed, in several cases, we know that this has not been their history. The key is man's power of accumulative selection: nature gives successive variations; man adds them up in certain directions useful to him. In this sense he may be said to make for himself useful breeds.

The great power of this principle of selection is not hypothetical. It is certain that several of our eminent breeders have, even within a single lifetime, modified to a large extent some breeds of cattle and sheep. In order to fully realise what they have done, it is almost necessary to read several of the many treatises devoted to this subject, and to inspect the animals. Breeders habitually speak of an animal's organisation as something quite plastic, which they can model almost as they please.

The same principles are followed by horticulturists; but the variations are here often more abrupt. No one supposes that our choicest productions have been produced by a single variation from the aboriginal stock. We have proofs that this is not so in some cases, in which exact records have been kept; thus, to give a very trifling instance, the steadily-increasing size of the common gooseberry may be quoted. We see an astonishing improvement in many florists' flowers, when the flowers of the present day are compared with drawings made only twenty or

thirty years ago. When a race of plants is once pretty well established, the seed-raisers do not pick out the best plants, but
merely go over their seed-beds, and pull up the "rogues," as they
call the plants that deviate from the proper standard.

Source: *On the Origin of Species by Means of Natural Selection, or the
Preservation of Favoured Races in the Struggle for Life* (London: John
Murray, 1859), 29–31, 32–33.

Document 10: *The Origin of Species*:
The Definition of a Species

The key to understanding Darwin's theory is in the first chapter
of *The Origin of Species*. The existence of a large number of varieties
of species, the fact that species mutate, and the fluid nature of variation are all posited in the first chapter. These ideas are based on the
ability of humans to change the structure of domesticated animals
and plants by selection.

Darwin recognized that his readers might wonder whether the
variability he described occurred in "the wild." The breeding of
domestic animals was something humans could control: did variation
and mutation occur in the natural world?

Darwin answered this question indirectly. In the second chapter
of *The Origin of Species*, Darwin discussed the definition of a species
and a variety. More particularly, he noted that naturalists found it
difficult to define either a species or a variety precisely. Furthermore,
even when naturalists could agree on these definitions, after applying
them to actual examples, naturalists might still disagree about classifying a particular plant as a species or a variety of a species.

The difficulty of distinguishing between species and varieties led
to a central proposition in Darwin's theory: everything in nature was
in a state of flux. Varieties were in the process of becoming subspecies, subspecies were becoming species, and species could become distinct families. In contemporary language, all organic life was evolving.

In this excerpt, Darwin explains the relationship between a species and a variety and the reason why this relationship is a clue to
the origin of species.

Certainly no clear line of demarcation has as yet been drawn
between species and sub-species—that is, the forms which in
the opinion of some naturalists come very near to, but do not
quite arrive at the rank of species; or, again, between sub-species
and well-marked varieties, or between lesser varieties and individual differences. These differences blend into each other in an

insensible series; and a series impresses the mind with the idea of an actual passage.

Hence I look at individual differences, though of small interest to the systematist, as of high importance for us, as being the first step towards slight varieties as are barely thought worth recording in works on natural history. And I look at varieties which are in any degree more distinct and permanent, as steps leading to more strongly marked and more permanent varieties; and at these latter, as leading to sub-species, and to species. The passage from one stage of difference to another and higher stage may be, in some cases, due merely to the long-continued action of different physical conditions in two different regions; but I have not much faith in this view; and I attribute the passage of a variety, from a state in which it differs very slightly from its parent to one in which it differs more, to the action of natural selection in accumulating ... differences of structure in certain definite directions. Hence I believe a well-marked variety may be justly called an incipient species; but whether this belief be justifiable must be judged of by the general weight of the several facts and views given throughout this work.

It need not be supposed that all varieties of incipient species necessarily attain the rank of species. They may whilst in this incipient state become extinct, or they may endure as varieties for very long periods, as has been shown to be the case by Mr. Wollaston with the varieties of certain fossil land-shells in Madeira.[5] If a variety were to flourish so as to exceed in numbers the parent species, it would then rank as the species, and the species as the variety; or it might come to supplant and exterminate the parent species; or both might co-exist, and both rank as independent species....

From these remarks it will be seen that I look at the term species, as one arbitrarily given for the sake of convenience to a set of individuals closely resembling each other, and that it does not essentially differ from the term variety, which is given to less distinct and more fluctuating forms. The term variety, again, in comparison with mere individual differences, is also applied arbitrarily, and for mere convenience sake.

Source: *On the Origin of Species by Means of Natural Selection, or the Preservation of Favoured Races in the Struggle for Life* (London: John Murray, 1859), 51–52.

Document 11: *The Origin of Species*: The Struggle for Existence

In the third chapter of *The Origin of Species,* Darwin discusses in more detail two of the most important components of his theory:

the struggle for existence and natural selection. Darwin worked out the idea of the struggle for existence after reading a book written by Thomas Malthus, a British economist and social commentator.

Malthus wrote *An Essay on the Principle of Population* (1798) in which he connected the problems of society with the availability of resources, particularly food. Malthus asserted that the human population was increasing geometrically while the amount of food was only increasing arithmetically. Such a discrepancy meant that conflict and war would inevitably occur among different groups of people struggling to acquire and control the resources they needed. Only checks on the population such as natural disasters, poverty, disease, and death eased the conflicts, Malthus argued. Darwin applied Malthus's theory about the shortage of resources to the whole natural world.

In this excerpt, Darwin explains what he means by "the struggle for existence" and its relationship to natural selection. Darwin also explains why Malthus's theory about population is an important clue to understanding the action of natural selection.

> I should premise that I use the term Struggle for Existence in a large and metaphorical sense, including dependence of one being on another, and including (which is more important) not only the life of the individual, but success in leaving progeny. Two canine animals in a time of dearth, may be truly said to struggle with each other which shall get food and live. But a plant on the edge of a desert is said to struggle for life against the drought, though more properly it should be said to be dependent on the moisture. A plant which annually produces a thousand seeds, of which on an average only one comes to maturity, may be more truly said to struggle with the plants of the same and other kinds which already clothe the ground. The missletoe is dependent on the apple and few other trees, but can only in a far-fetched sense be said to struggle with these trees, for if too many of these parasites grow on the same tree, it will languish and die. But several seedling missletoes, growing close together on the same branch, may more truly be said to struggle with each other. As the missletoe is disseminated by birds, its existence depends on birds; and it may metaphorically be said to struggle with other fruit-bearing plants, in order to tempt birds to devour and thus disseminate its seeds rather than those of other plants. In these several senses, which pass into each other, I use for convenience sake the general term of struggle for existence.
>
> A struggle for existence inevitably follows from the high rate at which all organic beings tend to increase. Every being, which during its natural lifetime produces several eggs or seeds,

must suffer destruction during some period of its life, and during some season or occasional year, otherwise, on the principle of geometrical increase, its numbers would quickly become so inordinately great that no country could support the product. Hence, as more individuals are produced than can possibly survive, there must in every case be a struggle for existence, either one individual with another of the same species, or with the physical conditions of life. It is the doctrine of Malthus applied with manifold force to the whole animal and vegetable kingdoms; for in this case there can be no artificial increase of food, and no prudential restraint from marriage.[6] Although some species may be now increasing, more or less rapidly, in numbers, all cannot do so, for the world would not hold them.

There is no exception to the rule that every organic being naturally increases at so high a rate, that if not destroyed, the earth would soon be covered by the progeny of a single pair. Even slow-breeding man has doubled in twenty-five years, and at this rate, in a few thousand years, there would literally not be standing room for his progeny. Linnæus[7] has calculated that if an annual plant produced only two seeds—and there is no plant so unproductive as this—and their seedlings next year produced two, and so on, then in twenty years there would be a million plants. The elephant is reckoned to be the slowest breeder of all known animals, and I have taken some pains to estimate its probable minimum rate of natural increase: it will be under the mark to assume that it breeds when thirty years old, and, goes on breeding till ninety years old, bringing forth three pair of young in this interval; if this be so, at the end of the fifth century there would be alive fifteen million elephants, descended from the first pair.

Source: *On the Origin of Species by Means of Natural Selection, or the Preservation of Favoured Races in the Struggle for Life* (London: John Murray, 1859), 62–64.

Document 12: *The Origin of Species*: The Mutation of Species

What exactly was natural selection? Following the ideas in the first chapter of *The Origin of Species*, natural selection should be related to artificial selection. If artificial selection was the choosing by humans of animals to breed and plants to cross that resulted in new varieties and species, then natural selection was the action of nature to produce the same effect, Darwin argued.

In Chapter III of *The Origin of Species*, Darwin began to explain how natural selection worked. In this excerpt, Darwin describes how the process of natural selection makes it possible for one species to mutate into a different species.

> Again, it may be asked, how is it that varieties, which I have called incipient species, become ultimately converted into good and distinct species, which in most cases obviously differ from each other far more than do the varieties of the same species? How do those groups of species, which constitute what are called distinct genera, and which differ from each other more than do the species of the same genus, arise? All these results, as we shall more fully see in the next chapter, follow inevitably from the struggle for life. Owing to this struggle for life, any variation, however slight and from whatever cause proceeding, if it be in any degree profitable to an individual of any species, in its infinitely complex relations to other organic beings and to external nature, will tend to the preservation of that individual, and will generally be inherited by its offspring. The offspring, also, will thus have a better chance of surviving, for, of the many individuals of any species which are periodically born, but a small number can survive. I have called this principle, by which each slight variation, if useful, is preserved, by the term of Natural Selection, in order to mark its relation to man's power of selection. We have seen that man by selection can certainly produce great results, and can adapt organic beings to his own uses, through the accumulation of slight but useful variations, given to him by the hand of Nature. But Natural Selection, as we shall hereafter see, is a power incessantly ready for action, and is as immeasurably superior to man's feeble efforts, as the works of Nature are to those of Art.[8]

Source: *On the Origin of Species by Means of Natural Selection, or the Preservation of Favoured Races in the Struggle for Life* (London: John Murray, 1859), 61.

Document 13: *The Origin of Species:* Natural Selection

Darwin devoted the fourth chapter of *The Origin of Species* to natural selection. Natural selection is Darwin's most important contribution to the theory of evolution. Darwin knew this and demonstrated it by making Chapter IV the longest in the book.

In Chapter IV, Darwin tried to answer several questions. What was natural selection? How did natural selection work? Why did natural selection occur? What was the effect of natural selection? For each question, the answer was partly based on ideas explained in the first three chapters of *The Origin of Species*—the mutability of domestic species, the flux between species and varieties, and the struggle for life. The following excerpt is one of several places in the chapter in which Darwin integrates all of these ideas.

Can it, then, be thought improbable, seeing that variations useful to man have undoubtedly occurred, that other variations useful in some way to each being in the great and complex battle of life, should sometimes occur in the course of thousands of generations? If such do occur, can we doubt (remembering that many more individuals are born than can possibly survive) that individuals having any advantage, however slight, over others, would have the best chance of surviving and of procreating their kind? On the other hand, we may feel sure that any variation in the least degree injurious would be rigidly destroyed. This preservation of favourable variations and the rejection of injurious variations, I call Natural Selection. Variations neither useful nor injurious would not be affected by natural selection, and would be left a fluctuating element, as perhaps we see in the species called polymorphic.[9]

As man can produce and certainly has produced a great result by his methodical and unconscious means of selection, what may not nature effect? Man can act only on external and visible characters: nature cares nothing for appearances, except in so far as they may be useful to any being. She can act on every internal organ, on every shade of constitutional difference, on the whole machinery of life. Man selects only for his own good; Nature only for that of the being which she tends. Every selected character is fully exercised by her; and the being is placed under well-suited conditions of life. Man keeps the natives of many climates in the same country; he seldom exercises each selected character in some peculiar and fitting manner; he feeds a long and short beaked pigeon on the same food; he does not exercise a long-backed or long-legged quadruped in any peculiar manner; he exposes sheep with long and short wool to the same climate. He does not allow the most vigorous males to struggle for the females. He does not rigidly destroy all inferior animals, but protects during each varying season, as far as lies in his power, all his productions. He often begins his selection by some half-monstrous form; or at least by some modification prominent enough to catch his eye, or to be plainly useful to him. Under nature, the slightest difference of structure or constitution may well turn the nicely-balanced scale in the struggle for life, and so be preserved. How fleeting are the wishes and efforts of man! how short his time! and consequently how poor will his products be, compared with those accumulated by nature during whole geological periods. Can we wonder, then, that nature's productions should be far "truer" in character than man's productions; that they should be infinitely better adapted to the most complex conditions of life, and should plainly bear the stamp of far higher workmanship?

It may be said that natural selection is daily and hourly scrutinising, throughout the world, every variation, even the slightest; rejecting that which is bad, preserving and adding up all that is good; silently and insensibly working, whenever and wherever opportunity offers, at the improvement of each organic being in relation to its organic and inorganic conditions of life. We see nothing of these slow changes in progress, until the hand of time has marked the long lapse of ages, and then so imperfect is our view into long past geological ages, that we only see that the forms of life are now different from what they formerly were.

Source: *On the Origin of Species by Means of Natural Selection, or the Preservation of Favoured Races in the Struggle for Life* (London: John Murray, 1859), 80–81, 83–84.

Document 14: *The Origin of Species*: The Power of Natural Selection

A key concept underpinning natural selection was uniformitarianism. The foremost proponent of uniformitarianism in the nineteenth-century British scientific community was the geologist Charles Lyell. According to Lyell, all geological formations came into existence over thousands or millions of years—in other words, very slowly and gradually.

Darwin applied Lyell's theory of uniformitarianism to organic life. Like the sea wearing away a cliff, so natural selection brought about persistent and permanent changes in species over thousands of generations.

In Chapter IV of *The Origin of Species*, Darwin stated explicitly his debt to Lyell. It is the slow action of natural selection that produces the wide range of diversity and complexity in the natural world. Again, with time on its side, Darwin argues that natural selection will produce changes in species far greater than that achieved by humans (even though the artificial changes are fairly impressive).

I am well aware that this doctrine of natural selection, exemplified in the above imaginary instances, is open to the same objections which were at first urged against Sir Charles Lyell's noble views on 'the modern changes of the earth, as illustrative of geology;' but we now very seldom hear the action, for instance, of the coast-waves, called a trifling and insignificant cause, when applied to the excavation of gigantic valleys or to the formation of the longest lines of inland cliffs. Natural selection can act only by preservation and accumulation of infinitesimally small inherited modifications, each profitable to the preserved being; and as modern geology has almost banished such views as the excavation of a great valley by a single diluvial wave, so will natural selection, if it be a true principle, banish the belief of the continued creation of new organic beings, or of any great and sudden modification in their structure.

That natural selection will always act with extreme slowness, I fully admit. Its action depends on there being places in the polity of nature, which can be better occupied by some of the inhabitants of the country undergoing modification of some kind. The existence of such places will often depend on physical changes, which are generally very slow, and on the immigration of better adapted forms having been checked. But the action of natural selection will probably still oftener depend on some of the inhabitants becoming slowly modified; the mutual relations of many of the other inhabitants being thus disturbed. Nothing can be effected, unless favourable variations occur, and variation itself is apparently always a very slow process. The process will often be greatly retarded by free intercrossing. Many will exclaim that these several causes are amply sufficient wholly to stop the action of natural selection. I do not believe so. On the other hand, I do believe that natural selection will always act very slowly, often only at long intervals of time, and generally on only a very few of the inhabitants of the same region at the same time. I further believe, that this very slow, intermittent action of natural selection accords perfectly well with what geology tells us of the rate and manner at which the inhabitants of this world have changed.

Slow though the process of selection may be, if feeble man can do much by his powers of artificial selection, I can see no limit to the amount of change, to the beauty and infinite complexity of the coadaptations between all organic beings, one with another and with their physical conditions of life, which may be effected in the long course of time by nature's power of selection.

Source: *On the Origin of Species by Means of Natural Selection, or the Preservation of Favoured Races in the Struggle for Life* (London: John Murray, 1859), 95–96, 108–109.

Document 15: *The Origin of Species*: Successful Species and Extinction

The phrases "the struggle for life" and "the struggle for existence," which Darwin used several times in *The Origin of Species*, imply intense competition between certain species and varieties. Why might a species or a variety of a species mutate? To take better advantage of the conditions around it compared with its competitors, a species has to modify and improve, otherwise it will not be able to withstand competition from other, improving, species. Ultimately, Darwin argued, the least-adaptable species could face extinction.

The origin of one species could mean the end of another species. While this process sounded rather ruthless, Darwin admitted, it also demonstrated an important fact about organic life: a person who traced backward through the variations and extinctions would find the original species, the first parent, of the existing species.

In these excerpts from the fourth chapter of *The Origin of Species*, Darwin explains why some species will be more successful than others. The action of natural selection and the resulting extinctions are the key to explaining the beginning of life.

Although I do not doubt that isolation is of considerable importance in the production of new species, on the whole I am inclined to believe that largeness of area is of more importance, more especially in the production of species, which will prove capable of enduring for a long period, and of spreading widely. Throughout a great and open area, not only will there be a better chance of favourable variations arising from the large number of individuals of the same species there supported, but the conditions of life are infinitely complex from the large number of already existing species; and if some of these many species become modified and improved, others will have to be improved in a corresponding degree or they will be exterminated. Each new form, also, as soon as it has been much improved, will be able to spread over the open and continuous area, and will thus come into competition with many others. Hence more new places will be formed, and the competition to fill them will be more severe, on a large than on a small and isolated area. Moreover, great areas, though now continuous, owing to oscillations of level, will often have recently existed in a broken condition, so that the good effects of isolation will generally, to a certain extent, have concurred. Finally, I conclude that, although small isolated areas probably have been in some respects highly favourable for the production of new species, yet that the course of modification will generally have been more rapid on large areas; and what is more important, that the new forms produced on large areas, which already have been victorious over many competitors, will be those that will spread most widely, will give rise to most new varieties and species, and will thus play an important part in the changing history of the organic world.

From these several considerations I think it inevitably follows, that as new species in the course of time are formed through natural selection, others will become rarer and rarer, and finally extinct. The forms which stand in closest competition

with those undergoing modification and improvement, will naturally suffer most. And we have seen in the chapter on the Struggle
for Existence that it is the most closely-allied forms,—varieties of
the same species, and species of the same genus or of related genera,—which, from having nearly the same structure, constitution,
and habits, generally come into the severest competition with
each other. Consequently, each new variety or species, during the
progress of its formation, will generally press hardest on its near-
est kindred, and tend to exterminate them. We see the same the
process of extermination amongst our domesticated productions,
through the selection of improved forms by man. Many curious
instances could be given showing how quickly new breeds of cattle, sheep, and other animals, and varieties of flowers, take the
place of older and inferior kinds. In Yorkshire, it is historically
known that the ancient black cattle were displaced by the long-
horns, and that these 'were swept away by the short-horns'
(I quote the words of an agricultural writer) 'as if by some mur-
derous pestilence.'[10]

Source: *On the Origin of Species by Means of Natural Selection, or the
Preservation of Favoured Races in the Struggle for Life* (London: John
Murray, 1859), 105–106, 110–111.

Document 16: *The Origin of Species*: The Transmission of Variations

Although Darwin was convinced that his theory was the best
explanation for the origin of species, he admitted that he could not
explain precisely every aspect of his theory. One of the questions
Darwin could not answer was why some species adapted and others
did not. What caused a species to start mutating? In several places
in *The Origin of Species*, Darwin concedes that "our ignorance of laws
of variation is profound."[11]

Nonetheless, in the fifth chapter of *The Origin of Species*, Darwin
postulated some reasons why variation or mutation might occur. (Typical of the nineteenth century, Darwin called these ideas laws.) In this
excerpt, Darwin suggests that the variation of a species is connected
with reproduction: this was the closest Darwin came to working out
that the mutation of genes was the cause of transmutation. Without
knowing about the action of genes, Darwin concludes that, whatever
caused the initial mutation, the accumulation of many mutations and
modifications ultimately led to the transmutation of species.

In the twentieth century, Neo-Darwinists such as the American
zoologist Theodosius Dobzhansky incorporating the work of early

twentieth-century geneticists, eventually provided the solution to the question Darwin could not answer.

> I have hitherto sometimes spoken as if the variations—so common and multiform in organic beings under domestication, and in a lesser degree in those in a state of nature—had been due to chance. This, of course, is a wholly incorrect expression, but it serves to acknowledge plainly our ignorance of the cause of each particular variation. Some authors believe it to be as much the function of the reproductive system to produce individual differences, or very slight deviations of structure, as to make the child like its parents. But the much greater variability, as well as the greater frequency of monstrosities,[12] under domestication or cultivation, than under nature, leads me to believe that deviations of structure are in some way due to the nature of the conditions of life, to which the parents and the more remote ancestors have been exposed during several generations. I have remarked in the first chapter—but a long catalogue of facts which cannot be here given would be necessary to show the truth of the remark—that the reproductive system is eminently susceptible to changes in the conditions of life; and to this system being functionally disturbed in the parents, I chiefly attribute the varying or plastic condition of the offspring. The male and female sexual elements seem to be affected before the union takes place which is to form a new being. In the case of 'sporting' plants, the bud, which in its earliest condition does not apparently differ essentially from an ovule, is alone affected.[13] But why, because the reproductive system is disturbed, this or that part should vary more or less, we are profoundly ignorant. Nevertheless, we can here and there dimly catch a faint ray of light, and we may feel sure that there must be some cause for each deviation of structure, however slight.
>
> Whatever the cause may be of each slight difference in the offspring from their parents—and a cause for each must exist— it is steady accumulation, through natural selection, of such differences, when beneficial to the individual, that gives rise to all the more important modifications of structure, by which the innumerable beings on the face of this earth are enabled to struggle with each other, and the best adapted to survive.

Source: *On the Origin of Species by Means of Natural Selection, or the Preservation of Favoured Races in the Struggle for Life* (London: John Murray, 1859), 131–132, 170.

Document 17: *The Origin of Species*: Darwin Defends His Theory

In the final chapter of *The Origin of Species*, Darwin repeated the major arguments of the book. This excerpt, which appears

virtually at the end of the book, contains the important ideas Darwin
has used in *The Origin of Species*. For example, Darwin explains that
species are "slowly changing by the preservation and accumulation
of successive slight favourable variations," which was one of his favorite phrases. Darwin also reiterates five themes of the book: the
impact of Lyell's work on his thinking; the necessity of drawing a les-
son from artificial selection; the variations of species and varieties
produced by humans; the recognition that natural selection repre-
sents a major change in scientific thinking (for which Darwin is responsible); and the "smallness" of humankind compared with the
vastness of time. (Notice that Darwin puts his arguments in the negative as if using the voices of his potential opponents.)

Darwin also acknowledges how difficult some naturalists and
geologists will find it to accept his ideas. Darwin even attempts to
stir up some evangelistic fervor on behalf of his theory. Even if older
scientists cannot accept his ideas, the younger ones will and they
should make a strenuous effort to convince the "unbelievers." Darwin
was passionate about his work and he was convinced that his theory
was the best explanation for the origin of species.

> I have now recapitulated the chief facts and considerations
> which have thoroughly convinced me that species have changed,
> and are still slowly changing by the preservation and accumula-
> tion of successive slight favourable variations. Why, it may be
> asked, have all the eminent living naturalists and geologists
> rejected this view of the mutability of species? It cannot be
> asserted that organic beings in a state of nature are subject to no
> variation; it cannot be proved that the amount of variation in
> the course of long ages is a limited quantity; no clear distinction
> has been, or can be, drawn between species and well-marked
> varieties. It cannot be maintained that species when intercrossed
> are invariably sterile, and varieties invariably fertile; or that ste-
> rility is a special endowment and sign of creation. The belief
> that species were immutable productions was almost unavoid-
> able as long as the history of the world was thought to be of
> short duration; and now that we have acquired some idea of the
> lapse of time, we are too apt to assume, without proof, that the
> geological record is so perfect that it would have afforded us
> plain evidence of the mutation of species, if they had undergone
> mutation.
>
> But the chief cause of our natural unwillingness to admit
> that one species has given birth to other and distinct species, is
> that we are always slow in admitting any great change of which
> we do not see the intermediate steps. The difficulty is the same
> as that felt by so many geologists, when Lyell first insisted that
> long lines of inland cliffs had been formed, and great valleys

excavated, by the slow action of the coast-waves. The mind cannot possibly grasp the full meaning of the term of a hundred million years; it cannot add up and perceive the full effects of many slight variations, accumulated during an almost infinite number of generations.

Although I am fully convinced of the truth of the views given in this volume under the form of an abstract, I by no means expect to convince experienced naturalists whose minds are stocked with a multitude of facts all viewed, during a long course of years, from a point of view directly opposite to mine. It is so easy to hide our ignorance under such expressions as the "plan of creation," "unity of design," &c., and to think that we give an explanation when we only restate a fact. Any one whose disposition leads him to attach more weight to unexplained difficulties than to the explanation of a certain number of facts will certainly reject my theory. A few naturalists, endowed with much flexibility of mind, and who have already begun to doubt on the immutability of species, may be influenced by this volume; but I look with confidence to the future, to young and rising naturalists, who will be able to view both sides of the question with impartiality. Whoever is led to believe that species are mutable will do good service by conscientiously expressing his conviction; for only thus can the load of prejudice by which this subject is overwhelmed be removed.

Source: *On the Origin of Species by Means of Natural Selection, or the Preservation of Favoured Races in the Struggle for Life* (London: John Murray, 1859), 480–482.

Document 18: Darwin on the Origin of Religion

Although Darwin shied away from controversy, particularly religious controversy, and did not debate his work or his findings in public meetings, he was aware of the implications of some of his ideas. Early in *The Descent of Man*, Darwin considered the origin of belief in a god or gods. Darwin suggested that religious ideas evolve in much the same way as species: from the simple to the complex, from a belief in spirits of nature to a Christian God. This apparent detour into the field of the sociology of religion is actually a discussion about philosophy; more particularly, an examination of the nature of humans. Darwin is less interested in stating his opinion than illustrating the importance of the power of reason. Humans are different from lower forms of animals because humans possess the higher faculty of reason; thus, humans have the ability to develop, evolve, much further than other species on the planet.

Belief in God—Religion.—There is no evidence that man was aboriginally endowed with the ennobling belief in the existence of an Omnipotent God. On the contrary there is ample evidence, derived not from hasty travellers, but from men who have long resided with savages, that numerous races have existed and still exist, who have no idea of one or more gods, and who have no words in their languages to express such an idea. The question is of course wholly distinct from that higher one, whether there exists a Creator and Ruler of the universe; and this has been answered in the affirmative by the highest intellects that have ever lived.

If, however, we include under the term "religion" the belief in unseen or spiritual agencies, the case is wholly different; for this belief seems to be almost universal with the less civilised races. Nor is it difficult to comprehend how it arose. As soon as the important faculties of the imagination, wonder, and curiosity, together with some power of reasoning, had become partially developed, man would naturally have craved to understand what was passing around him, and have vaguely speculated on his existence. . . .

But until the above-named faculties of imagination, curiosity, reason, &c., had been fairly well developed in the mind of man, his dreams would not have led him to believe in spirits, any more than in the case of a dog.

The tendency in savages to imagine that natural objects and agencies are animated by spiritual or living essences, is perhaps illustrated by a little fact which I once noticed: my dog, a full-grown and very sensible animal, was lying on the lawn during a hot and still day; but at a little distance a slight breeze occasionally moved an open parasol, which would have been wholly disregarded by the dog, had any one stood near it. As it was, every time that the parasol slightly moved, the dog growled fiercely and barked. He must, I think, have reasoned to himself in a rapid and unconscious manner, that movement without any apparent cause indicated the presence of some strange living agent, and no stranger had a right to be on his territory.

The belief in spiritual agencies would easily pass into the belief in the existence of one of more gods. For the savages would naturally attribute to spirits the same passions, the same love of vengeance or simplest form of justice, and the same affections which they themselves experienced. . . .

The same high mental faculties which first led man to believe in unseen spiritual agencies, then in fetishism, polytheism, and ultimately in monotheism, would infallibly lead him, as long as his reasoning powers remained poorly developed, to various strange superstitions and customs. Many of these are terrible to think of—such as the sacrifice of human beings to a blood-loving god; the trial of innocent persons by the ordeal or poison or fire; witchcraft, &c.—yet it is well occasionally to reflect on these superstitions, for they shew us what an infinite debt of gratitude we owe to the improvement of our reason, to science, and our accumulated knowledge. As Sir J. Lubbock has well observed, "it is not too much to say that the horrible dread of the unknown evil hangs like a thick cloud over savage life, and embitters every pleasure."[14] These miserable and indirect consequences of our highest faculties may be compared with the incidental and occasional mistakes of the instincts of the lower animals.

Source: Charles Darwin, *The Descent of Man, and Selection in Relation to Sex* (London: John Murray, 1871), I: 65–69.

Document 19: Darwin on the Origin of Humankind

Darwin concentrated on questions about biology in *The Origin of Species*; in *The Descent of Man*, he began to address the implications of his theory of descent by modification. An important conclusion, and one frequently ignored by Darwinists in the nineteenth century, was that humans were not the central characters in the natural world. In the concluding paragraphs of *The Descent of Man*, Darwin argues that humans have much in common with other animals and, because of their "humble origin," cannot consider themselves superior to their fellow creatures. (In an inversion of the expected prejudice, Darwin writes that he prefers a monkey for an ancestor rather than a "savage" Fuegian, a native of the southern part of South America.) Philosophically, Darwin was doing for human evolution and the science of biology what thinkers and scientists such as Galileo and Newton did for cosmology and physics in the seventeenth century. Humans are not at the center of the universe: they are simply a part of the universe.

> The main conclusion arrived at in this work, namely that man is descended from some lowly-organised form, will, I regret to think, be highly distasteful to many persons. But there can hardly be a doubt that we are descended from barbarians. The astonishment which I felt on first seeing a party of Fuegians on a wild and broken shore will never be forgotten by me, for the reflection at once rushed into my mind—such were our ancestors. These men were absolutely naked and bedaubed with paint, their long hair was tangled, their mouths frothed with excitement, and their expression was wild, startled, and distrustful. They possessed hardly any arts, and like wild animals lived on what they could catch; they had no government, and were merciless to every one

not of their own small tribe. He who has seen a savage in his native land will not feel much shame, if forced to acknowledge that the blood of some more humble creature flows in his veins. For my own part I would as soon be descended from that heroic little monkey, who braved his dreaded enemy in order to save the life of his keeper; or from that old baboon, who, descending from the mountain, carried away in triumph his young comrade from a crowd of astonished dogs—as from a savage who delights to torture his enemies, offers up bloody sacrifices, practises infanticide without remorse, treats his wives like slaves, knows no decency, and is haunted by the grossest superstitions.

Man may be excused for feeling some pride at having risen, though not through his own exertions, to the very summit of the organic scale; and the fact of his having thus risen, instead of having been aboriginally placed there, may give him hopes for a still higher destiny in the distant future. But we are not here concerned with hopes or fears, only with the truth as far as our reason allows us to discover it. I have given the evidence to the best of my ability; and we must acknowledge, as it seems to me, that man with all his noble qualities, with sympathy which feels for the most debased, with benevolence which extends not only to other men but to the humblest living creature, with his god-like intellect which as penetrated into the movements and constitution of the solar system—with all these exalted powers—Man still bears in his bodily frame the indelible stamp of his lowly origin.

Source: Charles Darwin, *The Descent of Man, and Selection in Relation to Sex* (London: John Murray, 1871), II: 404–405.

Document 20: Huxley on the Reception of *The Origin of Species*

Thomas Huxley was a close friend and confidante of Darwin's. In the 1880s, when Darwin's son, Francis, edited his father's letters and autobiography, Huxley wrote a short essay for the book on the impact of *The Origin of Species*. While Huxley tried to downplay Darwin's native or intuitive genius, he made clear that natural selection had already become the standard explanation for the origin of life on Earth and that the theory of evolution had become a viable philosophy as a result of Darwin's work.

Because Huxley was more concerned with the years just before and after 1859, he only dealt cursorily with the scientific objections to Darwin's theory of descent by modification. He did not mention the debate about natural selection—whether it was an adequate or accurate term to explain the process of evolution. For Huxley, the acceptance of evolution rather than supernatural or metaphysical explanations for the origin of life was the most important innovation of the nineteenth century.

To the present generation, that is to say, the people of a few years on the hither and thither side of thirty, the name of Charles Darwin stands alongside those of Isaac Newton and Michael Faraday; and, like them, calls up the grand ideal of a searcher after truth and interpreter of Nature. They think of him who bore it as a rare combination of genius, industry, and unswerving veracity, who earned his place among the most famous men of the age by sheer native power, in the teeth of a gale of popular prejudice, and uncheered by a sign of favour or appreciation from the official fountains of honour; as one who in spite of an acute sensitiveness to praise and blame, and notwithstanding provocations which might have excused any outbreak, kept himself clear of all envy, hatred, and malice, nor dealt otherwise than fairly and justly with the unfairness and injustice which was showered upon him; while to the end of his day, he was ready to listen with patience and respect to the most insignificant of reasonable objectors.

And with respect to that theory of the origin of the forms of life peopling our globe, with which Darwin's name is bound up as closely as that of Newton with the theory of gravitation, nothing seems to be further from the mind of the present generation than any attempt to smother it with ridicule or to crush it by vehemence of denunciation. "The struggle for existence," and "Natural selection," have become household words and everyday conceptions. The reality and the importance of the natural processes on which Darwin founds his deductions are no more doubted than those of growth and multiplication; and, whether the full potency attributed to them is admitted or not, no one doubts their vast and far-reaching significance. Wherever the biological sciences are studied, the 'Origin of Species' lights the paths of the investigator; wherever they are taught it permeates the course of instruction. Nor has the influence of Darwinian ideas been less profound, beyond the realms of Biology. The oldest of all philosophies, that of Evolution, was bound hand and foot and cast into utter darkness during the millennium of theological scholasticism. But Darwin poured new lifeblood into the ancient frame; the bonds burst, and the revivified thought of ancient Greece has proved itself to be a more adequate expression of the universal order of things than any of the schemes which have been accepted by the credulity and welcomed by the superstition of seventy later generations of men.

To any one who studies the signs of the times, the emergence of the philosophy of Evolution, in the attitude of claimant to the throne of the world of thought, from the limbo of hated and, as many hoped, forgotten things, is the most portentous event of the nineteenth century. But the most effective weapons of the modern champions of Evolution were fabricated by Darwin; and the 'Origin of Species' has enlisted a formidable body of combatants, trained in the severe school of Physical Science, whose ears might have long remained deaf to the speculation of *á priori* philosophers.

I do not think any candid or instructed person will deny the truth of that which has just been asserted. He may hate the very name of Evolution, and may deny its pretensions as vehemently as a Jacobite denied those of George the Second. But there it is—not only as solidly seated as the Hanoverian dynasty, but happily independent of Parliamentary sanction—and the dullest antagonists have come to see that they have to deal with an adversary whose bones are to be broken by no amount of bad words.

Even the theologians have almost ceased to pit the plain meaning of Genesis against the no less plain meaning of Nature. Their more candid, or more cautious, representatives have given up dealing with Evolution as if it were a damnable heresy, and have taken refuge in one of two courses. Either they deny that Genesis was meant to teach scientific truth, and thus save the veracity of the record at the expense of its authority; or they expend their energies in devising the cruel ingenuities of the reconciler, and torture texts in the vain hope of making them confess the creed of Science. But when the *peine forte et dure* is over, the antique sincerity of the venerable sufferer always reasserts itself. Genesis is honest to the core, and professes to be no more than it is, a repository of venerable traditions of unknown origin, claiming no scientific authority and possessing none.

Source: Thomas Huxley, "On the Reception of the 'Origin of Species,'" in *The Life and Letters of Charles Darwin, Including an Autobiographical Chapter*, ed. Francis Darwin (London: John Murray, 1887), II: 179–181.

Notes

1. A story about Columbus, probably apocryphal. At a royal banquet given in his honor, Columbus's genius was challenged by a Spanish nobleman. Anyone could have discovered the Indies with the resources Columbus had, the nobleman claimed. In reply, Columbus issued his own challenge: make an egg stand up without using breadcrumbs or salt. No one could do it. Columbus flattened the end of the egg by hitting it on the table. The principle he enunciated was that any task seems easy once the first person has done it.

2. Fuller's teasel is a weedlike plant found all over the United States but native to Europe. It has lavender flowers with four petals arranged in an egglike shape. Both the stem and the flower have hooked barbs. The head of all plants in the Dipsacaceae family looks like a pin cushion.

3. A terrierlike dog used in the nineteenth century to turn the wheel, which turned a spit over a fire, hence the name. The breed is now extinct.

4. A sheep with short, crooked legs and a long back. First "discovered" in Massachusetts in 1791, the legs and back are probably a genetic deformity.

5. Thomas Vernon Wollaston (1822–1878) was a British naturalist who wrote several books on the insects and shells of the Azores, Madeiran, and Canary Islands.

6. Malthus argued that freer access to marriage (and the concomitant possibility of having more children) was a significant factor in the increase in the human population.

7. Swedish naturalist (1707–1778).

8. "Art" here means "artificial" or "created by man" in contrast to something natural or created by nature.

9. Polymorphic means "many forms." See Glossary of Selected Terms.

10. Darwin is probably quoting William Marshall (1745–1818), a British agriculturist, whose book *The Rural Economy of Yorkshire* (1788) described the origins of cattle breeds in that county.

11. See *The Origin of Species*, 12, 13, 167, 198.

12. A nineteenth-century term for abnormalities. A monstrosity was any species that possessed a structure or organ with a substantial and visible deviation from the norm.

13. Nineteenth-century gardeners used the term "sporting plants" when a bud appeared on a plant that was different from the other buds. See *The Origin of Species*, 9–10.

14. Sir John Avery Lubbock (1834–1913), English banker, politician, and scientist. The quotation is from *Pre-Historic Times, as Illustrated by Ancient Remains, and the Manners and Customs of Modern Savages*, 2nd edition (London: Williams and Norgate, 1869), 571.

GLOSSARY OF SELECTED TERMS

Adaptation. A biological term that explains the relationship between an organism and its environment. The organism changes in response to its environment. The environment can be physical, such as climate, or societal, such as the immigration of new species into the habitat of the indigenous species, or functional, such as gills developing in fish so that they can process oxygen from water.

Big Bang Theory. The standard explanation given by contemporary cosmologists for the beginning of the universe. A very small particle, a singularity, expanded very rapidly to form the basic matter of the universe. Georgy Antonovich Gamow, a Russian-born American physicist, coined the term in the 1940s.

Biodiversity. Term used in biology to describe the number and distribution of living organisms in a particular area. The more species in an area the more diverse it is.

Catastrophism. A theory developed in the eighteenth century to explain the geology of the Earth. Catastrophists argued that natural phenomena such as mountains were formed by a series of global disasters such as floods and earthquakes.

Classification. In biology, it is the attempt by scientists to group similar organisms together in order to understand them better. Before the twentieth century biologists based classification on similarities in structure and the function of these structures. Today, genetic similarities are also used.

Coadaptation. A term coined by Darwin to explain the, usually beneficial, relationship between different species. In coadaptation, the skill, habits, actions, or form of one species matches and uses the skill, habits, actions, or form of another species. In Chapter III of *The Origin of Species*, The Struggle for Existence, Darwin states that the relationship between the woodpecker and mistletoe bush is an example of coadaptation. The pollen of the mistletoe needs to be carried by insects and the seed spread by birds; the sticky seeds of the mistletoe are picked up by woodpeckers who bore trees to search for insects to eat. The mistletoe is adapted to make maximum use of woodpeckers' habits.

Creationism. The belief that the description of the beginning of life as found in the biblical book of Genesis is an actual account of what occurred. Life on Earth—and for some creationists, in the universe—was created by God in six literal days.

Creation Science. The use of scientific data to support creationism. Also known as scientific creationism.

Divergence of Character. A term first used by Darwin and Alfred Wallace to explain how varieties of a species became new species. Each generation of the variety is slightly different from its parent as it adapts to its environment. Each mutation in the variety also makes it more different from the original species. After a number of generations, the difference between the variety and the original species is so great that the variety is a different species.

DNA (deoxyribose nucleic acid). A molecule found in the nuclei of cells that is a key component of heredity. In 1953, James Watson and Francis Crick demonstrated that the molecule was the shape of a double helix. The unwrapping of the two strands of the helix and the subsequent copying of each strand enables information about the cell and the whole organism to be passed on to the next generation.

Evolution. The idea that biological life on Earth developed from simple forms to more complex ones. (The development of inorganic matter is called chemical evolution.)

Evolutionary Theism. The attempt to combine belief in God and evolution. Evolutionary theists explain the origin of life by evolution but suggest that God is connected with the process—either by setting it in motion or by allowing it to occur. (Also known as theistic evolution.)

Fixity of the Species. The idea that species cannot change or mutate into other species. All species were created or came into existence exactly as they are at present. This was the most widely accepted theory about the origin of species before the spread of Darwin's theory.

Fundamentalism (Christian). An emphasis in Christianity begun by American Protestants in the early twentieth century. These Christians advocated a return to the basics of the religion, the fundamentals. Among these fundamental doctrines was biblical literalism, the idea that every statement in the Bible was true as written, which included the belief in a six-day creation as found in Genesis 1.

Gap Theory. This is a term used by some scientific creationists to explain why the geological data suggests that the Earth is much older than six thousand years. Although God created life on Earth in six literal days, there was a large amount of time between the days of creation.

Gene. The basic unit of heredity. Genes are located on chromosomes, which are found in the nucleus of each cell. Genes are a specific sequence of molecules, called nucleotides, in DNA (deoxyribose nucleic acid) or RNA (ribose nucleic acid). When a cell divides, the copying of the sequence of nucleotides enables information about the characteristics and functions of the cell to be transferred to the new cells.

Hermaphrodite. An animal or plant that has male and female sex organs. Most flowering plants are hermaphrodites. The stamen is the male organ and the pistil is the female organ. Flowering plants can self-pollinate.

Incipient Species. Darwin's term for varieties of a species. Darwin argued that every variety of a species was in the process of becoming a new species. Varieties became species by mutation and the process of natural selection.

Intelligent Design. The idea that organic life is too complex to have evolved by random mutation. The intricate and connected systems in organic life—for example, the processes necessary to keep the human body at the right temperature—must have been created by an intelligent being.

Irreducible Complexity. A term used by proponents of Intelligent Design to designate systems in organic life that are too complex and complementary to develop by evolution. One component of the system could not exist without or before the other. The eye and the maintenance of body temperature are examples of these systems.

Lamarckianism. A term that describes the process of evolution. New characteristics acquired by a species are passed on in total to the next and succeeding generations. (A bird acquiring a stronger beak in order to crack nuts better passes this characteristic to its progeny.) Named after the French zoologist Jean-Baptiste Lamarck, the theory was popular in the late-nineteenth century (as Neo-Lamarckianism); it was superseded by the Neo-Darwinist explanation of evolution developed in the 1950s.

Macroevolution. A major development in evolution, usually one species changing into another species. Macroevolution is synonymous with transmutation, the term familiar to Darwin. Generally, macroevolution is the process being referred to in discussions about evolution. The evolution of an organism from a common ancestor is macroevolution.

Microevolution. Changes or mutations in a species that do not result in transmutation. These changes can occur in a short period of time. The result of these changes or adaptations may be the formation of a new variety of the species. (Bacteria that become resistant to drugs have undergone microevolution.) Some creationists and proponents of Intelligent Design accept that microevolution occurs without conceding that macroevolution occurs.

Mutability. The ability of a species to change, particularly to evolve into another species. The opposite idea to the fixity of the species.

Mutation. The process of change in a species. In evolutionary theory, mutation occurs when genetic information in cells undergoing reproduction is copied incorrectly.

Naturalism. The idea that natural phenomena can and should only be explained by laws. In science, these laws must be testable by experimentation.

Natural Selection. A term coined by Darwin to describe the process that makes evolution occur. Members of a species acquire a new characteristic that enables them to adapt better to their surroundings than other species or other individuals in the same species. Those individuals with the new characteristic survive better, generally by producing more progeny. The process of adaptation and survival is natural selection.

Natural Theology. The idea that nature reveals the creative work of God. Particularly popular among Christians in Europe and the United States in the eighteenth century, proponents of natural theology believed people could learn all they needed to know about the character of God from studying nature.

natura non facit saltum. A Latin phrase meaning "nature does not make jumps." This idea was one of the major assumptions of Darwin's theory of descent by modification. Darwin argued that species changed slowly and gradually over a long period of time.

Neo-Darwinism. In the late nineteenth century, Neo-Darwinists were scientists who argued that natural selection was the only or the primary means of effecting evolution. In the twentieth century the same term was used to describe a different theory about evolution. From the 1950s onward, Neo-Darwinism has been the accepted scientific explanation of evolution. Twentieth-century Neo-Darwinists joined the genetic theory of heredity with the Darwinian idea of natural selection. Mutations in genes are passed from parent to progeny; those mutations that enable a species to adapt better to its environment than other species or other individuals in the same species are more likely to survive through natural selection.

Old Earth. Creationists who argued that the Earth was more than six thousand years old believed in an "Old Earth."

Polymorphic. A term that means "many forms." Darwin used this term in its botanical sense referring to plants that produce many varieties because of distinct differences in physical characteristics, such as the thickness of the leaf or the length of the stem. Orchids, one of Darwin's favorite plants, are polymorphic.

Pre-Implantation Genetic Diagnosis (PGD). Technique developed by molecular biologists (such as Mark Hughes) and reproductive endocrinologists (such as Jamie Grifo of New York University) that enables the genes of an embryo to be identified before implantation in the womb.

Scientists using this technique can ensure that specific character traits of the parents are passed on or eliminated from their offspring.

Progressionism. An idea developed in the eighteenth and nineteenth centuries to explain the relationship between different species. The species were fixed, they did not mutate or change, but they were all related to each other. The species belonged in an order that progressed from the simplest to the most complex. For example, a vertebrate animal such as a dog was a higher order of species than an invertebrate such a worm. Humans were the highest of species. Progressionism was a similar idea to Aristotle's Scale of Being.

Punctuated Equilibrium. An alternative explanation for the process of evolution. Scientists favoring punctuated equilibrium argue that evolution does not occur slowly and uniformly. The gaps in the fossil record are not gaps but a reflection of what occurred. Evolution occurs rapidly at some periods—hence the large number of fossil remains dating to particular era. Evolution does not occur or species change very little at other periods, hence the lack of fossils for some era. The American scientists Nils Eldredge (1943–) and Stephen Jay Gould (1941–2002) proposed the idea in 1971 because they were dissatisfied with the Neo-Darwinist explanation of evolution.

RNA (ribose nucleic acid). Related to DNA (deoxyribose nucleic acid), RNA carries the information about cell proteins from DNA, thus enabling new proteins and new cells to be built.

Saltationism. An alternative theory of evolution to Darwin's. Saltationists argue that species can arise suddenly as a result of significant mutation. Thomas Huxley favored a saltationist approach to evolution: he thought Darwin's theory of slow, gradual transformation was too restrictive. The early geneticists such as William Bateson (1861–1926) and Hugo de Vries (1848–1935) were the strongest proponents of saltationism.

Scale of Being. Aristotle's idea about the progression of species from the simplest to the most complex. Each species had a particular place in the hierarchy of nature that did not and could not change. Also known as the Chain of Being.

Sexual Selection. One of Darwin's explanations for evolution. Individuals of a species, usually females, chose a mate who is best able to help produce the most offspring. This selection enables species best adapted to their surroundings to survive. Darwin argued that natural selection played a much more significant role in evolution than sexual selection.

Social Biologists. Biologists who study the behavior of groups of animals. Pioneered by the American entomologist Edward O. Wilson (1929–), social biologists examine the relationship between the behavior of insects such as ants and that of other animal species such as humans.

Special Creation. A term used to describe the origin of organic life on Earth, particularly humans. Originally used by proponents of natural theology but now mainly used by creationists. The creation of human-kind is special because God did it at a particular time and place as part of a deliberate plan. This act of creation is described in the first two chapters of the book of Genesis.

Speciation. The process of change of a species into another species. Darwin used the term transmutation to describe this process.

Spontaneous Generation. A term that described how organic life and new species came into existence. Jean-Baptiste Lamarck was responsible for this theory. He argued that heat could cause the creation of simple forms of life from a mucus of inorganic matter. Lamarck also argued that new characteristics in a species appeared spontaneously; the parent then passed on these characteristics to the progeny.

Survival of the Fittest. A term coined by the British philosopher Herbert Spencer (1820–1903). The strongest individuals were the ones who survived and thrived. Spencer applied the idea universally: the individuals could be members of a species, companies, and even countries. Darwin used the term to explain natural selection in the fifth and sixth editions of *The Origin of Species*.

Taxonomy. The study and application of the rules of classification. These rules enable biologists to explain the relationship between various animals and plants. Of the major divisions in taxonomy, a kingdom contains the largest number of species and a subspecies the least. The major divisions are: Kingdom, Phylum, Class, Order, Family, Genus, Species, and Subspecies.

Transformism. A word used instead of evolution in the eighteenth and early nineteenth centuries, particularly in France. The word had a political connotation also. Transformists believed that society could change and progress in the same way that species did. The more society progressed the more egalitarian it would become. Transformist ideas were considered revolutionary, hence supporters of evolution before the publication of *The Origin of Species* were considered dangerous social radicals.

Transmutation. The theory that a species can change into a completely different species. The two species are related, but they are not the same. Evolution is a process that includes small changes, mutations, and large changes, transmutations.

Transmutationist. An adherent of the theory of transmutation; Charles Darwin was one such adherent.

Uniformitarianism. The theory that change in nature is slow, gradual, and occurs over a long period of time. The term was coined by the British geologist William Whewell (1794–1866) in a review of the second volume of *Principles of Geology*. Lyell was a uniformitarian as opposed to catastrophists such as Georges Cuvier. Darwin applied Lyell's ideas about uniformitarianism to speciation. In *The Origin of Species*, the transmutation of a species occurred after it underwent small changes or adaptations over a long period of time.

Woodwardian Hypothesis. The explanation suggested by the British natural historian John Woodward (1665/1668–1728) for the geology of the Earth. Woodward argued that the Earth had been destroyed by the flood described in the Bible; God suspended the law of gravitation, which enabled the flood to occur and alter the face of the Earth rapidly, in a few months. Fossils were living creatures killed in the flood.

Young Earth. The idea that the Earth is between 6,000 and 10,000 years old. The idea is based on a literal reading of the Bible, particularly the first chapter of Genesis and the genealogies found in books such as Numbers, Deuteronomy, Kings, and Chronicles. Creationists are the main proponents of a young Earth.

ANNOTATED BIBLIOGRAPHY

Darwin's Major Works

Books (in chronological order)

Darwin, Charles. *Journal of Researches into the Geology and Natural History of the Various Countries Visited by H.M.S. Beagle, under the Command of Captain Fitzroy, R.N. from 1832 to 1836.* London: Henry Colburn, 1839. Darwin's diary written during the *Beagle* voyage. The detailed entries reveal Darwin's acute powers of observation, a skill he had developed by the age of twenty-three. An excellent book to read to understand the way Darwin's mind worked (and would continue to work). In 1845, the publisher reversed "Geology" and "Natural History" in the title. In some editions published after 1860, the title is *Naturalist's Voyage Round the World.*

———, ed. *The Zoology of the Voyage of the H.M.S. Beagle, Under the Command of Captain Fitzroy, R.N., During the Years 1832 to 1836.* Part II: Mammalia. London: Smith, Elder and Co., 1839. The first of five companion volumes to "The Geology of the Voyage of the H.M.S. *Beagle.*" After 1843, the volumes were combined into one book, *The Zoology of the Voyage of the H.M.S. Beagle.* Each volume has descriptions and analysis of the zoological specimens Darwin collected during the *Beagle* voyage. Darwin did not classify the specimens: each volume was published whenever Darwin and the expert doing the classification had finished. (The parts were not published in order.) George R. Waterhouse, curator of the Zoological Society of London, did the classification for this volume.

———. *The Zoology of the Voyage of the H.M.S. Beagle, Under the Command of Captain Fitzroy, R.N., During the Years 1832 to 1836.* Part I: Fossil Mammalia. London: Smith, Elder and Co., 1840. The second volume published in the series. Richard Owen, professor of anatomy and physiology at the Royal College of Surgeons in London, did the classification work for this volume.

————. *The Structure and Distribution of Coral Reefs; Being the First Part of the Geology of the Voyage of the* Beagle, *Under the Command of Capt. Fitzroy R.N. During the Years 1832 to 1836.* London: Smith, Elder and Co., 1842. Better known by its shorter name, *The Structure and Distribution of Coral Reefs*, this is the first of three volumes summarizing Darwin's geological research while on the *Beagle*. Darwin was acknowledged as a world authority on coral reefs after the publication of this book.

————. *The Zoology of the Voyage of the H.M.S. Beagle, Under the Command of Captain Fitzroy, R.N., During the Years 1832 to 1836.* Part IV: Fish. London: Smith, Elder and Co., 1842. The third volume published in the series. The Reverend Leonard Jenyns, a fellow of the Linnean Society who turned down the opportunity to go on the *Beagle* voyage, did the classification work for this volume.

————. *The Zoology of the Voyage of the H.M.S. Beagle, Under the Command of Captain Fitzroy, R.N., During the Years 1832 to 1836.* Part III: Birds. London: Smith, Elder and Co., 1843. The fourth volume published in the series. John Gould, a fellow of the Linnean Society, did the classification work for this volume.

————. *The Zoology of the Voyage of the H.M.S. Beagle, Under the Command of Captain Fitzroy, R.N., During the Years 1832 to 1836.* Part V: Reptiles. London: Smith, Elder and Co., 1843. The last volume published in the series. Thomas Bell, professor of Zoology at King's College, London University, and future president of the Linnean Society, did the classification work for this volume.

————. *Geological Observations on the Volcanic Islands, Visited During the Voyage of H.M.S. Beagle, together with Some Brief Notices on the Geology of Australia and the Cape of Good Hope. Being the Second Part of the Geology of the Voyage of the* Beagle *Under the Command of Capt. Fitzroy, R.N. During the Years 1832 to 1836.* London: Smith, Elder and Co., 1844. The second of three volumes summarizing Darwin's geological research while on the *Beagle*. This book and the third volume were republished by Smith, Elder and Co. in 1876 as *Geological Observations on the Volcanic Islands and Parts of South America Visited During the Voyage of H.M.S. "Beagle."*

————. *Geological Observations on South America. Being the Third Part of the Geology of the Voyage of the* Beagle, *Under the Command of Capt. Fitzroy, R.N. During the Years 1832 to 1836.* London: Smith, Elder and Co., 1846. The last of three volumes detailing Darwin's geological research while on the *Beagle*. Better known by its shorter title *Geological Observations on South America*.

————. *A Monograph on the Fossil Lepadidae, or, Pedunculated Cirripedes of Great Britain*. London: The Palaeontographical Society, 1851. The first of Darwin's four books on barnacles. After their publication, Darwin was acknowledged as a world authority on barnacles.

————. *A Monograph on the Sub-Class Cirripedia, with Figures of All the Species: The Lepadidae; or, Pedunculated Cirripedes*. London: The Ray Society, 1851. The second of Darwin's four books on barnacles.

————. *A Monograph on the Sub-Class Cirripedia, with Figures of All the Species: The Balanidae, (or Sessile Cirripedes); The Verrucidae, etc., etc., etc.* London: The Ray Society, 1854. The third of Darwin's four books on barnacles.

————. *A Monograph on the Fossil Balanidae and Verrucidae of Great Britain*. London: The Palaeontographical Society, 1854. The last of Darwin's four books on barnacles.

————. *On the Origin of Species by Means of Natural Selection, or the Preservation of Favored Races in the Struggle for Life*. London: John Murray, 1859. The book that made Darwin the most prominent British scientist of the nineteenth century.

————. *On the Various Contrivances by which British and Foreign Orchids are Fertilised by Insects, and on the Good Effects of Intercrossing*. London: John Murray, 1862. Darwin describes the various ways orchids are fertilized in order to provide more evidence to support two major assertions he made in the *Origin of Species*: that organic beings must cross occasionally with another individual; and that no hermaphrodite organism fertilizes itself forever. Cross-fertilization produces progeny better able to adapt to their environment, a key idea in evolutionary theory.

————. *On the Movements and Habits of Climbing Plants*. London: Longman, Green, Longman, Roberts and Green and Williams and Norgate, 1865. The revision of a paper published in the *Journal of the Linnean Society*. Darwin explained how plants climbed after examining more than one hundred species. Darwin's son George drew the illustrations.

————. *The Variation of Animals and Plants Under Domestication*. 2 vols. London: John Murray, 1868. Darwin's description of the major characteristics of the domestic species he had observed. Darwin explains the effect of domestication on the ability of a species to mutate. Darwin includes additional evidence for his theory of evolution, which he could not fit in *The Origin of Species*.

————. *The Descent of Man, and Selection in Relation to Sex*. 2 vols. London: John Murray, 1871. Deals directly with the question of human origins (which Darwin did not address in *The Origin of Species*). Argues that humans are descended from a less complex form of species. Compulsory reading after *The Origin of Species*.

————. *The Expression of the Emotions in Man and Animals.* London: John Murray, 1872. The last of Darwin's published books on the evolution of animals. Darwin believed the behavioral sciences could prove that his theory of evolution was scientifically sound. He argued that the study of expression verified two important components of his theory of descent: first, the various races of humans descended from a single parent stock; and, second, humans descended from a simpler animal form.

————. *Insectivorous Plants.* London: John Murray, 1875. Explains in detail how certain plants have adapted so that they catch and digest insects. Darwin's sons Francis and George did some of the drawings.

————. *The Effects of Cross and Self Fertilisation in the Vegetable Kingdom.* London: John Murray, 1876. Complement to his book on orchids (1862). Darwin demonstrates why cross-fertilization is necessary and how plants are adapted to effect this. Darwin's skills as a statistician are evident. There are more than one hundred tables of measurements that Darwin took to verify his thesis that cross-fertilization was the most effective means for plants to produce the strongest progeny.

————. *The Different Forms of Flowers on Plants of the Same Species.* London: John Murray, 1877. A description of the characteristics of heterogonous plants. (Darwin called them "heterostyled.") These plants demonstrate the veracity of two assertions that Darwin made in *The Origin of Species*: first, classification is artificial; and, second, the male and female parts of these plants are organized in a way to produce the most number of seeds and pollen with the minimum expenditure of energy (which enables them to survive in their environment better than their competitors).

————. *The Power of Movement in Plants.* London: John Murray, 1880. A good example of Darwin's skill as an experimental botanist. Darwin invented a series of experiments that enabled him to observe how plants moved and under what conditions. His son Francis assisted in the research.

————. *The Formation of Vegetable Mould, Through the Action of Worms, with Observations on their Habits.* London: John Murray, 1881. Defense and revision of ideas presented in a paper to the Geological Society of London in 1837. Darwin argues that worms make a significant difference to the surface of the Earth. Concludes that the action of worms demonstrates that the sum of a large number of small effects is always great in nature. An argument for the principle of uniformitarianism in evolution.

Articles

Barrett, Paul H., ed. *The Collected Papers of Charles Darwin.* 2 vols. Chicago: University of Chicago Press, 1977. Darwin wrote more than 150 articles of various lengths. The two volumes contain all of the articles written by Darwin that Barrett could find. Each article is included in full (with a citation to the original journal or magazine). An invaluable resource for the study of Darwin.

Editions of Darwin's Manuscript Works

Barlow, Nora, ed. *The Autobiography of Charles Darwin, 1809–1882*. London: Collins, 1958. The autobiography Darwin wrote for his children, with commentary by Barlow. Includes the material removed by Darwin's son Francis for a published version of the autobiography and Darwin's letters (1887).

Burkhardt, Frederick, and Sydney Smith, eds. *The Correspondence of Charles Darwin*. 13 vols. Cambridge: Cambridge University Press, 1985–2002. Part of an ongoing project to publish all Darwin's correspondence, both sent and received. The volumes published cover the period 1821 to 1864. Each volume has useful appendixes, such as a brief biography of each correspondent.

———. *A Calendar of the Correspondence of Charles Darwin, 1821–1882*. New York and London: Garland Publishing, 1985. A supplement to *The Correspondence of Charles Darwin*. Lists all the known letters written by and to Darwin with a summary of the contents.

Darwin, Francis, ed. *The Foundations of the Origin of Species, Two Essays Written in 1842 and 1844 by Charles Darwin*. Cambridge: Cambridge University Press, 1909. The first two essays in which Darwin wrote out his theory. Darwin argues against the immutability of species and for a common ancestor for all species.

———. *The Life and Letters of Charles Darwin, Including an Autobiographical Chapter*. 3 vols. London: John Murray, 1887. First major biography and collection of Darwin's letters published after his death. Includes an edited version of Darwin's autobiography and reminiscences of Darwin by the editor, his son. Essential reading.

Herbert, Sandra, ed. *The Red Notebook of Charles Darwin*. Ithaca, NY: Cornell University Press, 1980. Edited version of the notebook Darwin wrote while on the *Beagle* voyage.

Stauffer, R. C., ed. *Charles Darwin's Natural Selection: Being the Second Part of His Big Species Book Written from 1856 to 1858*. Cambridge: Cambridge University Press, 1975. The book on the origin of species that Darwin began to write but never finished.

Books on Darwin

Barrett, Paul H., Donald J. Weinshank, and Timothy T. Gottleber, eds. *A Concordance to Darwin's* Origin of Species, *First Edition*. Ithaca, NY:

Cornell University Press, 1981. Lists all the words that occur in the first edition of *The Origin of Species* and the pages on which they appear. Invaluable resource for the study of *The Origin of Species*, particularly the language Darwin used.

Barrett, Paul H., Donald J. Weinshank, Paul Ruhlen, and Stephan J. Ozminski, eds. *A Concordance to Darwin's* The Descent of Man, and Selection in Relation to Sex. Ithaca, NY: Cornell University Press, 1987. Lists all the words in the first edition of *The Descent of Man* and the pages on which they appear.

Brent, Peter. *Charles Darwin*. London: Heinemann, 1981. Very imaginative biography of Darwin. Brent makes readers feel as though they are present at the events described. Detailed coverage of Darwin's life up to 1861: not as good for the later years.

Browne, Janet. *Charles Darwin*. Vol. 1: *Voyaging*. London: Jonathan Cape, 1995; Vol. 2: *The Power of Place*. London: Jonathan Cape, 2002. Excellent and detailed biography of Darwin. Browne describes Darwin's life in the context of his time: as a Victorian middle-class Englishman and a Victorian scientist.

Clark, Ronald W. *The Survival of Charles Darwin*. New York: Random House, 1984. Makes the connection between Darwin's life and the development of the theory of evolution.

Colp, Ralph. *To Be an Invalid: The Illness of Charles Darwin*. Chicago: University of Chicago Press, 1977. Excellent book giving a summary and the dates of Darwin's illnesses. Discusses the strengths and weaknesses of the numerous theories commentators have suggested as the cause of Darwin's illnesses.

de Beer, Gavin. *Charles Darwin: Evolution by Natural Selection*. London: Thomas Nelson and Sons, 1963. Easy-to-read biography written for an audience that knows little about Darwin.

Desmond, Adrian J., and James R. Moore. *Darwin*. London: Michael Joseph, 1991. Excellent biography of Darwin aimed at a popular audience. Easy-to-read, detailed account of Darwin's life. Very useful bibliography.

Healey, Edna. *Emma Darwin: The Inspirational Wife of a Genius*. London: Headline, 2001. Definitive biography of Darwin's wife; includes information about the Darwins' domestic life at Down House.

Herbert, Sandra. *Charles Darwin, Geologist*. Ithaca, NY: Cornell University Press, 2005. Argues convincingly that Darwin was an accomplished geologist long before he developed his theory of evolution. Focuses on an area frequently neglected by Darwin's biographers.

Keynes, Randal. *Annie's Box: Charles Darwin, His Daughter, and Human Evolution*. London: Fourth Estate, 2001. Excellent study of the life of Darwin and the relationship between his family life and his scientific research. Argues that the premature death of Darwin's daughter had a profound effect on his thinking about the origin of life.

Keynes, Richard. *Fossils, Finches, and Fuegians: Charles Darwin's Adventures and Discoveries on the* Beagle, *1832–1836.* London: HarperCollins, 2002. Very readable retelling of Darwin's *Beagle* voyage. Keynes used the notes Darwin made on the voyage, some of which are used for the first time. Excellent resource on the *Beagle* voyage.

Mattson, Mark T., James L. Marra, and Stephen C. Zelnick. *A Student Introduction to Charles Darwin,* revised printing. Dubuque, IA: Kendal/Hunt Publishing, 1999. Excellent, simple introduction to the *Origin of Species.* Has a helpful commentary on the argument in the *Origin of Species* and good thought-provoking questions about Darwin's work and the theory of evolution.

Miller, Jonathan, and Borin Van Loon. *Introducing Darwin and Evolution.* New York: Totem Books, 2000. A simple introduction to the theory of evolution, Darwin's life and work, and the immediate impact of Darwin's ideas. Written in nontechnical language and interspersed with a large number of amusing illustrations and cartoons. Originally published as *Darwin for Beginners* (1982).

Oxford Dictionary of National Biography. Oxford: Oxford University Press, 2004. Best source for biographical information on British figures, including scientists and nonscientists, who lived in the eighteenth to twentieth centuries. This is an updated version of the *Dictionary of National Biography,* which is referred to in some libraries as the DNB. (There is an online version.)

Peckham, Morse, ed. *The Origin of Species by Charles Darwin: A Variorum Text.* Philadelphia: University of Pennsylvania Press, 1959. Documents all of the changes Darwin made to *The Origin of Species* between the first and sixth editions. The changes are listed sentence by sentence (which makes the text a little difficult to follow). Has useful information about the publication of *The Origin of Species,* such as the cost of each edition and the numbers printed and sold.

Tort, Patrick. *Charles Darwin: The Scholar Who Changed Human History.* London: Thames and Hudson, 2001. Excellent introduction to Charles Darwin, his ideas, and the theory of evolution. Has simple and clear explanations accompanied by numerous diagrams and pictures, all in color, to illustrate Darwin's life and times as well as evolutionary theory.

University of Cambridge, University Library. *Handlist of Darwin Papers at the University Library, Cambridge.* Cambridge: Cambridge University Press, 1960. The University Library at Cambridge has the largest collection of material written by Darwin in his own handwriting. This book lists the material held at the Library.

Wilson, Louise, ed. *Down House: The Home of Charles Darwin.* Edenbridge, Kent: Westerham Press Ltd., 2000 (first published as *Charles Darwin at Down House* in 1998). Guide to the life of Charles Darwin published by English Heritage, the organization responsible for the maintenance of Down House. Has a detailed history of Down House from 1842 to the present and includes pictures, plans of the house, and maps of the grounds.

The History of Science

Bowler, Peter J., and Iwan Rhys Morus. *Making Modern Science: A Historical Survey*. Chicago: University of Chicago Press, 2005. Excellent introduction to the major discoveries and debates in science since the sixteenth century. Particularly good on the history of the biological sciences but also deals with the Scientific Revolution, and the history of the physical and social sciences. Second half of the book deals with important topics such as popular science, science and religion, science and gender, and science and technology.

Crick, Francis. *What Mad Pursuit*. New York: Basic Books, 1988. The story of the discovery that DNA is a double-helix molecule by one of the discoverers. Crick also reflects on the impact of the study of genetics on the study of science and humankind.

Hawking, Stephen. *The Universe in a Nutshell*. New York: Bantam Books, 2001. Hawking discusses the philosophical and religious implications of scientific theories such as the Big Bang and evolution. Good, popular science written by one of Britain's foremost physicists. Has many color illustrations.

Rees, Martin. *Just Six Numbers: The Deep Forces That Shape the Universe*. New York: Basic Books, 2000. Explains some of the major theories about the universe by showing the importance of the mathematical ideas underpinning them. Dark matter, black holes, the expansion of the universe, the Big Bang theory, and the number of dimensions in the universe are all discussed as well as their relationship to the origin of life. Makes clear the connection between cosmology and biology.

Wynn, Charles, and Arthur W. Wiggins. *The Five Biggest Ideas in Science*. New York: John Wiley and Sons, 1997. Explains the relationship between Darwin's theory about natural selection and other major scientific theories in physics, chemistry, astronomy, and geology in very simple language. The illustrations and cartoons make the complex ideas discussed easy to understand.

The History of Evolution

Bateson, William. *Mendel's Principles of Heredity: A Defence*. Cambridge: Cambridge University Press, 1902. One of the first books in English to support Mendelianism as an alternative to natural selection. Has a translation of the paper Gregor Mendel wrote on plant hybridization, which outlined his theory of heredity.

Bratchell, Dennis Frank. *The Impact of Darwinism: Texts and Commentary Illustrating Nineteenth Century Religious, Scientific, and Literary Attitudes*. London: Avebury Publishing, 1981. A good introduction to the topic. Explains why evolution was a controversial idea in the nineteenth century and why scientists supported or opposed Darwin's ideas. Has examples of poetry and prose written in reaction to the theory of evolution.

Bryan, William Jennings. *The Menace of Darwinism*. New York: Fleming H. Revell Company, 1921. Bryan was a good example of an early twentieth-century public figure who believed that Darwinism and evolution were a danger to civilized society: Bryan explains this point in a simple, easy-to-understand style.

Chambers, Robert. *Vestiges of the Natural History of Creation*. London: John Churchill, 1844. Best-known effort in English to popularize a theory of evolution before *Origin of Species*. Chambers attempted to work out a universal theory for the origin of life; argues that complex life developed from simple forms.

Davies, Merryl W. *Darwin and Fundamentalism*. Duxford, Cambridgeshire: Icon Books, 2000. Excellent short introduction to the evolution versus creationism debate. Argues that evolutionary scientists can be just as fundamentalist as creationists who believe that God created the world in six days. Has a useful history of Western philosophy before Darwin.

Davis, Percival, and Dean H. Kenyon. *Of Pandas and People: The Central Question of Biological Origins*. Dallas, TX: Haughton Publishing, 1989. First book published by proponents of Intelligent Design for non-scientists. The first section provides an overview of the main topics in evolutionary theory; the second section deals with evolution in more detail. Each chapter is designed to form the basis of lectures for high school teachers. The authors argue that facts about nature may be interpreted differently. Using one perspective, a person may decide that the origin of life occurred via evolution; using another perspective, a person may decide that an intelligent designer is responsible for life on Earth. Essential reading on the subject of Intelligent Design.

Desmond, Adrian J. *Huxley: From Devil's Disciple to Evolution's High Priest*. London: Michael Joseph Ltd., 1994. Excellent, readable biography of Huxley. Shows Huxley as a typical Victorian and as a man who changed the thinking of nineteenth-century society.

de Vries, Hugo. *The Mutation Theory: Experiments and Observations on the Origin of Species in the Vegetable Kingdom*, trans. J. B. Farmer and

A. D. Darbishire. Vol. I: *The Origin of Species by Mutation*; Vol. II: *The Origin of Varieties by Mutation*. Chicago: Open Court Publishing, 1909. English translation of de Vries's famous *Die Mutationstheorie* (1901), a significant work in the development of the Neo-Darwinist synthesis. de Vries argues that his mutation theory, based on the action of genes, can solve the problem that Darwin could not—the precise mechanism that makes natural selection occur.

Dobzhansky, Theodosius. *Genetics and the Origin of Species*. New York: Columbia University Press, 1937. Groundbreaking book in the development of the Neo-Darwinist synthesis. Argues that the mutation of genes is an essential component of speciation.

Gray, Asa. *Darwiniana: Essay and Reviews Pertaining to Darwinism*. New York: D. Appleton and Company, 1876. Collection of articles by the foremost nineteenth-century American apologist for Darwin. Discusses the connection between religious faith, Christianity, and the theory of evolution. Argues that evolution is not antithetical to Christianity.

Gribbin, John, and Mary Gribbin. *Fitzroy: The Remarkable Story of Darwin's Captain and the Invention of the Weather Forecast*. New Haven, CT: Yale University Press, 2004. Fascinating biography of Robert FitzRoy, the captain of the *Beagle*, which highlights his contributions to the development of marine safety and meteorology.

Huxley, Julian. *Evolution: The Modern Synthesis*. London: George Allen and Unwin Ltd., 1942. First book to recognize the development of a Neo-Darwinist synthesis. Describes the ways the theory of evolution changed as a result of new research by biologists, particularly in the area of genetics. Explains why Neo-Darwinism is a better explanation of evolution than Darwin's or Mendel's theory.

King-Hele, Desmond. *Erasmus Darwin*. London: Giles de la Mare Publishers Ltd., 1999. Very detailed and readable biography of Charles Darwin's grandfather. Explains the connection between Erasmus Darwin's and Charles Darwin's ideas about evolution. Updated version of an earlier biography (1977).

Knight, David, ed. *The Evolution Debate, 1813–1870*. 9 vols. London: Routledge, 2003. Each volume is a reprint of a significant work of nineteenth-century science. Noteworthy volumes: I—Georges Cuvier, *Essay on the Theory of the Earth*; II/III—William Buckland's Bridgewater Treatise *Geology and Mineralogy Considered with Reference to Natural Theology*; VII—Thomas Huxley, *Man's Place in Nature*; VIII—Charles Lyell, *The Geological Evidences of the Antiquity of Man*; and XIV—Alfred Russel Wallace, *Contributions to the Theory of Natural Selection* and the two papers presented jointly to the Linnean Society by Wallace and Darwin entitled "On the Tendency of Species to Form Varieties." Each volume has a helpful introduction.

Lamarck, Jean Baptiste. *Zoological Philosophy: An Exposition with Regard to the Natural History of Animals*, trans. Hugh Elliot. Chicago: University of Chicago Press, 1984 (first published 1809). Translation of Lamarck's classic work on natural history, *Philosophie zoologique*.

Larson, Edward John. *Summer for the Gods: The Scopes Trial and America's Continuing Debate over Science and Religion*. New York: Basic Books, 1997. Best scholarly study of the Scopes Trial. Discusses the continuing impact of the Trial on contemporary American culture.

Livingstone, David N. *Darwin's Forgotten Defenders*. Grand Rapids, MI: William B. Eerdmans Publishing, 1987. Examines the reaction of nineteenth-century evangelical Christians in Britain and the United States to *The Origin of Species* and the theory of evolution. Argues that these reactions varied from passionate defenders to outspoken opponents.

Lyell, Charles. *Principles of Geology*. 3 vols, ed. James A. Secord. London: Penguin, 1997 (First published 1830–1833). Classic and standard work of the nineteenth century arguing that geology is a science that should only consider naturalistic explanations of geological phenomena.

Malthus, Thomas Robert. *An Essay on the Principle of Population, As It Affects the Future Improvement of Society. With Remarks on the Speculations of Mr. Godwin, M. Condorcet, and Other Writers*. London: J. Johnson, 1798. Classic book on the problem caused by geometric population increase and arithmetic increase in the availability of food. Argues that only natural disasters, disease, and war will check the competition for food and related resources.

McIver, Tom. *Anti-Evolution: A Reader's Guide to Writings before and after Darwin*. Baltimore: Johns Hopkins University Press, 1992 (originally published 1988). Lists and describes most of the major works, books, and pamphlets written in opposition to the theory of evolution since the 1960s as well as a few important works from the 1920s onward. Indispensable reference work.

Moran, Jeffrey P. *The Scopes Trial: A Brief History with Documents*. Boston: Bedford/St. Martin's, 2002. Very useful introduction to the Scopes Trial. Has a portion of the transcripts from each day of the trial, a diverse range of contemporary commentaries on the Trial and the impact of the theory of evolution on American society, and a selection of contemporary cartoons.

Numbers, Ronald. *Darwinism Comes to America*. Cambridge, MA: Harvard University Press, 1998. Excellent analysis of the reception of Darwin's ideas and the theory of evolution in the United States. Describes the different reactions of Christians to Darwinism and explains why there was such a wide range of attitudes about evolution. Has a useful biographical appendix of naturalists in the National Academy of Sciences between 1863 and 1900.

Roberts, Jon H. *Darwinism and the Divine in America: Protestant Intellectuals and Organic Evolution, 1859–1900.* Madison: University of Wisconsin Press, 1988. Explains why American Protestants concentrated on attacking the science in *The Origin of Species* up to 1875 and then attacked the theological implications of the theory of evolution after 1875.

Secord, James H. *Victorian Sensation: The Extraordinary Publication, Reception, and Secret Authorship of Vestiges of the Natural History of Creation.* Chicago: University of Chicago Press, 2002. Definitive study of Robert Chambers's *Vestiges of the Natural History of Creation.* Explains why *Vestiges* was such a controversial book and why there was a hunt to find the author. Excellent introduction to the social context of *Vestiges* and *The Origin of the Species.* Has an extensive bibliography.

Uglow, Jenny. *The Lunar Men: Five Friends Whose Curiosity Changed the World.* New York: Farrar, Straus and Giroux, 2002. Story of the Lunatics, the group of men (which included Darwin's grandfathers Erasmus Darwin and Josiah Wedgwood) who had a major influence on scientific and technological ideas in eighteenth-century Britain. Explains the connection between the British Industrial Revolution and the scientific innovations of men such as Charles Lyell and Charles Darwin.

Wilson, Edward O. *Sociobiology: The New Synthesis.* Cambridge, MA: Belknap Press, 1975; reissued 2000 with a new preface. Argues that it is possible to learn and understand human evolution and behavior better by studying other social animals, particularly ants. A groundbreaking book.

The Science and Significance of Evolution

Beer, Gillian. *Darwin's Plots: Evolutionary Narrative in Darwin, George Eliot, and Nineteenth-Century Fiction.* 2nd edition. Cambridge: Cambridge University Press, 2000. Groundbreaking book on Darwin as a creative writer. Argues that Darwin's writing style is difficult to categorize: his arguments are unique and exhibit the influence of Victorian culture. *The Origin of Species* was and is influential because the writing was both Victorian and new.

Behe, Michael J. *Darwin's Black Box: The Biochemical Challenge to Evolution.* New York: Free Press, 1996. This prominent figure in the Intelligent Design Movement argues that the complexity of organic life precludes evolution as an explanation for the origin of life.

Chaisson, Eric J. *Cosmic Evolution: The Rise of Complexity in Nature.* Cambridge, MA: Harvard University Press, 2001. Argues that it is possible to discuss complexity in nature without invoking God or an intelligent designer.

Dawkins, Richard. *The Blind Watchmaker.* New York: W. W. Norton, 1996 (first published 1986). Discusses the significance of Darwin and Wallace's theory. Written for a popular audience, argues that the theory of evolution proves that the universe does not have a designer.

———. *The Selfish Gene.* New York: Oxford University Press, 1976. Groundbreaking study of the importance of genes in evolution. Argues that the desire by genes to preserve themselves is the driving force in evolutionary change.

Dembski, William A. *The Design Inference: Evaluating Change Through Small Probabilities.* Cambridge: Cambridge University Press, 1998. Argues that the complexity of biochemical systems suggests that it is extremely unlikely that such systems developed by small changes; a simpler explanation is that complex biological systems were designed by an intelligence.

Himmelfarb, Gertrude. *Darwin and the Darwinian Revolution.* London: Chatto and Windus, 1959. Discusses the historical and social context of Darwin's research, and the writing and reception of *The Origin of Species.* Good introduction to the social and philosophical impact of Darwin's work.

Johnson, Philip E. *Darwin on Trial.* Washington, DC: Regnery Gateway, 1991. Examines the flaws in logic in the theory of evolution and argues that these problems fatally undermine the theory. Very readable critique.

Jones, Steve. *Darwin's Ghost: The Origin of Species Updated.* New York: Ballantine Books, 2000. First published as *Almost Like a Whale* (1999). Jones uses twentieth-century examples to explain the major ideas of *The Origin of Species.*

Kohn, David, ed. *The Darwinian Heritage.* Princeton, NJ: Princeton University Press, 1985. Wide-ranging and scholarly group of essays discussing the impact of Darwin's work. Deals with the development of Darwin's ideas, Darwin as a Victorian, and the reception of Darwin's theory of natural selection.

Pinker, Steven. *How the Mind Works.* New York: W. W. Norton, 1997. Good, readable, and scholarly introduction to evolutionary psychology, the study of evolution, and the development of the brain. Pinker discusses a wide range of topics from the difficulties of building a robot to human attitudes to happiness.

Tattersall, Ian, Eric Delson, and John Van Couvering, eds. *Encyclopedia of Human Evolution and Prehistory.* New York: Garland, 1988. Comprehensive encyclopedia on the evolution of humankind. Covers a very wide range of subjects from evolutionary theory to primate paleontology. Quite technical but an excellent resource.

Places

Cambridge University Library, West Road, Cambridge. CB3 3DR, UK

www.lib.cam.ac.uk

A large portion of Darwin's handwritten manuscripts are housed in this library. Some highlights include Darwin's religious views written for his autobiography; proofs of the sixth edition of *The Origin of Species*; and photographs of the Darwin family.

Christ's College, Cambridge University, Cambridge, CB2 3BU, UK

www.christs.cam.ac.uk

Darwin's room while he attended Christ's College is Number 6. The College has left the room exactly as it was when Darwin occupied it; special permission is needed to see it.

Down House, Luxted Road, Downe, Kent, BR6 7JT, UK

www.english-heritage.org.uk/server/show/ConProperty.102

Darwin's home (and estate) for forty years is maintained by English Heritage. Usually, there is an exhibition about the *Beagle* voyage and about some aspect of Darwin's home life. The study, dining room, and drawing room look as they did during Darwin's life. Definitely worth visiting.

National Portrait Gallery, St. Martin's Place, London WC2H OHE, UK

www.npg.org.uk

Features portraits of most of the well-known Victorian figures. Has several portraits and prints of Darwin, including a replica of the last portrait painted by John Collier (1850–1934) in 1883—the original is in Down House.

The Natural History Museum, Cromwell Road, London SW7 5BD, UK

www.nhm.ac.uk

The museum was the brainchild of the distinguished scientist Richard Owen, the first director. The marble statue of Darwin presented to Prince Edward in 1885 by the Royal Society is in this museum. The Darwin Center houses some of the specimens Darwin collected on his *Beagle* voyage.

Shrewsbury, Shropshire, UK

www.visitshrewsbury.com

The town where Darwin was born and spent his childhood. By following the Darwin Trail, a mapped walk around the town, it is possible to see most of the major sites associated with Darwin's early life: St. Chad's, the church where Darwin was christened; the home of Reverend Case, Darwin's first school; the Unitarian Church Darwin attended with his mother; the building where Robert Darwin practiced; and the

Shrewsbury School (now a library). A ten-minute walk from the center of town in the district of Framwell is The Mount, Darwin's birthplace. (The Mount is privately owned: visitors need permission to enter.)

Westminster Abbey, Westminster, London SW1P 3PA, UK

www.westminster-abbey.org

Darwin is buried in this famous church in Central London. Darwin's grave is on the left side of the Nave next to the monument to Isaac Newton (near the end of the guided tour).

Magazines

Note: Each of these magazines has an online edition.

Astronomy

www.astronomy.com

Has excellent articles on astrophysics and cosmology.

Natural History

www.naturalhistorymag.com

One of the best popular magazines covering the biological sciences. The articles are usually written so that a nonscientist can understand the ideas being discussed.

Science

www.sciencemag.org

Regularly publishes articles on evolution, biology, genetics, and paleontology.

Scientific American

www.scientificamerican.com

Regularly publishes articles on evolution, genetics, and cosmology.

Journals

Note: All journals have online editions.

Journal of the History of Biology

www.springerlink.com (go to "Browse Publications" and enter journal name)

The premier scientific journal on biology: especially good on developments in the nineteenth and twentieth centuries and the philosophical and social implications of those developments.

Nature

> www.nature.com

One of the premier scientific journals. Always has good articles on the biological and evolutionary sciences, particularly in genetics and paleontology.

Theology and Science

> www.tandf.co.uk/journals (go to "Alphabetical Listing" and enter journal name)

Useful articles on the interaction and connection between religion and science; particularly good for articles on Intelligent Design.

Articles

Briggs, Robert, and Thomas J. King. "Transplantation of Living Nuclei from Blastula Cells into Enucleated Frogs' Eggs." *Proceedings of the National Academy of Sciences of the United States of America* vol. 38, no. 5 (15 May 1952): 455–463. Briggs and King announced that they had developed a technique for transplanting the nucleus of a mature cell to an egg cell. A version of the technique was used to clone animals forty years later. Uses technical language.

Brown, P., et al. "A New Small-bodied Hominin from the Late Pleistocene of Flores, Indonesia." *Nature* vol. 431 (28 October 2004): 1055–1061. Researchers from the University of New England in New South Wales, Australia, and the Indonesian Centre for Archaeology in Jakarta, Indonesia, announced that they had found the skeletal remains of a new species of hominid *Homo floresiensis* or Flores Man. The researchers suggest the new species is related to modern humans even though it is half the size of one ancestor, *Homo erectus*.

Browne, Janet. "Darwin in Caricature: A Study of the Popularisation and Dissemination of Evolution." *Proceedings of the American Philosophical Society* vol. 145, no. 4 (December 2001): 496–509. Excellent article on the impact and effect of cartoons about Darwin and *The Origin of Species*. Browne argues that these cartoons expressed society's fears about the implications of the theory of evolution as well as providing a succinct summary of Darwin's major ideas. The cartoons were one reason why the theory of evolution spread so rapidly.

International Human Genome Sequencing Consortium. "Initial Sequencing and Analysis of the Human Genome." *Nature* vol. 409 (15 February 2001): 860–921. The Human Genome Project, led by Eric S. Lander of the Whitehead Institute for Biomedical Research, published its findings on the human genome. The two-color pullouts analyze each of the twenty-two human chromosomes, including details such as the gene sequence and the site of each gene.

Quammen, David. "Was Darwin Wrong?" *National Geographic* vol. 206, no. 5 (November 2004): 4–35. Excellent, nontechnical introduction to the major ideas of evolution. Also has excellent pictures to illustrate the ideas discussed.

Venter, J. Craig, et al. "The Sequence of the Human Genome." *Science* vol. 291 (16 February 2001): 1304–1351. The team led by J. Craig Venter of Celera Genomics published its findings on the human genome sequence. Contains a color pullout of the history of mapping the human genome from 1953 to 2001 and brief biographies of people who made small but significant contributions to the mapping of the human genome.

Watson, James D., and Francis H. C. Crick, "A Structure for Deoxyribose Nucleic Acid." *Nature* vol. 171 (25 April 1953): 737–738. Watson and Crick announced that they had evidence to show that DNA is a double-helix molecule.

———. "Genetical Implications of the Structure of Deoxyribonucleic Acid." *Nature* vol. 171 (30 May 1953): 964–967. Watson and Crick's famous article in which they describe the structure of the DNA molecule and explain how the structure enables genetic information to be transmitted. They suggest that mutation occurs during cell division when the two chains of DNA uncoil and pull apart: a split in the "wrong" part of the chain is a mutation.

Videos/DVDs

Cosmos, 2000, executive producers Ann Druyan and Joe Firmage. Studio City, CA: Cosmos Studios. Updated version of *Cosmos*, a thirteen-part television series (1989). Carl Sagan, an American physicist and cosmologist who was interested in making science understandable to nonscientists, is the narrator. Although mainly about cosmology, there are some very good episodes on evolution. Episode II, which includes a visual rendering of evolution from a single-celled organism to a human, is particularly good. (Running time: 780 minutes)

Inherit the Wind, 1991, produced by Stanley Kramer. Lomitas Productions, Inc., 1960; MGM/United Artists Home Video, 1991. Originally a play, the film is based on perceptions of the Scopes Trial rather than the trial itself. Science and open-mindedness are opposed by religion and intolerance. The depiction of the controversy the theory of evolution sparked makes the film compulsory viewing. (Running time: 128 minutes)

Neanderthals on Trial, 2002, produced by Mark J. Davis. Boston: A NOVA Production by MDTV Productions, Inc for WGBH Boston. Excellent program on human evolution. Different scientists discuss whether humans and Neanderthals are related and the philosophy at the foundation of evolutionary science. (Running time: 60 minutes)

Web Sites

http://www.aboutdarwin.com
Excellent site dedicated to the life and times of Darwin. Contains a time line, pictures, and a series of maps of the *Beagle* voyage.

http://darwin.lib.cam.ac.uk
Web site of Darwin Correspondence Online project at Cambridge University. Fully searchable by putting in a name, place, or theory. Has lists of all of Darwin's correspondents with brief biographies; all the books and journals referred to in Darwin's letters; all letters cataloged by the project and the archives or libraries in which they are held.

http://www.darwinfoundation.org
Web site of the Charles Darwin Foundation (CDF) and the Charles Darwin Research Station, which is operated by the CDF. Has excellent photographs of the animal and plant life of the Galapagos and the research being conducted by the scientists, educators, and volunteers who work at the Station. Has summaries and references to articles written about the Galapagos, including some about Darwin's work there.

http://www.discovery.org/csc
Web site of the Discovery Institute's Center for Science and Culture (CSC). A good site for the latest information on the Intelligent Design Movement.

http://www.english-heritage.org.uk/days-out/places
Enter "Down House" in the search engine and it will find information on Darwin's home, including opening times, price, exhibitions, and directions.

http://evolution.berkeley.edu
The Understanding Evolution Web site. Very useful for basic information on contemporary evolutionary theory, the evidence for evolution, the history of the theory of evolution, and ways to teach evolution. Updated regularly with features on the latest research in evolution.

http://www.gct.org
Web site of the Galapagos Conservation Trust (GCT). The site is designed as a resource for schoolchildren and people who know little about botany and zoology. Has good photographs of the flora and fauna of the Galapagos

Islands and information on the history of the islands, including Darwin's visit there.

http://www.hawking.org.uk

Web site of the British physicist and cosmologist Stephen Hawking. Hawking is very good at explaining the origin of the universe in simple, nontechnical language. The site has full text of his better-known lectures on the subject.

http://www.natcenscied.org

Web site of the National Center for Science Education. Excellent resource for information on the Evolution versus Creation debate. Has a history of the evolution/creation controversy, links to the full text of court cases concerning creationism, reviews of books and DVDs dealing with evolution and creationism, and updated news on debates about the teaching of evolution in schools.

http://pages.britishlibrary.net/charles.darwin

Site of The Writings of Charles Darwin on the Web. Pilot Web site with digitized versions of American or later editions of Darwin's published works. An invaluable resource. (Completed site will be known as "The Complete Works of Charles Darwin Online.")

http://www.royalsoc.ac.uk

Web site of the Royal Society, the premier scientific society of Britain. Has a history of the society, a biography of the past and present members/fellows of the society, a list of past presidents and officers, and lists of the recipients of the awards and medals given by the society. Very good source of information on the prominent scientists working during and after Darwin's life.

http://www.stephenjaygould.org

Web site of The Unofficial Stephen Jay Gould Archive. As Gould was a prominent evolutionary biologist and promoter of science, the site has links to important articles dealing with various topics in science and evolution. This includes Gould's testimony in the *McLean v. Arkansas* case (on whether creation science could be taught in American schools); the text of interviews with Gould and other evolutionary biologists such as Richard Dawkins and Ernst Mayr; and biographical sketches of figures such as Charles Darwin, Charles Lyell, and Joseph Hooker.

http://www.ucmp.berkeley.edu

Web site of the University of California, Berkeley Museum of Paleontology. Excellent resource for information on all aspects of evolution. The search engine is particularly useful for finding information about the life and ideas of scientists in the nineteenth and twentieth centuries.

http://www.victoriaweb.org

Excellent Web site on Victorian history. Has background essays on nineteenth-century developments such as the Industrial Revolution. Has brief biographies of all the significant figures in Victorian Britain.

INDEX

About the Author

KEITH A. FRANCIS is associate professor of history at Baylor University. He teaches and researches in nineteenth- and twentieth-century British history. His main areas of focus are politics, particularly women's issues, religion, and science. He was born in London and educated in England but has spent most of his teaching career in the United States.